T0393902

Greek Employment Relations in Crisis

Greece's economy and society have undergone important structural changes in recent years as a result of the financial crisis and consequent austerity policies that have been implemented. The Greek labour market and employment relations system have been subject to immense pressures, leading to fundamental changes both in the structure of institutions and in the behaviour of the main employment relations actors.

The present volume constitutes a first attempt to appreciate the consequences of a decade of austerity politics on the Greek labour market. Offering a multidisciplinary perspective and building on original research by leading Greek scholars in the fields of labour economics, employment relations and the sociology of work, it will discuss the impact of the crisis and the resulting policies on the Greek labour market and employment relations.

This volume will be of interest to policy makers, researchers and students interested in the past, present and future of Greek employment relations and the impact of austerity on Greece.

Horen Voskeritsian is a Lecturer in Management at Birkbeck College, University of London. He has written extensively on the condition of Greek Employment Relations during the crisis and his work has appeared in numerous international conferences and international publications, such as *Economic and Industrial Democracy, International Journal of HRM, Relations Industrielles/Industrial Relations* and *Labour History.*

Panos Kapotas is a Senior Lecturer in Law at the University of Portsmouth. His research interests range from equality and anti-discrimination law to labour law, European human rights law and European Union law. His work has been published in English and Greek in edited volumes and in leading law journals, including the *European Law Review,* the *European Constitutional Law Review* and the *International Labor Rights Case Law.*

Christina Niforou is a Lecturer in Human Resource Management at the University of Birmingham Business School. Her work has been published in leading academic journals, including the *British Journal of Industrial Relations, Human Resource Management* and the *Journal of Business Ethics.*

Routledge Studies in the European Economy

For a full list of titles in this series, please visit www.routledge.com/series/
SE0431

Greek Employment Relations in Crisis

Problems, Challenges and Prospects

Edited by Horen Voskeritsian, Panos Kapotas and Christina Niforou

 Routledge
Taylor & Francis Group

LONDON AND NEW YORK

First published 2019
by Routledge
2 Park Square, Milton Park, Abingdon, Oxon OX14 4RN

and by Routledge
52 Vanderbilt Avenue, New York, NY 10017

Routledge is an imprint of the Taylor & Francis Group, an informa business

British Library Cataloguing-in-Publication Data
A catalogue record for this book is available from the British Library

Library of Congress Cataloging-in-Publication Data
Names: Voskeritsian, Horen, editor. | Kapotas, Panos, 1978- editor. | Niforou, Christina, editor.
Title: Greek employment relations in crisis : problems, challenges, and prospects / edited by Horen Voskeritsian, Panos Kapotas and Christina Niforou.
Description: 1 Edition. | New York : Routledge, 2019. | Series: Routledge studies in the European economy | Includes bibliographical references and index.
Subjects: LCSH: Industrial relations–Greece. | Collective bargaining–Greece. | Greece–Economic conditions–21st century.
Classification: LCC HD8650.5 (ebook) | LCC HD8650.5 .G744 2019 (print) | DDC 331.8809495–dc23
LC record available at https://lccn.loc.gov/2018057080

ISBN: 978-1-138-20735-6 (hbk)
ISBN: 978-1-315-46249-3 (ebk)

Typeset in Times New Roman
by Integra Software Services Pvt. Ltd.

Printed and bound in Great Britain by
TJ International Ltd, Padstow, Cornwall

Contents

Figures

Tables

Contributors

Rebekka Christopoulou is an Assistant Professor at the Economics Department of the University of Macedonia, Greece. She was trained as an economist at the University of Cambridge (PhD), the University of York (MSc) and the University of Crete (undergraduate degree). Prior to joining the University of Macedonia, she held research positions at the Ohio State University and Cornell University. She has also worked for the Wage Dynamics Network at the European Central Bank (2007–2008) and as Greek Ministry of National Economy Research Fellow at the London School of Economics (2008–2009). Her research interests fall within the areas of labour economics, health economics and economic demography.

Nicholas Giannakopoulos is an Associate Professor of Applied Economics at the Department of Economics of the University of Patras, Greece, where he completed his PhD in economics in 2006. His research interests include wage formation, labour supply, unemployment, educational outcomes and social economics. He teaches microeconomics, labour economics and empirical methods in economics.

Christos A. Ioannou, an economist (PhD), has research work in the areas of labour markets, human resources, collective bargaining, wage and employment policies. His latest published work refers to public sector employment relations in Greece – adjustment and reforms – in *Public Service Management and Employment Relations in Europe; Emerging from the Crisis?* Bach Stephen and Bordogna Lorenzo (editors), Routledge, London, 2016. His current research focuses on paradigm change in wage formation, productive reforms in the Greek economy and the Future of Work in Greece in the context of the ILO Centenary initiative. He has acted as advisor, consultant and director for a variety of both government and private sector organisations, national and international. He has served as Mediator and Arbitrator with the Organisation for Mediation and Arbitration (OMED) in Greece since 1991 and as Deputy Greek Ombudsman in charge of social protection, health and welfare issues since 2013.

Christina Karakioulafis is an Assistant Professor at the Department of Sociology, University of Crete, Greece. She teaches courses related to industrial relations and the sociology of work. Her main research interests concern unemployment and employment precariousness, trade unionism, industrial relations trends and theory, as well as subjects related to working conditions (workplace violence) and sociology of professions (artistic work). She is the author of one book in Greek and has co-authored and co-edited others. She has also published articles, mainly in francophone journals, regarding Greek trade unionism and industrial relations during the period of the crisis.

Andreas Kornelakis is a Senior Lecturer in International Management at King's Business School, King's College London, UK. He was awarded a PhD from the London School of Economics and has won several prizes, grants and scholarships for his work. He worked as a researcher at the LSE, taught at the University of London and the University of Sussex, and held visiting research posts at the European University Institute, Florence and the National University of Ireland, Galway. His research interests dwell on the changing political-economic environment in Europe with a focus on comparative employment relations and HRM. He is an Editorial Board member of the journal *Work, Employment and Society*. He has published in a wide range of journals such as: *Work, Employment & Society; British Journal of Industrial Relations; Business History; Journal of Common Market Studies; International Journal of Human Resource Management; European Journal of Industrial Relations; New Technology, Work & Employment* and *Economic & Industrial Democracy*.

Ioannis Laliotis is a Research Fellow at the School of Economics of the University of Surrey, UK. He received his PhD from the Department of Economics at the University of Patras in 2014, where he studied the structure of wages and the institutional framework of the Greek labour market. After that, he joined the University of Surrey as a working package leader on a research project, investigating the relationship between workforce and productivity in public sector labour markets, with a special focus in the English National Health System. His research interests lie within the intersection of labour economics, health economics, and applied microeconometrics. His work has examined issues such as the institutional aspects of the wage formation process, the relationship between wages and economic conditions, the relationship between health outcomes and economic conditions, the relationship between crime and economic conditions, and the provision of healthcare services. His papers have been published in academic outlets such as the *British Journal of Industrial Relations*, the *Journal of Labor Research, Health Economics, Empirical Economics* and *The Lancet*. Parts of his work have been presented in prestigious conferences such as the European Economic

Association, the European Association of Labour Economists and the European Health Economics Association.

Ilias Livanos is an Expert on Skills and Labour Markets at the European Centre for the Development of Vocational Training (Cedefop). He has worked towards the development of and is currently leading, Cedefop's work on Future Skills Demand and Supply. He has been a core team member responsible for developing the Skills Panorama and he has also been the lead expert for constructing the European Skills Index and developing a system for monitoring occupational shortages, namely the Mismatch Priority Occupations. Livanos is an economist by training, with a PhD in Employment Research from the University of Warwick, where he worked for a number of years prior to joining Cedefop. His expertise is in the wider area of Applied Economics, in particular, Labour Economics, Education Economics and Industrial Relations. His research activities focus on applied micro-econometrics using socio-economic datasets, such as the European Union Labour Force Survey. He has contributed to a number of books and edited volumes and has been published in various top ranked journals, including *Industrial Relations: A Journal of Economy and Society, Regional Studies, Industrial and Economic Democracy, Journal of Economic Studies, Education Economics, Applied Economics Letters, Higher Education*, the *International Journal of Manpower, Personnel Review* and *the Journal of Labour Research.*

Vassilis Monastiriotis is an Associate Professor of Political Economy at the London School of Economics. He holds a PhD in Economic Geography from the London School of Economics. His research spans across three disciplinary areas, including Economics, Geography and Political Economy. His main research interests are regional and national labour markets, regional and local socio-economic disparities, labour market flexibility and labour relations, macroeconomic policy and the political economy of reform. He is currently working on a number of projects on labour market flexibility and regional economic disparities, while he has attracted funding from various sources, including the Economic and Social Research Council, the Royal Geographical Society and the Department of Trade and Industry.

Maria Pantalidou is a PhD candidate at the Department of International European Economic Studies in the Athens University of Economics and Business (AUEB), Greece. She received her undergraduate and master's degree in Economics from the University of Macedonia in Thessaloniki, Greece. Her master's thesis focused on youth unemployment in Greece and the family as a social safety net for youths who are unemployed or work in poorly paid jobs. Her research interests are within the fields of applied and empirical microeconomics and social policy implementation, with a specific focus on the redistributive role of the state in Greece and other European countries. She is currently engaged in research on school systems and the transition from school to work and the role of the family and public institutions in the transition from youth to adulthood. In parallel with her research, Maria serves her department as a tutor for undergraduate courses.

Konstantinos Pouliakas is an Expert on Skills and Labour Markets at the European Centre for the Development of Vocational Training (Cedefop). He is the agency's lead researcher on skill mismatch and the future of work projects and coordinator of its country's support programme "Governance of EU skills anticipation and matching". Konstantinos has developed, managed and analysed the first European Skills and Jobs Survey. He has been a member of the steering committees of high profile European Commission skills and VET projects, consultant for the World Economic Forum and author of influential policy contributions on skill mismatch and unemployment (Employment and Social Developments in Europe, New Skills Agenda for Europe). He has represented Cedefop at high-level international conferences on skills and VET in Europe, USA, and Latin America. Before joining Cedefop, he held posts at the University of Aberdeen (UK) and the University of Cyprus and briefly worked for the Bank of Greece and the UK's HM Treasury. He has been widely published in peer-reviewed journals on Economics. He holds an MPhil from the University of Oxford (St. Antony's College) and a DPhil from the Scottish Graduate Program in Economics. He is an Honorary Lecturer at the University of Aberdeen Business School, Invited Professor at Universita Degli Studi Roma TRE and an IZA Research Fellow.

Michail Veliziotis is a Lecturer in Human Resource Management at the Southampton Business School, University of Southampton, UK. He studied economics at the Athens University of Economics and Business in Greece. He holds a PhD from the University of Essex. His main research interests are in the field of employment studies, doing research on topics related to trade unions and labour market institutions, comparative people management, job quality and employee well-being. He is an Editorial Board member of *Work, Employment and Society*, and he has published in journals such as *Journal of Vocational Behavior; Environment and Planning A; Work, Employment & Society; Social Science and Medicine*; and *The International Journal of Human Resource Management*.

Horen Voskeritsian is a Lecturer in Management at Birkbeck College, University of London. He has written extensively on the condition of Greek Employment Relations during the crisis and his work has appeared in numerous international conferences and international publications, such as Economic and Industrial Democracy, International Journal of HRM, Relations Industrielles/Industrial Relations and Labour History.

Introduction

The story of Greece in the last decade is a story of crises. One would struggle to find an area of public life that has remained unscathed by the economic, political, and social crises that redrew the political and legal landscape and profoundly affected the psyche of the Greek people. Against this backdrop, it is fair to say that the changes to the Greek labour market and the employment relations system have been cataclysmic, both from an institutional and a normative point of view.

As the worst of this crisis should hopefully be behind us, it is time to reflect on where we are and where we go from here. Identifying what old problems remain or what new problems have been created by austerity policies and deregulatory interventions and figuring out what challenges lie ahead for regulators and social partners are the key aims of the present volume. The safest – if not the only – way to gauge the future prospects of the Greek labour market is to have a clear understanding of the political context of the crisis that has shaped the present state of affairs.

Towards the end of 2009, the sustainability of the Greek debt made international headlines. With its government gross debt standing at 126.7% of the GDP, Greece was considered by the international markets as a liability that, sooner or later, would have to face the consequences of running extensive public debts. This line of analysis was, of course, not new; already in January 2009, less than a year after the 2008 financial crisis that would determine the political and economic realities of the following decade, Greece was considered by international observers as a critical case (Gourinchas et al. 2016).

It is true that the country was not hit by the global economic downturn as heavily as most of its EU counterparts – primarily due to the fact that its banking sector was not as exposed to the international markets and toxic debts as other European countries. Yet, the global financial crisis found Greece in a vulnerable position, and its public debt and budget deficit seemed to grow at a rate faster than that of other EU countries, culminating in what Gourinchas et al. (2016: 14) call the "three shocks" in the Greek economy: a sovereign debt crisis, a banking crisis, and a "sudden stop," with foreign investors unwilling to lend to Greece. The revelation by the newly elected PASOK government in September 2009 that the country's actual debt and deficit was much larger than what had officially been reported to the EU authorities opened Pandora's box. For the first time since 1932, the prospect of defaulting was once again on the horizon (Tsoulfidis and Zouboulakis 2016).

In reality, the Greek economy was showing some disconcerting signs since the late 2008s–early 2009s, with consumption in slight decline – largely as a response to the 2008 global crisis – and Greek businesses feeling an unfamiliar pressure on their finances after more than two decades of relative economic tranquillity. Nevertheless, and despite these turbulences, this was still a period of belief in the dynamic potential of the Greek economy. This belief was fuelled by the bubble of economic prosperity created in the past decade due to the cheap money that both businesses and households had access to after the country's entry into the Eurozone (Theodoropoulou 2016).

It was only in late 2009 – early 2010 – not long after the international rating agencies downgraded Greece's long-term debt from (A-) to (BBB+) – that public mood started to shift. It was then gradually becoming apparent that Greece's liquidity problems rendered the country's public debt unsustainable and the prospect of defaulting more real than ever. Against this backdrop, George Papandreou's PASOK government turned to its EU partners for assistance. As it turned out, little could be immediately achieved on that front, as the EU was equally unprepared (both institutionally and politically) to deal with a prospective default of a Eurozone member state. The absence of a support mechanism emerged as a potential Trojan horse that could derail the Euro project and revealed the political and economic "black holes" at the heart of the EU's monetary system.

Since the ECB and other EU member state banks were holding a lion's share of the country's sovereign debt, finding a solution to the Greek case became a matter of utmost urgency in order to avoid a new round of financial crises that could shake the very foundations of the European project. As a result, and after a long round of negotiations with its European partners, in May 2010, the Greek government signed the first (of three) Memorandum of Understanding (MoU) with the European Commission, the European Central Bank, and the IMF (the three institutions that would thereafter be infamously known as the Troika) (European Commission 2010, 2012, 2015). In return for financial assistance of €110 billion, the Greek government agreed to implement a series of fiscal and structural changes to the Greek economy and society. Unsurprisingly, the demands of the Troika obeyed the same neoliberal logic and were inspired by the same austerity rationale that dominated responses to the 2008 crisis and defined the political trajectory of the IMF and the European Commission in the last decade.

In 2010, therefore, Greece found itself in the midst of a *double crisis* that struck at the very foundations of its economy, its society, and its political establishment. A *fiscal crisis*, on the one hand, that quickly evolved to a *financial crisis*, leading to high levels of unemployment, closure of businesses, rise in poverty, and emigration of capital (both human and otherwise). And an *institutional crisis*, on the other hand, that radically transformed the identity and function of deeply embedded institutions that governed the Greek life.

Although the severity of the measures introduced by the MoU came both as a surprise and a shock to the Greek citizenry, the new direction of travel was, in reality, not at all new. Policies of a similar or of the same "spirit" had been introduced across the EU since the early 1990s. As Hyman (2015: 5) has argued, "EU policy has moved increasingly towards the economists' orthodoxy that employment protection is a source of labour market rigidity, creating a dichotomy between privileged 'insiders' and the socially excluded". Fiscal consolidation, the retreat of the state, and the deregulation of employment relations were common features of policies that became part of the normative picture across Europe (Crouch 2011), but especially in the UK and Germany (Traxler 1995) as well as in the (then) new EU member states (Soulsby et al. 2017).

Still, and despite appearances, the Greek case is somewhat different – and in more than one way. Contrary to (de)regulatory interventions elsewhere, the measures introduced in Greece came at a time of economic stagnation and were reflective of a top-down approach with questionable democratic pedigree. Crucially, the inclusion of a non-European actor in the Troika was, both symbolically and substantively, an admission that the handling of the situation was no longer a European "family matter". Even more importantly, however, the Memoranda policies were introduced abruptly and in bulk, thus leading to a deep and profound shock for the economy and the Greek society, as neither had the necessary time to adjust to the new reality through a process of smooth institutional change.

Despite the profound shock, the new policies were not left uncontested. The Greek public reacted to the threat that the double crisis posed for their livelihood in a variety of ways: politically, socially, and psychologically. Unsurprisingly, much of the reaction converged in or around the workplace. Industrial conflict rose exponentially, and strikes (especially political strikes) became an everyday reality in the post-MoU environment (Hamann et al. 2013; Lindvall 2013; Vandaele 2016). The strikes were accompanied by mass demonstrations in the big urban centres (especially in Athens and Thessaloniki), and many were characterised by severe violence. On May 5, 2010, during one of the most massive demonstrations in recent history, unknown individuals burned a subsidiary of a bank in Athens, resulting in the death of three employees who were trapped inside.[1] This event, together with the violent nature that many demonstrations tended to acquire, led to a search for alternative means of protest. Inspired by the Spanish *Indignados Movement*, as well as from the Arab spring events, a call to occupy Syntagma square – the main square in the centre of Athens, just opposite the Houses of Parliament – on May 25, 2011, attracted increasing support from diverse segments of the population (Simiti 2014).

At the same time, a large portion of the electorate, disappointed by the failure of mainstream politics to protect their standards of living and motivated by nationalist feelings fused by what was perceived to be an outside interference in Greek life, turned slowly towards radical politics. Nothing demonstrates this tendency better than the meteoric rise of the extreme right-wing Golden Dawn party in public life. Until the 2009 elections, Golden Dawn commanded a mere 0.3% of the vote, but during the 2012 elections, it managed to secure its place in the Greek parliament with 7% of the vote (Halikiopoulou et al. 2016; Vasilopoulou and Halikiopoulou 2013). Finally, disillusioned by the emerging new reality, the destruction of their hopes, and the pressure on their well-being, many Greeks opted for the "exit" route: migration, especially among the young and highly skilled workforce, rose (Labrianidis 2014; Labrianidis and Vogiatzis 2013), as did the number of suicides and attempted suicides among the general population (Branas et al. 2015; Economou et al. 2013).

The signing of the first MoU took place under conditions of extreme pressure. Despite the provisions in the original agreement for the initiation and carrying out of social dialogue regarding issues related to the labour market at least, little – if any –dialogue took place. Moreover, the "one-size-fits-all" model that was introduced by the Troika meant that no research regarding the possible consequences of the adopted policies on the economy and society was ever conducted. In the end, the Greek government appeared as a passive recipient of policies dictated to it by the Troika, with little or no power to alter the course or content of the proposed measures.

Under the cover of "urgency", the MoU put forward a series of actions that radically altered public management, the role of the state, and employment relations (Kouzis 2010). Even after the signing of the Memorandum, during the long implementation period that followed the original agreement, and up to the signing of the Second MoU in 2012, the same *modus operandi* was followed: social dialogue was marginalised, evidence-based policy was inexistent, and the justification for the adoption of said policies rested on a familiar discourse of urgency, crisis, and catastrophe, which reinforced and replicated the hegemonic role the creditors had now assumed in the Greek public sphere. The marginalisation or exclusion of social partners from the process of decision making was not something unique to the case of Greece. Similar trends that had been observed in Europe in previous years (Heyes and Lewis 2014; Heyes et al. 2012) and would be observed in subsequent years in other countries forced the introduction of structural adjustments to their employment relations systems (Armingeon and Baccaro 2012; Culpepper and Regan 2014; Hyman 2015; Ioannou and Sonan 2017).

Whether the trajectory of change would have been different if a more democratic and evidence-based approach had been adopted, or whether the Troika would indeed be open to such a prospect, is a counterfactual question that is impossible to address. Yet, the fact that all social partners complained about the lack of consultation and their exclusion from the decision-making process is quite telling (Voskeritsian et al. 2017). Such an inclusion might have seemed immaterial, or even counter-productive, to the government and Greece's creditors, but this assessment could not have been further from the truth. If one appreciates that resurfacing from a crisis calls for the extensive support and collaboration of all productive forces, the *process of change* becomes as important (if not more) as the *content* of change.

Unfortunately, all subsequent MoUs failed to make this realisation. Breaking with years of tradition, and with deeply embedded institutions and behaviours, they implemented generic "readymade" policies without properly considering the institutional context and its underlying dynamics. Inevitably, the MoUs and their drafters failed to accumulate popular and institutional support, which in turn led to a variety of socio-economic problems, conflict being just the tip of that particular iceberg.

All the MoUs were constructed with a simple, and quite straightforward, dual objective: first, to reduce public expenditure and increase taxation to help balance the budget, and second, to create an environment that would help businesses survive and attract investments. Hence, following the classical neo-liberal rationale, flexibility was introduced in the labour market and wage determination was disconnected from sectoral- and occupational-level collective bargaining through a process of gradual decentralisation (Kornelakis and Voskeritsian 2014; Koukiadaki and Kretsos 2012). Although national- and industry-level collective bargaining continued to exist, their function, especially in the first couple of years after the signing of the first MoU, became almost entirely marginalised (Grimshaw and Koukiadaki 2016). The logic behind this exercise of internal devaluation was that a decentralised and flexible labour market would allow companies to adjust their costs and labour processes to the new economic realities, thereby avoiding a spike in unemployment, gradually improving their productivity and competitiveness and helping create a welcoming investment environment. Thus, in a series of policies from 2010 until 2012, the Greek institutional context was transformed from a protective one to an extremely deregulated and flexible one, resembling very much a Liberal Market Economy, albeit in a disorganised fashion (Kornelakis and Voskeritsian 2014).

The adopted measures severely impacted various labour market indices. In the two years following the signing of the first MoU, wages plummeted – especially after the curtailing, in 2012, of the National Minimum Wage (MNW) by 22% (32% for workers under the age of 25), the marginalisation of sectoral collective bargaining, and the consequent rise of firm-level wage determination (Christopoulou and Monastiriotis 2016, Daouli et al. 2013, Ioannou and Papadimitriou 2013, Koukiadaki and Kokkinou 2016, Laliotis et al. 2014). Moreover, flexible forms of employment (such as part time employment, compressed hours and flexitime) replaced the more stable and full-time contracts that characterised the labour market until then (Gialis et al. 2017; Kretsos 2011).

However, only one part of the equation seemed to function as envisaged: for although wage and employment flexibility were firmly established, their effects on productivity and competitiveness were not discernible. Greek businesses, especially the small and medium ones, continued to close, big capital started to migrate to more stable economic and political environments, the balance of trade remained in deficit, and unemployment continued to erupt, reaching levels that the country had not witnessed since the Second World War.

On top of that, several unintended consequences started to emerge. Faced with increased taxation, increased non-wage costs, and the dissolution of the welfare state, employers and employees reverted to the shadow economy to complement their income and to survive. Undeclared work and other illegal practices (such as under-declared employment, under-payment or non-payment of wages, illegal firing of employees, suppression of trade union activities, etc.) started to become a norm in the labour market (ILO 2016). Moreover, many companies opted for the opportunities that the new institutional framework provided to unilaterally determine the terms and conditions of employment in their establishments, giving rise to a labour process and a working environment characterised by authoritarianism and exploitation. Faced with increased unemployment, weak trade unions in the private sector, the absence of robust statutory protection, and a crumbling social protection system, many employees had no choice but to embrace the new realities of work.

Greece, being an inward-looking economy that historically relied on internal consumption and internal investments for its growth and on the presence of a multitude of SMEs (almost 97% of Greek businesses employ fewer than 10 employees), failed to overcome its chronic structural problems and become more competitive in the international markets. A contributing factor was that product prices remained quite inelastic despite the reduction in production costs (primarily due to the lower labour costs). This inelasticity was attributable both to the currency, as euro fluctuations in line with Eurozone performance did not allow massive changes in prices and overall cost of living within a single country, and to the fact that Greek companies used the savings they made on labour costs to maintain or, in some cases, increase their profits (Ioakeimoglou 2018). Eventually, this trend was partially addressed through the functioning of the market, but that did not happen overnight, and it allowed enough time for serious negative social consequences to play out. Moreover, the focus on labour cost reduction – and not on improving labour productivity through training or investment in the development of human resources – as a means to increase competitiveness further accentuated the negative climate that characterised the labour market.

Structure of the book

As is the case with any radical change, the new employment relations environment generated more questions about the future than answers about the present. What effects, for example, did the decentralisation of collective bargaining have on the structure of the employment relations system, the balance of power between the actors, competitiveness and productivity, motivation, and job satisfaction? How did the Greek companies respond to the changes in law, and how was the organisation of the labour process influenced? What effects did these changes have on day-to-day employment relations, managing conflict, and enhancing productivity? How did unemployment and under-employment impact human capital development, and what are the longitudinal consequences for Greece's employees? What are the implications of institutional change for equality and diversity, and especially gender equality, in the labour market? How did the dual crisis impact the labour mobility of young employees? How did the new realities of work impact work-life balance, job quality, and overall happiness? What challenges and opportunities did the new institutional environment create for the social partners, and how have they responded to them?

This is just a small sample of the questions that are bound to dominate research on employment relations in Greece for years to come. The purpose of the present volume is to contribute to the ongoing debates about the impact of the crisis and the post-crisis future of Greece by exploring some of the most significant facets of the Greek labour market. It goes without saying that the multifaceted nature of the relevant issues entails that one cannot, and indeed should not, attempt to engage with them from a single disciplinary perspective. Identifying, understanding, and addressing inherently complex social situations that are dynamic and involve multiple social and institutional actors can only be done through an inter-disciplinary and multi-disciplinary analytical lens. As a first step in that direction, the present volume contains contributions from scholars from various disciplinary backgrounds, including labour economics, employment relations, and sociology of work. Despite the different analytical tools and theoretical starting points, all the contributions share a common denominator: their objective is to enable us to better understand the consequences of the double crisis in the Greek labour market in a broadly defined manner.

To better appreciate the direction of change and the effects of the adjustment policies, one should consider the impact the institutional changes and the economic crisis had on the power dynamics in the employment relations system. In the first chapter, therefore, Voskeritsian and Kornelakis examine how the new institutional environment led to a redistribution of power across all levels of the employment relations environment. By doing so, they also consider the effects of this power redistribution on capital and labour strategies in determining the employment relations realities at the firm and industry levels. The authors argue that apart from the obvious alteration in the two actors' bargaining power, the crisis also changed the legitimacy framework in which the power of the two actors was exercised. Consequently, the way the demands of capital were perceived (and accepted) by individual labour was also altered. Moreover, the structural and institutional dependency of organised labour on the state over the past decades created a space that prevented the development of an effective resistance to capital's demands. Hence, capital was able to take advantage of the legal tools provided by the institutional changes and transform collective bargaining into a zero-sum game. The redistribution of power in the employment relations arena and its concentration at the hands of capital explains the way the MoUs policies impacted employment relations practices.

One such important impact concerns the effects the crisis had on the structure of collective bargaining and the level of wages. Indeed, as previously mentioned, the downward adjustment of wages was among the cornerstones of all successive MoUs. In the second chapter, Ioannou reviews the effects the changes had across Greece's bargaining structure. Sectoral and occupational agreements, which determined the terms and conditions of employment for most private sector employees up to 2011, suffered a decisive blow. From 2011 onwards, a radical decentralisation of collective bargaining started taking place, and the once dominant sectoral agreements gave way to firm-level agreements. A major characteristic of the latter, especially those signed by a new negotiating body that was introduced into the employment relations system (the Association of Persons), was that they led to a steep decline in wages. Hence, the implication of these changes was the rapid and extensive disconnection of wage determination from pre-existing collective bargaining structures. These changes have been so profound that even if the "old" system of wage determination returns, Ioannou argues, we may not necessarily observe a return to the "old" habits.

Despite the fact that wages declined in general, this was not the case across all sectors. In the third chapter, Christopoulou and Monastiriotis explore this issue further by studying how inter-sectoral wage differentials evolved in Greece before and during the crisis. Using data from the Greek Labour Force Survey, they demonstrate that sectoral wage premia are directly linked with the availability of rents in a specific sector rather than with the sector's potential for rents or the ability of workers to extract such rents. They also show that the market inefficiency in the allocation of premia increased instead of declining, as envisaged by the MoU policies: although the crisis coincided with a lowering of the extent to which premia may be attributable to the availability of rents, it also led to a widening of gross and net sectoral wage differentials. Thus, the reforms did not necessarily lead to a more competitive market environment, as firms continued to offer wage premia when they could.

This may, of course, be a reality in certain sectors and for certain firms, but the conditions in companies that utilised the provisions for decentralised, firm-level bargaining were quite different. As Giannakopoulos and Laliotis argue in Chapter 4, the 2011 reforms on collective bargaining had profound implications for firm-level employment relations. By analysing almost 900 firm-level agreements, the authors conclude that decentralised bargaining was used by companies as a tool to minimise pressure within the workplace and reduce wages to the level of the national minimum wage. However, the effects of decentralisation differed depending upon the negotiating party. Hence, all firm-level agreements signed by Associations of Persons led to severe wage decreases, whereas agreements signed by firm-level trade unions had more moderate wage effects.

Wage moderation and decline was, of course, an expected result of the internal devaluation policies. However, the profound institutional changes had an important impact on other labour market indices as well. All the Memoranda emphasised the *quantitative* element of adjustment, be it an increase in competitiveness through wage adjustment to reflect labour prod-uctivity, or the further flexibilisation of the labour market to reduce, among other things, unemployment. Yet the double crisis had an important *qualita-tive* dimension as well, as reflected in the quality of available jobs or the effi-cient utilisation of human capital, for instance.

Moving beyond the question of quantity, in Chapter 5, Veliziotis and Korne-lakis discuss an under-explored issue in Greek employment relations – job quality. Utilising data from successive European Working Conditions Surveys, they provide a detailed account of the overall quality of jobs in Greece during the past two decades, adopting a comparative European perspective. Their findings reveal a "twin gap" in the Greek labour market: on the one hand, a quantity gap – as reflected in the high levels of unemployment – and on the other, a quality gap – as reflected in the diachronically low levels of reported job quality among Greek employees. Interestingly, Greek employees were gen-erally unhappy about the quality of their jobs even before the crisis, although as expected, the crisis magnified these experiences. Compared to other EU countries of similar institutional and economic characteristics, Greece seems to be constantly occupying one of the lowest places in the relevant rankings.

The issue of job quality is linked, in one way or another, to the type of job one has. Although the adjustment programmes further enhanced flexibility in the Greek labour market, thus creating a vast market for atypical employment, not everyone participating in this market did so voluntarily. Even though spe-cific demographics – such as students or women with children – seized the new opportunities to their benefit, others found themselves in non-standard employment out of need. As appreciated, involuntary employment has import-ant implications for one's performance, productivity, and general well-being, but it also begs the question of efficient utilisation of the country's human cap-ital. If employees cannot effectively utilise their skills, then there is a high possi-bility of skills obsolescence, brain-drain, and an increasingly discouraged workforce. Livanos and Pouliakas deal with this important issue in Chapter 6 by focusing on the extent, trend, and determinants of involuntary non-stand-ard employment during the crisis. Their findings are suggestive of a general deterioration in the quality of workplace employment relations. People in this type of employment receive lower wages, have higher chances of not being covered by any type of health or social insurance, and are often involved in occupations characterised by low job quality. The authors argue that if Greece is to recover from the crisis, the issue of under-employment must be addressed in parallel to the issue of unemployment.

Although the under-employed may face a series of social and economic problems, their struggle is somewhat easier than that of the unemployed. Since 2010, unemployment levels in Greece quadrupled, reaching a peak of 27% in the general population (and almost 51% among young workers). Unemployment put a huge strain on the Greek society, challenging the state's capacity to address the problem as well as the society's ability to sup-port the unemployed. Greece being a traditional Mediterranean society meant that the family played an important role in substituting the state in providing for, and supporting, the unemployed. However, the experience of unemployment came as a shock to many, influencing the way they perceived themselves, the world, and their future. The book's final section deals with the experience of unemployment and the coping strategies the unemployed developed to overcome the stigma of unemployment.

In Chapter 7, Karakioulafis explores how the unemployed experience and cope with the loss of work and how they perceive their present and future situation. Although different individuals develop different strategies to cope with the condition of unemployment, a generalised pessimism about the future and the ability to find a job is observed. Discouragement, therefore, prevails among other significations of unemployment. However, contrary to the pre-crisis years, the stigma of unemployment seems to be more manageable due to the shared experience of unemployment across all levels of society. Being unemployed in Greece is no longer the exception but a common experience; it is a reality, no matter how harsh, which has been normalised. Knowing that one is not alone helps mitigate the feelings of incompetence or guilt that burden many of the unemployed. In their struggle to survive, the family (especially the parents and, in some cases, the grandparents) has become an unofficial social security mechanism. Yet, this assistance also comes at a psychological cost, since the unemployed carry the guilt of being a burden to their equally struggling parents.

The role of the family as a safety net became more prominent among the young adults – unemployed or not – during the crisis. As Christopoulou and Pantalidou point out in the final chapter (Chapter 8), the two-way intergenerational dependency that characterised Greek society before the crisis has now assumed a one-way direction, with young people becoming the recipients rather than the providers of support. During these difficult times, families responded by providing either housing or monetary transfers, although due to the pressures on their finances, housing became the prominent way to support the young. Using data from the Greek Labour Force Survey, the authors paint a comprehensive picture of the kind of support young people received during the crisis. Among other interesting findings, they reveal that parents "rescued" more young men than women, something that also reflects the paternalistic structure of the Greek society, since young women were already safely "protected" by the family, conforming to their traditional gender roles.

Before leaving our readers to delve into the relevant chapters, it is worth offering some final thoughts on how to approach this book and what (not) to expect.

As with any edited volume, there is no pressing need to read the book from cover to cover. It is true, of course, that the particular order of the chapters reveals how they fit together into a single narrative, and we are hoping that this will become evident to those who choose to read the book in a linear fashion. But interdisciplinary endeavours such as this one are bound to attract attention from readers of different disciplinary backgrounds and diverse academic persuasions. With this in mind, we believe that inter-active engagement with the book should also be encouraged. Starting with a chapter that "speaks" one's own disciplinary language before diving into deeper and, perhaps, hitherto unknown waters may be a perfectly legitimate way into the book, enabling the reader to appreciate how the different discip-linary outlooks shed light on different facets of the subject matter.

We must also concede one caveat that comes with the territory of works of this nature. We are not claiming that this book offers a comprehensive picture of the Greek labour market, Greek employment relations, and the changes that have reshaped them over the last few years. What we are con-sciously aiming for, rather, is to provide a snapshot of the current state of affairs and instigate substantive discussions on present challenges and future prospects. We have no ambition to persuade our readers that this book is telling the whole story –we are not convinced that any book on a volatile and politically charged topic could ever claim to do that. More than any-thing else, then, this book should be seen as an inspiration for further, rigorous, interdisciplinary research and as an invitation to engage with a substantive and constructive academic, institutional, and political dialogue. We are confident that this book will become part of a literature keen on *reimagining, redesigning*, and *rebuilding* Greek employment relations for a post-crisis labour market, and we hope that many of our readers will join the fray.

The Editors,
July 2018

Note

1 www.theguardian.com/world/gallery/2010/may/06/greece-crisis-protest-killed (link correct as of July 2018).

References

Armingeon, K. and Baccaro, L. (2012). 'Political Economy of the Sovereign Debt Crisis: The Limits of Internal Devaluation'. *Industrial Law Journal*, 41(3): 254–275.

Branas, C. C., Kastanaki, A. E., Michalodimitrakis, M., Tzougas, J., Kranioti, E. F., Theodorakis, P. N., Carr, B. G., and Wiebe, D. J. (2015). 'The Impact of Economic Austerity and Prosperity Events on Suicide in Greece: A 30-Year Interrupted Time-Series Analysis'. *BMJ Open*, 5(1). www.ncbi.nlm.nih.gov/pmc/articles/PMC4316557/ (accessed 3 May 2018).

Christopoulou, R. and Monastiriotis, V. (2016). 'Public-Private Wage Duality during the Greek Crisis'. *Oxford Economic Papers*, 68(1): 174–196.

Crouch, C. (2011). *The Strange Non-Death of Neoliberalism*. London: Polity Press.

Culpepper, P. D. and Regan, A. (2014). 'Why Don't Governments Need Trade Unions Anymore? The Death of Social Pacts in Ireland and Italy'. *Socio-Economic Review*, 12(4): 723–745.

Daouli, J., Demoussis, M., Giannakopoulos, N., and Laliotis, I. (2013). 'Firm-Level Collective Bargaining and Wages in Greece: A Quantile Decomposition Analysis'. *British Journal of Industrial Relations*, 51(1): 80–103.

Economou, M., Madianos, M., Peppou, L. E., Theleritis, C., Patelakis, A., and Stefanis, C. (2013). 'Suicidal Ideation and Reported Suicide Attempts in Greece during the Economic Crisis'. *World Psychiatry*, 12(1): 53–59.

European Commission. (2010). *The Economic Adjustment Programme for Greece.* Brussels: European Commission, Directorate-General for Economic and Financial Affairs.

European Commission. (2012). *The Second Economic Adjustment Programme for Greece.* Brussels: European Commission, Directorate-General for Economic and Financial Affairs.

European Commission. (2015). *Memorandum of Understanding between the European Commission Acting on Behalf of the European Stability Mechanism and the Hellenic Republic and the Bank of Greece.*

Gialis, S., Tsampra, M., and Leontidou, L. (2017). 'Atypical Employment in Crisis-Hit Greek Regions: Local Production Structures, Flexibilization and Labour Market Re/Deregulation'. *Economic and Industrial Democracy*, 38(4): 656–676.

Gourinchas, P.-O., Philippon, T., and Vayanos, D. (2016). *The Analytics of the Greek Crisis.* London: Hellenic Observatory, LSE.

Grimshaw, D. and Koukiadaki, A. (2016). *Evaluating the Effects of the Structural Labour Market Reforms on Collective Bargaining in Greece.* Geneva: ILO.

Halikiopoulou, D., Nanou, K., and Vasilopoulou, S. (2016). *Changing the Policy Agenda? The Impact of the Golden Dawn on Greek Party Politics.* London: Hellenic Observatory, LSE.

Hamann, K., Johnston, A., and Kelly, J. (2013). 'Unions against Governments Explaining General Strikes in Western Europe, 1980–2006'. *Comparative Political Studies*, 46(9): 1030–1057.

Heyes, J. and Lewis, P. (2014). 'Employment Protection under Fire: Labour Market Deregulation and Employment in the European Union'. *Economic and Industrial Democracy*, 35(4): 587–607.

Heyes, J., Lewis, P., and Clark, I. (2012). 'Varieties of Capitalism, Neoliberalism and the Economic Crisis of 2008–?' *Industrial Relations Journal*, 43(3): 222–241.

Hyman, R. (2015). 'Austeritarianism in Europe: What Options for Resistance?' In: *Institute for New Economic Thinking Conference, 'Liberté, egalité, fragilité'*, 2015, Paris.

ILO. (2016). *Diagnostic Report on Undeclared Work in Greece.* Geneva: ILO.

Ioakeimoglou, I. (2018). *Labour Cost and Profit Margins during the Memoranda Years (Κόστος Εργασίας και Περιθώρια Κέρδους στα Χρόνια των Μνημονίων).* Athens: Labour Institute, GSEE – Observatory of Economic and Social Developments.

Ioannou, C. and Papadimitriou, K. (2013). *Collective Bargaining in Greece during 2011–2012: Trends, Changes and Prospects (In Greek).* Athens: OMED.

Ioannou, G. and Sonan, S. (2017). 'Trade Unions and Politics in Cyprus: A Historical Comparative Analysis across the Dividing Line'. *Mediterranean Politics*, 22(4): 484–503.

Kornelakis, A. and Voskeritsian, H. (2014). 'The Transformation of Employment Regulation in Greece: Towards a Dysfunctional Liberal Market Economy?' *Relations Industrielles/Industrial Relations*, 69(2): 344–365.

Koukiadaki, A. and Kokkinou, C. (2016). 'The Greek System of Collective Bargaining in (The) Crisis'. In: A. Koukiadaki, I. Tavora and M. M. Lucio (eds.). *Joint*

Regulation and Labour Market Policy in Europe during the Crisis. Brussels: ETUI, pp. 135–203.

Koukiadaki, A. and Kretsos, L. (2012). 'Opening Pandora's Box: The Sovereign Debt Crisis and Labour Market Regulation in Greece'. *Industrial Law Journal*, 41(3): 276–304.

Kouzis, Y. (2010). 'The Neoliberal Restructuring of Labour and the Crisis Alibi'. In: K. Vergopoulos (ed.). *The Map of the Crisis, the End of the Illusion.* Athens: Topos, pp. 82–98.

Kretsos, L. (2011). 'Union Responses to the Rise of Precarious Youth Employment in Greece'. *Industrial Relations Journal*, 42(5): 453–472.

Labrianidis, L. (2014). 'Investing in Leaving: The Greek Case of International Migration of Professionals'. *Mobilities*, 9(2): 314–335.

Labrianidis, L. and Vogiatzis, N. (2013). 'The Mutually Reinforcing Relation between International Migration of Highly Educated Labour Force and Economic Crisis: The Case of Greece'. *Southeast European and Black Sea Studies*, 13(4): 525–551.

Laliotis, I., Daouli, J., Demoussis, M., and Giannakopoulos, N. (2014). 'Firm-Level Contracting and Wages in Greek Manufacturing'. In: *Crises, Institutions and Labour Market Performance: Comparing Evidence and Policies.* Italy: University of Perugia.

Lindvall, J. (2013). 'Union Density and Political Strikes'. *World Politics*, 65(3): 539–569.

Simiti, M. (2014). *Rage and Protest: The Case of the Greek Indignant Movement.* London: Hellenic Observatory, LSE.

Soulsby, A., Hollinshead, G., and Steger, T. (2017). 'Crisis and Change in Industrial Relations in Central and Eastern Europe'. *European Journal of Industrial Relations*, 23(1): 5–15.

Theodoropoulou, S. (2016). 'Severe Pain, Very Little Gain: Internal Devaluation and Rising Unemployment in Greece'. In: M. Myant, S. Theodoropoulou, and A. Piasna (eds.). *Unemployment, Internal Devaluation and Labour Market Deregulation in Europe.* Brussels: ETUI, pp. 25–57.

Traxler, F. (1995). 'Farewell to Labour Market Associations: Organised versus Disorganised Decentralisation as a Map for Industrial Relations'. In: C. Crouch and F. Traxler (eds.). *Organised Industrial Relations in Europe: What Future?* Aldershot: Ashgate, pp. 3–19.

Tsoulfidis, L. and Zouboulakis, M. (2016). *Greek Sovereign Defaults in Retrospect and Prospect.* Munich: Munich Personal RePEc Archive. https://mpra.ub.uni-muenchen.de/71588/1/MPRA_paper_71588.pdf.

Vandaele, K. (2016). 'Interpreting Strike Activity in Western Europe in the past 20 Years: The Labour Repertoire under Pressure'. *Transfer: European Review of Labour and Research*, 22(3): 277–294.

Vasilopoulou, S. and Halikiopoulou, D. (2013). 'In the Shadow of Grexit: The Greek Election of 17 June 2012'. *South European Society and Politics*, 18(4): 523–542.

Voskeritsian, H., Veliziotis, M., Kapotas, P., and Kornelakis, A. (2017). *Between a Rock and a Hard Place: Social Partners and Reforms in the Wage Setting System in Greece under Austerity.* London: Hellenic Observatory, LSE.

1 Power, institutional change and the transformation of Greek employment relations

Horen Voskeritsian and Andreas Kornelakis

1 Introduction

The institutions governing the Greek labour market have undoubtedly gone through a period of sustained and comprehensive change in the course of the Greek crisis. Although institutional change in the pre-crisis era followed the pattern of incremental erosion and path-dependence, the period of the crisis has been marked by a significant shift in this pattern. The changes that were engineered in the institutional framework of employment relations were abrupt, severely contested by labour market actors, and unilaterally imposed by the state, which in turn was compelled to abide by the conditions of the bailout agreements. The purpose of this chapter is to examine the changes in the employment relations institutions against the backdrop of literature and theories on institutional change and emphasise the new power dynamics unleashed by these changes.

The literature on institutional change has focused primarily on the way institutions are transformed and on the reasons behind such transformations (Hall and Thelen 2009; Streeck and Thelen 2005; Thelen 2009). Yet, the question of how institutional change impacts the actual behaviour of actors is still underdeveloped. It is generally assumed that the changing institutional structure will trigger some feedback responses from the actors, who will adjust their strategies and behaviour to the new environment. Path dependency is promoted as the main explanation for the observed changes: prior institutional experiences, and the paths that these have carved into the social nexus, largely determine the direction and path of change. However, sometimes, the inductive nature of this approach cannot be reconciled with some empirical observations. For instance, the transformation of German industrial relations in the early 1990s diverged from the path that had been followed up until then (Doellgast and Greer 2007; Hassel 1999).

Moreover, institutional change may generate a variety of responses, some of which may not have been anticipated by the change instigators themselves. This depends on the type of intervention said change introduces in the institutional framework. Thus, some institutional changes may be of a compulsory nature and have universal applicability, whereas others may widen the range of options available and leave the final choice of their implementation to the discretion of the actors. In this latter case, the take-up of the changes by individual actors depends on the actors' needs and a recalculation of their expected benefits. For example, a change in the redundancy regulations (e.g. the procedure that needs to be followed or the level of severance payment) has immediate and direct effects on a firm's redundancy strategy. In other words, a company cannot choose not to follow these regulations, as they replace previous regulations and there are no other options. On the other hand, the flexibilisation of the labour market through the broadening of the range of atypical forms of employment does not mean that firms will necessarily move towards hiring more employees on atypical contracts. Instead, this change will widen the range of options, but the take-up will vary from firm to firm. Whether employment will become more flexible or not, therefore, depends not only on the institutional framework but on other factors as well.

The different ways in which institutional change is perceived and interpreted by societal actors is, therefore, an open question. Institutional change may, in theory at least, generate a variety of actors' responses. The main argument of this chapter is that the actors' responses to institutional changes will be mediated through the power dynamics in a specific employment relations system. In other words, the two main employment relations' actors (capital and labour in this case) renegotiate the transition from one institutional arrangement to another as a function of their relative power in the employment relationship.

Although we do not view capital and labour as monolithic actors, we follow Korpi (2006) in assuming that the class-related interests of the two actors are more important analytically than the intersectional conflicts. Thus, although different interests may exist in between and within different employers and employees, what matters is the general class-related interest. Analytically, we employ a *power resources model* (Korpi 2006; Wright 2015) to account for the strategic behaviour of the two actors in the labour market. We argue that the institutional changes impacted employment relations practices through a modification of the parties' interests and a reallocation of power from labour to capital. The reallocation concerned not only the possession of power resources, but also the quality of the actors' resources, the actors' ability to exercise this power, as well as the effectiveness of their power. Against the backdrop of these institutional changes and power dynamics, new strategic games in the workplace were triggered, which eventually led to new (albeit temporary) *equilibria* in the employment relations system.

Overall, the aim of this chapter is twofold: first, to develop a conceptual framework that integrates the power dynamics in the theories and analyses of institutional change, and second, to show how the economic crisis and the institutional changes that were initiated as a result of the adjustment programmes altered the power dynamics in Greek employment relations and highlighted the behaviour of the employment relations actors both at the sectoral and firm levels. To this end, the chapter is structured as follows. The second section introduces a novel conceptual framework of power relations that emphasises the inter-dependence between institutional change and power dynamics in the employment relations system. The third section considers institutional changes in the Greek employment relations' framework through the lens of the power-based framework. The fourth section is the conclusion.

2 Power, institutional change, and employment relations: towards a conceptual framework

Power has been central in the study of employment relations since the 1970s, usually discussed in relation to conflict. Hyman (1975) was among the first to elaborate on the importance of power struggles in understanding the industrial relations phenomena, in contradistinction with the then predominant systemic view of industrial relations (Clegg 1972; Flanders 1970). Recent research has focused on trade union power (Gumbrell McCormick and Hyman 2013), especially in the context of mobilisation (Kelly 1998) and the revitalisation of the trade union movement (Frege and Kelly 2003; Heery et al. 2003). In what follows, we expand our focus to appreciate the relationship between institutions and power in the employment relations arena. We adopt the classic definition of power as an actor's ability to pursue its interests by controlling or limiting other actors' actions (Dahl 1957; Korpi 2006; Reed 2013). Moreover, we define *power dynamics* as the inter-relationship between the allocation of power in the employment relations' arena and its possession by the relevant actors, the ability to exercise power, and the decision to deploy power to pursue one's interests. In this sense, power is a relational concept, as its successful deployment depends on how power will be received by the party towards which it is being deployed.

Furthermore, the relational character of power dynamics implies that power does not have an *a priori* transformational essence, in the sense that power deployment does not necessarily guarantee a change in another actor's behaviour. More specifically, the level of power an actor holds and the quality of its resources depend on the societal structure and the institutional framework in which power is being manifested. Hence, changes in the external environment and institutional framework governing the relations between labour market actors may alter any of the three components of power dynamics (i.e. the allocation of power, the ability to exercise power, and the decision to deploy power). However, a change in the components does not guarantee a change in behaviour, because a change in behaviour depends both on each actor's interests and on how each actor evaluates the power resources of the other actor. To better understand how this relational concept can be utilised, we now turn to define the components of power dynamics.

2.1 The allocation and possession of power in the context of employment relations

According to Mann (1986), the sources of an actor's power can be economic, political, cultural, or (in the case of states) military. *Economic power* stems from one's structural characteristics and the position one occupies in a certain social structure. In employment relations, the economic power of capital depends on its structural characteristics (e.g. the size of the company and its capital base) and its position in the economy and society (the industry in which it operates, its monopolistic position, or its importance in the functioning of the economy). Similarly, labour's economic power depends on its structural characteristics, such as organised versus unorganised labour, the size of organised labour (what Gumbrell McCormick and Hyman (2013) call "associational power"), its financial strength, the internal coherence of the labour movement, its scarcity (i.e. low supply of labour), or its skills (Kimeldorf 2013). Finally, labour's position in the labour process is important, as it may increase its "disruptive potential," which is the possibility of creating a disruption that will be considered important enough to merit counter-action by the other party – see Perrone et al. (1984).

Political power, on the other hand, depends on the networking structure one controls, or has access to, at the state level. There is an interdependency between the economic and political sphere, as people who occupy a certain class position have better access to the corridors of power than others (Savage 2015). Although this is true for individuals, it may not necessarily be true for collective organisations, such as trade unions or employers' associations. The economic power of a trade union or an employers' association may facilitate the "access to the state," but the type of state and the political orientation of the ruling party may guarantee privileged access to actors with political power.

The power each actor enjoys depends on the historical context in which this power is exercised. The socio-historical environment provides *social legitimacy* (Haugaard 2008) to the allocation and use of power, and hence, it provides meaning to it, whereas the legal environment provides *normative legitimacy* (or *legality* or *lawfulness*) to an actor's actions. Social and normative legitimacy define the limits one's power may reach. This depends on the dominant values in a specific society and on the consequent rights that one enjoys within this structure. Thus, acts of power that were considered legitimate in the past may have lost their legitimacy in the present, without this necessarily implying that the sources of power have changed as well. Legitimacy is important as it *empowers* the actor (i.e. provides them with a *power to* act in a specific way [Göhler 2013]). For example, collective bargaining could not take place, and would not be meaningful, if any of the parties did not enjoy the legitimacy prescribed to them by the socio-historical and legal context in which they operate. Similarly, the use of child labour or forced labour lacks legitimacy in the current historical period, but this was not the case in other eras. Legitimacy is what differentiates the use of power, as discussed here, from the use of violence – i.e. the exercise of physical power determined primarily by a party's natural power (Haugaard 2008).

2.2 The ability to exercise power

Possessing power is different from *the ability to exercise* power (Perrone et al. 1984). This ability depends on one's possession of power as well as on *the context* in which this power is exercised. In other words, the broader environment (social, economic, political and technological) and, specifically, the institutional framework create legal rules and conditions that may either constrain or enhance the ability to exercise power. For instance, workers may possess power depending on their structural position in the labour process or in the market (Wallace et al. 1989). However, as Griffin argues, "the disruptive potential of workers in 'central' industries may be thwarted, at least in the short run and during periods of economic slack, by the prior stockpiling of non-perishable goods" (cited in Perrone et al. 1984: 425). This is an example of labour not being able to successfully exercise its potential power due, first, to the power of capital to shape the production process in such a way as to undercut labour's power and, second, due to external circumstances (i.e. the economic slack) that define the context in which power is exercised. In practical terms, the ability to exercise power refers to an actor's opportunities to successfully mobilise its power sources to achieve an outcome. Successful mobilisation depends on an actor's organisational capacity (i.e. on its ability to successfully utilise and deploy the power sources – see Gumbrell McCormick and Hyman 2013; Kelly 1998) – and on the sphere (or spheres) in which power will be exercised. Wright (2015) identifies three such spheres: the *sphere of politics*, the *sphere of exchange*, and the *sphere of production*.

In the sphere of politics, capital and labour may try to influence the formation and implementation of policies through access to the corridors of power. As previously mentioned, the state tradition and the ideological orientation of the political party in government shape the historical evolution of national industrial relations systems (Crouch, 1993). Exercising power at this level changes the institutional restrictions on the function of the capitalist economy and the labour market more specifically. The sphere of exchange refers to the market in which capital and labour interact and collectively regulate the industrial relations system (through national, sectoral, or occupational collective bargaining or through their participation in social dialogue initiatives). Finally, the sphere of production refers to the firm level and it is the only sphere where capital may interact with individual and unorganised labour.

Overall, labour market actors pursue their interests and exercise their power across all three spheres, which operate at different levels and provide access to different sources of power. The choice of the sphere in which power will be exercised depends largely on the strategic choices of the actors and their perceived likelihood to achieve the desired outcomes. Hence, if an option exists, an actor will choose to operate in a sphere where it has or can accumulate more power or where it can inhibit the effectiveness of its opponent's power. This decision is shaped by the institutional framework that defines the actors that may participate in a specific sphere and the extent of this participation. For example, a firm may wish to determine wages in the sphere of production, but this may not be possible due to institutional constraints (e.g. the structure of collective bargaining may not allow firm-level wage determination). If, however, such an option exists, a firm may decide to engage into the sphere of production instead of the sphere of exchange because it may enjoy greater power in the former. Moreover, the firm's interlocutor in the sphere of production may be less powerful than the one in the sphere of exchange, hence making the choice of the former sphere more attractive.

2.3 The decision to deploy power

Possessing power, retaining the ability to exercise power, and eventually deciding to deploy power are three different things. Deploying one's power resources depends on one's evaluation of the possibility of satisfying one's interests by using their power (what Leap and Grigsby 1986: 205 refer to as potential *versus* enacted power). The value one attributes to this possibility depends on several factors, one of which is the legal, social, economic, and political environment one operates in. Changes in this environment may alter an actor's interests and priorities, thus leading to a decision to act in order to satisfy the new set of interests. Moreover, changes in the environment may also alter the power sources of an actor, thus creating new expectations regarding the achievement of one's interests (Korpi 1974a). Another factor is an actor's perception about the other party's power potential and the possibility of exercising said potential to undermine the first actor's interests. As Wright (2015: 209) argues, "the intensity of class struggle ... is not simply a function of the relative balance of power of different classes, but also of the intensity of the threat posed to dominant interests by subordinate class power." Finally, the deployment of power depends on an evaluation of the *costs and benefits* of this action and *the probability of satisfying* one's interests (Korpi 1974b: 104).

In the case of employment relations, a change in the external environment – for example, an economic crisis, a change in government, or the introduction of new technology – may provide incentives to exercise power with a view to create a situation where an actor's interests will continue to be satisfied. A firm, for example, may decide to invest in new technology to replace labour and hence reduce labour costs and gain more control over the production process. However, having an incentive to act does not necessarily entail that one will act. Whether action will occur depends on how one evaluates the possible resistance and the potential consequences stemming from the deployment of power. For instance, a firm will need to consider how organised labour will react in an attempt to alter the terms and conditions of employment, and it will need to evaluate whether sacrificing long-term cooperation with a trade union to achieve short-term gains is really worth the price.

The emerging question in this case concerns the way an actor will behave towards its interlocutor. When the decision to deploy power has been reached, a *strategic game* is being initiated. Depending on the institutional context, different strategies may be available for an actor to follow. These range from complete domination to complete accommodation, and whether one strategy will be chosen over another depends on the relative power of the two actors (Ibsen 2015; Wright 2015) as well as on the legitimacy a specific strategy enjoys within the given socio-historical context.

It is inferred from the preceding analysis that if an actor has the opportunity to choose the sphere in which the game will be played, then the sphere with the weakest opponents will be selected. Since labour's power is very much dependent on its collective organisation, the sphere of production – where organised labour may be weak or non-existent – can be considered the sphere of choice for capital to pursue its interests. In other words, if capital has the option to deploy its power in the sphere of production rather than in the sphere of exchange, then we can expect that it will push for a strategic game to be initiated in the former. The opposite is true for labour, which will aim to bring the game up to a sphere where organised labour is strong (such as the industry level – i.e. the sphere of exchange). Finally, these strategic games are not static but dynamic, since power relations may change during the game.

In sum, introducing power-based explanations to examine trajectories and paths of institutional change in contemporary capitalism (see also Ibsen 2015) can go a long way towards improving our understanding of the causes, transmission mechanisms, and consequences of institutional changes on employment relations' practices and outcomes. To this end, the next section will examine the case of Greece and the transformation of its employment relations institutional framework during the Greek crisis. It will apply the preceding conceptual framework as a heuristic device to shed light on the reallocation of power between labour and capital and the broader implications for the Greek economy and society.

3 The transformation of power dynamics and institutional change in the Greek employment relations system during the crisis

The signing of the Memorandum of Understanding (MoU) between the Greek government and the Troika in May 2010 initiated a series of changes in the industrial relations institutions that radically altered the morphology of the labour market and the behaviour of the industrial relations actors (Kornelakis and Voskeritsian 2014; Koukiadaki and Kokkinou 2016; Koukiadaki and

Kretsos 2012; Voskeritsian et al. 2017). As stipulated in the first loan agreement as well as in the subsequent ones (in 2012 and 2015), the measures aimed to help companies survive the crisis, improve competitiveness, and create an environment that would attract foreign investments (European Commission 2010, 2012, 2015). To achieve that, the Memoranda focused on two major axes: first, on the flexibilisation of the labour market, and second, on the reduction of labour costs through a process of internal devaluation.

The changes were introduced in *three distinct waves*, from 2010 to 2012, aiming to gradually adjust the labour market environment to the demands of the loan agreements. The *first wave*, introduced in a series of legislative reforms in 2010 and 2012, aimed at enhancing flexibility in the labour market by deregulating employment protection legislation (EPL) and providing incentives for the use of atypical forms of employment. Laws 3846/ 2010 and 4093/2012 introduced elements of the "Flexicurity" model in Greece: overtime pay rates were significantly reduced, and sub-minimum wages for apprentices and young employees were established (apprentices aged 15–18 could be hired at rates of 30% of the NMW, while workers aged 18–25 could be hired at rates of 84% of the NMW). At the same time, part time employment, temporary contracts, and the use of agency workers became cheaper and easier for employers to implement. Finally, the working week was extended from five to six days, and working time could be increased without an increase in compensation for retail employees.

To further assist the employers in implementing these changes, the law provided the right to negotiate changes in working time to a body that, up until then, remained dormant in the legislative framework – the so-called "Association of Persons". Although this body existed in law since 1982 (Law 1264/1982), it had never emerged in practice. Workplace representation remained the prerogative of the trade unions or (from 1988 onwards) the works councils. However, its resurrection in the practice of industrial relations during these years provided employers with an overriding mechanism that allowed them to introduce policies that would otherwise be difficult to negotiate with trade unions. Finally, changes in the employment protection legislation (EPL) rendered dismissals easier and cheaper dismissals for the employers, whilst the collective redundancies framework was simplified and the upper limits for collective dismissals increased.

Although these measures created the conditions for the flexibilisation of the labour process and labour cost reductions, wages could not be downwardly adjusted easily. To save on labour costs, the employer had to either alter the composition of the workforce (e.g. hiring young workers or apprentices instead of older employees) or modify the structure of the labour process (e.g. introduce atypical forms of employment or substitute full-time employees with precarious workers). The question of internal devaluation, therefore, remained open.

The main reason for this was that wages in Greece were linked to sectoral and occupational collective agreements. According to Law 1876/1990, a strict hierarchy of collective agreements ruled wage determination in Greece. At the top of this hierarchy, the National General Collective Agreement (signed by the tertiary social partners) set the level of the national minimum wage. Below the National Agreement were the sectoral agreements – signed by sectoral trade unions and the respective employers' associations – and the occupational agreements (see Ioannou, in this volume, for a detailed discussion on the role of the sectoral and occupational collective agreements in Greece's wage structure).

The sectoral agreements also determined wages in most of the firms through the *erga omnes* principle. According to this principle, an agreement signed by employers representing 50% of the sector's workforce could also be implemented in the rest of the sector (i.e. it could be extended across the sector) irrespective of whether other employers had signed it or not. The extension of the collective agreement took place through a Ministerial Decree, and although – at least in theory – the Minister of Labour should confirm whether the above threshold had indeed been reached, in practice, most of the requests for the extension of an agreement submitted to the Ministry of Labour were granted.

The third level of bargaining results in firm-level agreements, signed by a firm's trade union and the management. Usually, firm-level collective agreements took the sectoral collective agreement as a benchmark and offered better terms and conditions of employment. However, firm-level agreements were the exception rather than the rule in the structure of the Greek collective bargaining system for reasons that had to do both with the right to form a trade union and the structure of Greek capitalism. The establishment of a trade union requires at least 20 signatories, and, at that time, a minimum of 50 employees was necessary for a trade union to be able to participate in firm-level collective bargaining. Greece being an economy dominated by small and very small enterprises (about 97% of Greek businesses employ fewer than 20 employees), these conditions practically meant that only 3% of Greek companies had the potential to have a firm-level trade union, and even less to have an established right for collective bargaining. Therefore, firm-level collective agreements were restricted to a handful of big firms, mainly in traditional manufacturing industries and the service sectors (e.g. banking; see Kornelakis 2014).

The above complex collective bargaining structure sometimes meant that an employee could be covered by more than one collective agreement. For instance, an accountant working in a bank could be covered by three different collective agreements: the sectoral agreement for the banking sector, the occupational agreement for the accountants, and the collective agreement signed by the bank's trade union. In such cases, the favourability principle applied, according to which the best agreement for the worker was implemented. Usually, this was the sectoral agreement or the firm-level agreement in the workplaces where it existed. If a firm-level agreement contained terms and conditions of employment that were worse than the sectoral one, then the latter applied.

The above system functioned well in periods of economic growth, as it ensured common standards across a sector and the avoidance of unfair competition and social dumping. However, when the crisis erupted, an important issue came to the fore. Companies that wanted to downwardly adjust wages to reflect the new market conditions found it difficult to do so, as wages were linked to sectoral agreements. The *second wave* of changes, therefore, aimed at disconnecting wage determination from sectoral and occupational bargaining, hence promoting the logic of internal devaluation. The underlying assumption was that sectoral wages are "sticky" and do not reflect productivity, and the rationale behind the policies was to provide companies with enough flexibility to determine the level of wages at the firm level.[1]

To achieve this, a way had to be found to override the hold that sectoral agreements had on firm-level wages. In 2010, Law 3899/2010 initiated an attempt towards this end by introducing a new kind of collective agreement – the Special Operational Collective Agreement (SOCA) – which could be signed in a company that faced financial difficulties by a firm-level or a sectoral trade union. Contrary to the traditional firm-level collective agreements, the SOCA could derogate from the sectoral collective agreement's wage rates, thus agreeing on sub-minimum wages.

The introduction of the SOCA was an attempt by the PASOK socialist government to strike a balance between the increasing pressures it was facing from the trade unions and the demands of the Troika for the flexibilisation of collective bargaining. Thus, although some flexibility was introduced in the determination of wages, the Troika still pressed for further deregulation. The main reason for this was that the SOCA could not guarantee a fully fledged wage adjustment, as its successful implementation was dependent on three factors: first, the company had to prove that it was facing financial difficulties; second, in practice, the agreement could only be signed in companies that had a firm-level trade union because although the law allowed sectoral unions to engage in such bargaining, it was highly improbable that this would ever take place; and third, and perhaps most importantly for the Troika, the implementation of the agreement rested on its ratification by the Greek Labour Inspectorate. These provisions, therefore, introduced both a practical restriction in the number of companies that could legitimately sign such an agreement and an administrative restriction that could delay, or even cancel, the implementation of such an agreement. Under pressures from the Troika, in 2011, Law 4024/2011 introduced changes that would eventually result in the full deregulation of the collective bargaining system and radically change the structure of Greek industrial relations.

First, Law 4024/2011 allowed firm-level bargaining to take place in all firms, even those employing fewer than 50 employees, as previously stipulated. However, the question of who would negotiate on behalf of the workers in companies with fewer than 20 employees (the legal minimum required to set up a firm-level trade union) was still unanswered. To address this gap, the law allowed the Association of Persons to assume this role. As previously mentioned, the Association of Persons was a dormant body that existed in law but never acquired any real substance in practice. Moreover, it did not enjoy any of the standard trade union rights, such as the right to strike or the protection of its executive members from dismissal. Nevertheless, the new law provided the opportunity to Associations of Persons representing three-fifths of a company's employees to negotiate a firm-level collective agreement with the management.

Allowing the extension of collective bargaining to a larger percentage of firms was not enough, however, to address the institutional hold that sectoral agreements had in wage determination. To this end, a *second change* was the suspension of the favourability principle, thus allowing firm-level agreements to derogate from the sectoral agreement, even if the former included worse terms and conditions than the latter. The *third change* was the freezing of the *erga omnes* principle, which ensured that wage determination at the firm level would be completely dissociated from any sectoral or occupational agreements. Under the new provisions, a sectoral agreement would apply only to the signatory parties, thus allowing companies that were not members of an employers' association to negotiate their own agreements. The combination of these three changes provided companies with the ability to derogate from sectoral collective bargaining and sign firm-level agreements with sub-minimum wages, thus ensuring that the process of internal devaluation would be properly implemented.

The *third wave* of changes guaranteed wage restriction for the duration of the loan agreement: in 2012, the statutory regulation of the NMW was introduced, together with a steep decrease in its level (by 32% for young employees [16–25 years old] and by 22% for the rest of the population) (Act 4046/2012 and Cabinet Decision 6/2012), leading to a "remaking of the wage-setting system" in Greece (Karamessini and Grimshaw 2017). At the same time, a provision allowed firms to unilaterally reduce the level of wages to the NMW level if they were not covered by a collective agreement.

Power dynamics in the Greek industrial relations system changed radically and decisively during this period. The allocation of power in the industrial relations arena was redistributed to capital's benefit, leaving trade unions incapable of reacting and unorganised labour left to fend for itself. The rising unemployment, the flexibilisation of the labour market, the dissociation of wage determination from sectoral bargaining, the introduction of the Associations of Persons as a legitimate interlocutor in firm-level bargaining, and the ability of employers to unilaterally decide the level of wages provided capital with the necessary armoury to control the labour process to their benefit.

At the same time, organised labour was dealt a decisive blow, as the traditional role of sectoral unions as guarantors of wage determination across the sector was undermined, and trade unions failed to support workers where they needed them more: at the firm level. This was not only a result of the opportunities the new framework provided to the employers, but also a consequence of the trade unions' organising inertia. Greece's unionisation rate fluctuated between 38% in the early 1980s to 25% in the early 2010, following the general downward trend observed across the EU (Visser 2013). Most of this percentage, however, represented public sector unionisation, while the private sector remained largely non-unionised. The main reason for this low unionisation rate rested on the fact that the Greek trade unions were not as dependent on membership levels for their institutional survival as their counterparts in Europe. This had to do both with the structure of the system, which provided institutional power to unions at the sectoral levels through the prevalence of the sectoral collective agreement in the determination of wages as well as the fact that Greek trade unions had an organic relationship with the state and the ruling political parties (Kouzis 2007; Zambarloukou 2006).

Trade unions were dependent for many years on financial contributions from an organisation called *Ergatiki Estia*, a public body that managed employees' contributions towards the support of the working population. These contributions were automatically paid to the state via one's salary, and they financed various programmes of social support. However, *Ergatiki Estia* was also used to fund trade unions' activities, resulting in a structural and paternalistic dependence between trade unions and the state (Koukoules 1994).

Moreover, trade unions had strong links to the various political parties through the various fractions that operated within the trade union movement (Kouzis 2007; Lavdas 2005). This interrelationship between unions and parties functioned in two opposite ways: on the one hand, the trade unions might have been guaranteed access to the corridors of power, thus influencing industrial relations outcomes via the sphere of politics, but in many cases, the fractions could also be acting antagonistically to the trade union itself, leading to internal conflicts and democratic deficits.

Since the trade unions could utilise a system that provided them with institutional power, access to the sphere of politics, as well as to the sphere of exchange and guaranteed their financial viability, there was little incentive to engage with organising the shop floor. Although firm-level unions could only exist in establishments of more than 20 employees, in theory, local sectoral and occupational unions could engage in organising workers into their ranks in their respective geographical regions. This rarely occurred, however. A partial exception to this trend was the rise, from the early 2000s onwards, of some small radical trade unions in urban centres, representing workers in precarious employment, such as couriers and cleaners (Kretsos and Vogiatzoglou 2015). Although their presence and actions during the crisis years were substantial, and some of them managed to bring about positive changes for their members, they did not manage to develop a momentum that could cut across the labour market. Characterised by a radical nature and a geographical focus that made it difficult to expand outside their small urban circle, they were usually in conflict with the established trade unions and eventually remained on the fringes of the trade union movement.

In this economic and institutional context, capital's ability to exercise its newly accumulated power was substantially improved. Labour was unable to successfully resist the managerial initiative due to high unemployment levels and the lack of effective representation at the firm level. The sphere of production acquired an importance in the bargaining structure that was hitherto reserved for a handful of central industries (such as shipbuilding, steel, the banking sector, etc.). At the same time, the sphere of exchange lost much of its former glory, and the sphere of politics became almost obsolete and inaccessible – apart for some big companies that could manipulate developments behind the scenes. Indeed, a major characteristic of this period was that any attempt to initiate or engage in tripartite social dialogue failed. The hearty resistance through general strikes (Hamann et al. 2013) that trade unions engaged in every time a new measure was voted in the Greek parliament, although spectacular and grandiose, had little effect either on the Parliamentary endorsement of the policy or on its implementation in practice.

Faced with these conditions, the decision of capital to exercise its power to control the labour process and reduce labour costs was almost unavoidable. Employers quickly opted to bring the bargaining game down to the sphere of production and interact with weak labour. This was supported by the emergence of a crisis discourse that helped legitimise the managerial offensive (Kouzis 2010). Most employers were not particularly concerned with resistance, as the high availability of labour ensured that any such attempt could be eradicated by the threat of dismissals. Furthermore, the use of the Association of Persons in the first year of its implementation not only ensured a reduction in wages by allowing management to manipulate the outcomes of collective bargaining as they saw fit (see the chapter by Giannakopoulos and Laliotis in this volume for a detailed analysis), but also introduced an element of pseudo-representation and pseudo-legitimacy into its actions. In the firms where firm-level agreements were not signed, employers used their discretion to unilaterally reduce wages to the level of the national minimum wage.

4 Conclusions

At the beginning of this chapter, we suggested that the different ways in which institutional change is perceived and interpreted by social actors is an open question and, therefore, the main task that this chapter set out to undertake was twofold. The first task was to develop a conceptual framework that integrates the power dynamics in the theories and analyses of institutional change. The second task was to show how the economic crisis and the institutional changes that were initiated as a result of the adjustment programmes in the Greek labour market altered the power dynamics in the system and highlighted the behaviour of the employment relations actors both at the sectoral and firm levels.

The main argument of this chapter is that actors' responses to institutional changes will be mediated through the power dynamics in a specific employment relations system. In other words, the two main employment relations' actors (capital and labour) renegotiate the transition from one institutional arrangement to another as a function of their relative power in the employment relationship. To this end, we loosely employed a *power resources model* (Korpi 2006; Wright 2015) to account for the strategic behaviour of the two societal actors (capital and labour) in the labour market. We argued that the institutional changes altered day-to-day employment relations' practices through a redistribution and reallocation of power from labour to capital. Analytically, we distinguished between different components of power, and thus, the reallocation concerned not only the possession of power resources, but also the actors' ability to exercise this power as well as their decisions to deploy this power. Thus, the conceptual framework expected that institutional changes would trigger new strategic games in the workplace, which would eventually lead to new equilibria in the three main spheres of politics, market exchange, and production.

Indeed, the review of changes in the institutional framework of the labour market pinned down how these power dynamics played out during the Greek crisis. The Greek employment relations system changed radically and decisively during this period. The allocation of power in the employment relations' arena was recalibrated in favour of capital, leaving the trade unions incapable of reacting and unorganised labour weak and unprotected. On the one hand, contextual changes in the economic environment, such as the rising unemployment, the flexibilisation of the labour market, and the deep recession provided a fertile ground for employers to abuse their power at the workplace. On the other hand, institutional changes, such as the dissociation of wage determination from sectoral bargaining, the introduction of weak representative bodies such as the Associations of Persons, and the ability of employers to unilaterally decide the level of wages, provided capital with a wider range of options to modify working practices and intensify the labour process. At the same time, organised labour suffered a decisive blow, as the traditional role of sectoral unions as guarantors of wage determination across the collective bargaining system was undermined. The trade unions failed to support workers where they needed such support most: at the shop floor level. Admittedly, this was not only a result of the options and opportunities that the new institutional framework provided to employers, but also a consequence of the trade unions' organising inertia.

In conclusion, the chapter argued in favour of introducing power-based explanations to examine trajectories and paths of institutional change in contemporary capitalism (see also, Ibsen 2015). Synthesising insights from the power resources models (Korpi 2006; Wright 2015) to advance power-based explanations instils more dynamism in extant theories of institutional change (Hall and Thelen 2009; Streeck and Thelen 2005; Thelen 2009). Even more, power-based explanations are more likely to shed light on and improve our understanding of the causes, transmission mechanisms, and consequences of institutional changes on employment relations' practices and outcomes. The case of Greece was indicative of how institutional changes are mediated by the power dynamics, reallocating power from one actor to another and thereby triggering new strategic games and equilibria in different spheres of the labour market.

Note

1 Interestingly, this assumption was not adequately supported by empirical evidence at the time. Ioannou in Chapter Two attempts a first approach to this question by comparing the tradable and non-tradable sectors; however, more research is required on this topic.

References

Clegg, H. A. (1972). *The System of Industrial Relations in Great Britain*. Totowa, NJ: Rowman & Littlefield.

Crouch, C. (1993). *Industrial Relations and European State Traditions*. Oxford, New York: Clarendon Press.

Dahl, R. (1957). 'The Concept of Power'. *Behavioral Science*, 2(3): 201–215.

Doellgast, V. and Greer, I. (2007). 'Vertical Disintegration and the Disorganization of German Industrial Relations'. *British Journal of Industrial Relations*, 45(1): 55–76.

European Commission (2010). *The Economic Adjustment Programme for Greece*. Brussels: European Commission, Directorate-General for Economic and Financial Affairs.

European Commission. (2012). *The Second Economic Adjustment Programme for Greece*. Brussels: European Commission, Directorate-General for Economic and Financial Affairs.

European Commission (2015). *Memorandum of Understanding between the European Commission Acting on Behalf of the European Stability Mechanism and the Hellenic Republic and the Bank of Greece*. https://ec.europa.eu/info/sites/info/files/01_mou_20150811_en1.pdf.

Flanders, A. (1970). *Management and Unions: The Theory and Reform of Industrial Relations*. London: Faber and Faber.

Frege, C. M. and Kelly, J. (2003). 'Union Revitalization Strategies in Comparative Perspective'. *European Journal of Industrial Relations*, 9(1): 7–24.

Göhler, G. (2013). '"Power to" and "Power over"'. In: S. R. Clegg and M. Haugaard (eds.). *The Sage Handbook of Power*. London: Sage, pp. 27–39.

Gumbrell McCormick, R. and Hyman, R. (2013). *Trade Unions in Western Europe: Hard Times, Hard Choices*. Oxford: Oxford University Press.

Hall, P. A. and Thelen, K. (2009). 'Institutional Change in Varieties of Capitalism'. *Socio-Economic Review*, 7(1): 7–34.

Hamann, K., Johnston, A. and Kelly, J. (2013). 'Unions Against Governments Explaining General Strikes in Western Europe, 1980–2006'. *Comparative Political Studies*, 46(9): 1030–1057.

Hassel, A. (1999). 'The Erosion of the German System of Industrial Relations'. *British Journal of Industrial Relations*, 37(3): 483–505.

Haugaard, M. (2008). 'Power and Habitus'. *Journal of Power*, 1(2): 189–206.

Heery, E., Kelly, J. and Waddington, J. (2003). 'Union Revitalization in Britain'. *European Journal of Industrial Relations*, 9(1): 79–97.

Hyman, R. (1975). *Industrial Relations: A Marxist Introduction*. London: Macmillan.

Ibsen, C. L. (2015). 'Three Approaches to Coordinated Bargaining: A Case for Power-based Explanations'. *European Journal of Industrial Relations*, 21(1): 39–56.

Karamessini, M. and Grimshaw, D. (2017). 'Minimum Wages and the Remaking of the Wage-Setting Systems in Greece and the UK'. In: D. Grimshaw, C. Fagan, G. Hebson and I. Tavora (eds.). *Making Work More Equal: A New Labour Market Segmentation Approach*. Oxford: Oxford University Press, pp. 330–355.

Kelly, J. (1998). *Rethinking Industrial Relations: Mobilization, Collectivism and Long Waves*. London: Routledge.

Kimeldorf, H. (2013). 'Worker Replacement Costs and Unionization Origins of the U.S. Labor Movement'. *American Sociological Review*, 78(6): 1033–1062.

Kornelakis, A. (2014). 'Liberalization, Flexibility and Industrial Relations Institutions: Evidence from Italian and Greek Banking'. *Work, Employment and Society*, 28(1): 40–57.

Kornelakis, A. and Voskeritsian, H. (2014). 'The Transformation of Employment Regulation in Greece: Towards a Dysfunctional Liberal Market Economy?' *Relations Industrielles/Industrial Relations*, 69(2): 344–365.

Korpi, W. (1974a). 'Conflict, Power and Relative Deprivation'. *The American Political Science Review*, 68(4): 1569–1578.

Korpi, W. (1974b). 'Conflict and the Balance of Power'. *Acta Sociologica*, 17(2): 99–114.

Korpi, W. (2006). 'Power Resources and Employer-Centered Approaches in Explanations of Welfare States and Varieties of Capitalism: Protagonists, Consenters, and Antagonists'. *World Politics*, 58(2): 167–206.

Koukiadaki, A. and Kokkinou, C. (2016). 'The Greek System of Collective Bargaining in (the) Crisis'. In: A. Koukiadaki, I. Tavora and M. M. Lucio (eds.). *Joint Regulation and Labour Market Policy in Europe during the Crisis*. Brussels: ETUI, pp. 135–203.

Koukiadaki, A. and Kretsos, L. (2012). 'Opening Pandora's Box: The Sovereign Debt Crisis and Labour Market Regulation in Greece'. *Industrial Law Journal*, 41(3): 276–304.

Koukoules, Y. (1994). *Greek Trade Unions, Financial Independence and Dependence, 1938–1984*. Athens: Odysseas.

Kouzis, Y. (2007). *The Characteristics of the Greek Trade Union Movement*. Athens: Gutenberg.

Kouzis, Y. (2010). 'The Neoliberal Restructuring of Labour and the Crisis Alibi'. In: K. Vergopoulos (ed.). *The Map of the Crisis, the End of the Illusion*. Athens: Topos, pp. 82–98.

Kretsos, L. and Vogiatzoglou, M. (2015). 'Lost in the Ocean of Deregulation? The Greek Labour Movement in a Time of Crisis'. *Relations Industrielles/Industrial Relations*, 70(2): 218–239.

Lavdas, K. (2005). 'Interest Groups in Disjointed Corporatism: Social Dialogue in Greece and European "Competitive Corporatism"'. *West European Politics*, 28(2): 297–316.

Leap, T. L. and Grigsby, D. W. (1986). 'A Conceptualization of Collective Bargaining Power'. *ILR Review*, 39(2): 202–213.

Mann, M. (1986). *The Sources of Social Power*. Cambridge: Cambridge University Press.

Perrone, L., Wright, E. O. and Griffin, L. J. (1984). 'Positional Power, Strikes and Wages'. *American Sociological Review*, 49(3): 412–426.

Reed, I. A. (2013). 'Power Relational, Discursive, and Performative Dimensions'. *Sociological Theory*, 31(3): 193–218.

Savage, M. (2015). *Social Class in the 21st Century*. London: Pelican, An Imprint of Penguin Books.

Streeck, W. and Thelen, K. (2005). 'Introduction: Institutional Change in Advanced Political Economies'. In: W. Streeck and K. Thelen (eds.). *Beyond Continuity: Institutional Change in Advanced Political Economies*. Oxford: Oxford University Press, pp. 1–39.

Thelen, K. (2009). 'Institutional Change in Advanced Political Economies'. *British Journal of Industrial Relations*, 47(3): 471–498.

Visser, J. (2013). *Database on Institutional Characteristics of Trade Unions, Wage Setting, State Intervention and Social Pacts, 1960–2011 (ICTWSS)*.

Voskeritsian, H., Veliziotis, M., Kapotas, P. and Kornelakis, A. (2017). *Between a Rock and a Hard Place: Social Partners and Reforms in the Wage Setting System in Greece under Austerity*. London: Hellenic Observatory, LSE.

Wallace, M., Griffin, L. J. and Rubin, B. A. (1989). 'The Positional Power of American Labor, 1963–1977'. *American Sociological Review*, 54(2): 197–214.

Wright, E. O. (2015). *Understanding Class*. London: Verso.

Zambarloukou, S. (2006). 'Collective Bargaining and Social Pacts: Greece in Comparative Perspective'. *European Journal of Industrial Relations*, 12(2): 211–229.

2 Collective bargaining decentralisation and wage adjustment for internal devaluation

Christos A. Ioannou

1 Introduction

In December 2010, during the first stages of the economic adjustment in Greece, total employment amounted to 4.3 million, of which 2.7 million were in salaried and wage employment. For the one million employed in the public sector, collective agreements were frozen and annulled in March 2010, and in 2011, their wage-setting was removed from the jurisdiction of collective bargaining (Ioannou 2016: 299). Only the 1.7 million salary and wage earners employed in the private sector had the right to determine their pay through collective bargaining. This chapter explains how, after eight years of adjustment and reforms, the relationship between collective bargaining and wage determination has been subjected to radical changes affected by, and evolved under, the new regulatory framework for collective bargaining. Moreover, it explores the changing collective bargaining structure and its underpinning rationale as well as its impact on wage levels and relativities.

Three successive, ill designed, and ill implemented adjustment programmes (2010–2012, 2012–2014, 2015–2018) were aimed at reducing macroeconomic and fiscal imbalances and restoring competitiveness and fiscal sustainability in Greece. At their core rested the valid assumption that during Greece's first decade in the Eurozone, real wage growth consistently outpaced productivity gains, in part reflecting spillovers from excessive public wage increases. The resulting increase in unit labour costs eroded external competitiveness. Greece's real effective exchange rate appreciated by some 10–20%, depending on the deflator used, over 2000–2009. According to the Commission services' calculations, it was overvalued by 10 to 20% in 2009 (EC 2010: 3–5). Overvaluation implies the need for devaluation, which in conditions of common currency can only take the form of internal devaluation.

The first programme (2010–2012) did not include a conditionality about the private sector's wages, as the idea of imposing an across-the-board cut in private sector wages was not retained (EC 2010: 21). Instead, the programme provided for strengthening wage-setting mechanisms that would support adjustment through normal market forces and changes in the wage bargaining system and the social partners bargaining behaviour (Ioannou

2011b). Reforms in the product markets, the business environment, and public institutions were supposed to contribute to competitiveness improvements to compensate for excessive labour costs. The social partners were supposed to introduce wage moderation for a long period and allow opt-outs from sectoral agreements at the regional and the company level. However, this strategy did not work. None of these reforms were implemented, and public finance adjustment was attempted mainly by raising taxes even though fiscal imbalances had come mainly from the public expenditure side (Giannitsis and Zografakis 2015: 16; Ioannou 2016: 50–53), which in turn fed into higher inflation, further deterioration of competitiveness, and soaring unemployment.

Not surprisingly, the second adjustment programme (2012–2014) moved towards the initially dropped idea of imposing an across-the-board cut in private sector wages to implement internal devaluation (EC 2012; Ioannou 2012a, IMF, 2012). This implied radical change in the regulatory framework for collective bargaining, which had an impact on the collective bargaining structure and accelerated the process of corrections and adjustments on wage levels and wage relativities.

The role of labour law and associated reforms in the formation of country structures of collective bargaining has been commonly accepted in literature (e.g. Sciarra 2006). It has been also recognised long ago (Clegg 1976; Cordova 1987; Guigni 1967; Windmuller et al. 1987) that the bargaining behaviour of trade unions and employers' associations forge the links between the existing legislation and the wage determination procedures and thus shape the collective bargaining structures. Visser (2016: 3) distinguishes between regulatory and non-regulatory changes, acknowledging that change can either result from a modification of the rules or government policies under which collective bargaining operates, or it can occur through behavioural changes within unions, firms, and employers' associations and the interactions between them. This chapter examines the changing bargaining structure and the reshaped relationship between collective bargaining and wage determination in Greece as the outcome of the changing bargaining behaviour of employers and their associations and workers and their trade unions under the new regulatory framework. Section 2 outlines the changes in collective bargaining structures and processes since 2012. Section 3 presents the processes of wage internal devaluation and their outcomes. The final section concludes and sets the findings in perspective.

2 The collapse of the collective bargaining structure and bargaining decentralisation

Collective bargaining institutions and processes in Greece saw a major reform in 1990 with Law 1876/1990. Company and sectoral/industry collective agreements were included in the legal framework for the first time, next to the pre-existing and dominant occupational collective agreements. The

National General Collective Agreement (EGSSE) setting minimum wage standards at the national level covering all employees remained focal. State controlled compulsory arbitration, which dominated the national collective bargaining system since 1955, was substituted by a new system of mediation and quasi compulsory arbitration. The EGSSE set minimum wage standards at the national level, covering the unskilled workers and operating as the guideline for topup wage increases in the industry and occupational and company collective agreements. There was a hierarchy of bargaining levels through the "favourability principle": lower levels of bargaining could only improve the standards set at a higher bargaining level. Collective agreements could be extended by the Ministry of Labour if an agreement already covered 50% of the employees in the respective bargaining unit (sector or occupation). If bargaining failed, one side of the social partners had the right to call on the Organisation for Mediation and Arbitration (OMED) for mediation and then for compulsory arbitration. This system of Law 1876/1990 operated for two decades (1992–2012).

Table 2.1 provides an overview of the bargaining structure in Greece. It includes the number of collective agreements by type (sectoral, occupational, company) and by source of regulation (collective agreements or arbitration awards) for the period 1992–2016. It reflects the collective agreements and the arbitration awards as registered with the Ministry of Labour based on the date of their registration, not on the date they were signed or the period they cover. It represents the flow of collective agreements and only indicates the stock of collective agreements in force. The table also distinguishes sub-periods defined by reforms to the regulatory framework for collective bargaining.

The collective bargaining structure in Greece in 1992–2012 consisted of 100 collective agreements on average, classified as sectoral/industry agreements, 90 classified as occupation collective agreements, and around 150 company collective agreements (Ioannou 2011a), operating under the umbrella of the EGSSE. In reality, there were only few (less than 10) encompassing sectoral/industry collective agreements, i.e. covering all or the great majority of the employees, jobs, and specialties in a certain sector/industry (e.g. the banking sector collective agreement). Most of the so-called sectoral/industry collective agreements only covered the main specialty, job, or occupation in a certain sector (Ioannou 2011a: 774–775). For instance, the "meat and sausage industry collective agreement" in a meat and sausage company only covered meat workers' specialties, and the company had to apply another 20 sectoral and occupational collective agreements (or arbitration awards) to its personnel (e.g. to also cover food technologists, engineers, industry chemists, electricians, agronomists, technicians, drivers, salesmen, sales office personnel, IT personnel, guards, cleaners, accountants, administrative staff, etc.).

This set of sectoral and occupational collective agreements constituted a rather fragmented collective bargaining structure for wage determination in Greece. The numbers and the jurisdictions of that structure of sectoral

Table 2.1 The collective bargaining structure under Law 1876/1990 (1992–2016) and its reforms

Year	NGCA		Occupational				Sectoral		Company		Total			%	
			National		Regional -Local										
	CA	AA	CA	AA	CA	AA	CA	AA	CA	AA	CA	AA	CA + AA	CA	AA
							Law 1876/1990								
1992			28	12	14	5	66	8	63	7	171	32	203	84,2	15,8
1993	1		50	11	26	2	98	15	105	2	280	30	310	90,3	9,7
1994	1		44	14	26	2	99	17	117	4	287	37	324	88,6	11,4
1995	1		41	14	25	4	64	13	108	2	239	33	272	87,9	12,1
1996	1		46	16	20	6	76	18	242	3	385	43	428	90	10,1
1997			44	14	25	8	69	96	143	4	281	52	333	84,4	15,6
1998	1		51	13	16	10	87	28	137	7	292	58	350	83,4	16,6
1999			23	20	18	9	70	19	115	3	228	51	279	81,7	18,3
2000	1		54	15	22	4	98	17	122	6	297	42	339	87,6	12,4
2001			34	12	24	1	60	22	146	5	263	40	303	86,8	13,2
2002	2		43	19	32	6	96	20	175	11	348	56	404	86,1	13,8
2003			28	25	26	8	52	26	168	5	274	64	338	81.1	18.9
2004	1		37	16	43	4	101	22	216	10	398	52	450	88,4	11,6
2005			37	18	24	8	84	15	234	20	379	61	440	86,2	13,8
2006	1		42	17	34	6	100	24	224	7	401	54	455	88,1	11,9
2007			23	14	20	3	73	19	202	7	318	43	361	88,1	11,9

2008	1	43	17	27	2	117	25	215	15	403	59	462	87,2	12,8
2009		15	11	12	5	47	30	215	12	289	58	347	83,3	16,7
2010	1	33	8	14	6	31	21	227	11	306	46	352	86.9	13.1
Law 3899/17–12-2010 art. 14 and Law 4024/27–10-2011 art. 37 para. 3														
2011		15	5	7	1	23	12	170	9	215	27	242	88,9	11,1
Law 4046/14–2-2012 art. 1 para. 6 and Government Council decree 6/28–2-2012														
2012		4	1	6		19	7	976		1005	8	1013	99,2	0,8
2013	1	4	-	10		8		410		433		433	100	0,0
Law 4303/17–10-2014 art. 4 para 1														
2014	1	3		5		10	2	286		305	2	307	99.3	0.7
2015	1	5		7		6	4	263	1	282	5	287	98.3	1,7
2016	1	2	3	6		7	7	318	4	334	14	348	96	4

Notes: CA Collective Agreement – AA Arbitration Award. The numbers of CAs and AAs and the dates are based on the date of their registration and not on the date they are signed or even the period they cover. Therefore, a CA signed in 2010 but registered in 2011 is counted in 2011. Similarly an AA issued in 2012 but referring to a collective bargaining procedure and a period of coverage for 2010 or 2011 is counted as part of the bargaining structure in 2012. In Ioannou et al. (2011) and Ioannou and Papadimitriou (2013), there are analytical proposals for improving the monitoring of developments in the bargaining structure. Sources: Ministry of Labour, OMED, Ioannou et al. (2011), Ioannou and Papadimitriou (2013).

and occupational collective agreements have been rather stable despite some gradual changes during the 1990s and 2000s up to 2008. There was a slow upward trend in the number of sectoral agreements (which were not legally permissible before the 1990 reform) and a gradual decline in the number of occupational agreements, the dominant tradition of which goes back to the 1950s and even the late 1930s. In parallel, there was an upward trend in the number of company collective agreements (Ioannou 2011a: 767, 782–785). However, many company collective agreements were rather unstable as their flow was irregular. Beyond a "core" of some 150 company collective agreements that survived during most of the period (1990–2008) and appear on a regular basis in the annual or biannual flow of company collective agreements, a greater number of company collective agreements were registered with the Ministry of Labour but were short-lived. Their discontinuity relates to factors such as the lack of bargaining power to renew the company collective agreement, the company unions' reliance on the sectoral collective agreements, discontinued activities of company unions, and company-plant mergers or exits from the market (Ioannou 2011a: 780–785).

The bargaining structure outlined in Table 2.1 was, for the period 1992–2010, the outcome of a sequence of procedures whereby one side (mainly the trade union) would initiate collective bargaining to renew an existing collective agreement after, or near, its expiry date or to conclude a new agreement; resort to mediation (mainly from the trade union side) in case of failure of collective negotiations; or resort to compulsory arbitration, with the precondition that either the other side "denied the mediation procedure" or the applicant side had accepted the mediator proposal rejected by the other side.

The right to unilateral access to compulsory arbitration has been critical for the reproduction of the bargaining structure that prevailed until 2012, as it functioned as a secure fallback mechanism. Although the share of arbitration awards in the total number of collective agreements registered per year ranged between 10% and 19% in 1992–2010 (see Table 2.1) and was in the lower band of 12–15% in recent years prior to the crisis, arbitration was critical for the reproduction and the survival of most sectoral and occupational collective agreements in 1992–2012. On average, more than half of the sectoral and occupational collective agreements necessitated recourse to mediation, where part of them were led successfully to a mediated but voluntary collective agreement. Further, on average, a third of the occupational collective agreements and a quarter of the sectoral collective agreements necessitated the unilateral recourse to arbitration in order to be settled (Ioannou 2012b). Indeed, as indicated in Table 2.2, in the early years of the crisis, in 2009–2010, the need for recourse to mediation and then to compulsory arbitration became necessary in a much higher and increasing percentage (81.4% in 2010) of occupational and sectoral collective agreements in dispute.

Table 2.2 The share of sectoral and occupational collective agreements and arbitration awards concluded under mediation and arbitration services

Year	Under OMED	National total	OMED share %
		Law 1876/1990	
1992	54	133	40,6
1993	79	202	39,1
1994	86	202	42,6
1995	82	161	50,9
1996	91	182	50,0
1997	105	256	41,0
1998	113	205	55,1
1999	92	159	57,9
2000	123	210	58,6
2001	78	153	51,0
2002	93	216	43,1
2003	89	165	53,9
2004	96	223	43,0
2005	84	186	45,2
2006	98	223	43,9
2007	71	152	46,7
2008	99	231	42,9
2009	73	120	60,8
2010	92	113	81,4
	Law 3899/17–12-2010 art. 14 and Law 4024/27–10-2011 art. 37 para. 3		
2011	23	63	36,5
	Law 4046/14–2-2012 art. 1 para. 6 and Government Council decree 6/28–2-2012		
2012	9	37	24,3
2013	2	23	8,7
	Law 4303/17–10-2014 art. 4 para 1		
2014	6	20	30,0
2015	11	22	50,0
2016	14	26	53.8
Total	1.749	3.665	48,9

Sources: Ioannou et al. (2011), OMED Annual reports 2009–2016, Ministry of Labour.

The continuous reproduction of the bargaining structure comprising those 100 sectoral and 90 occupational collective agreements that shaped wage determination in the Greek private sector over two decades (1992–2012) relied heavily on the regulatory framework that established two fundamental rights:

first, the right to unilateral recourse to compulsory arbitration procedures, which has been considered by the ILO incompatible with free collective bargaining[1], and second, the right to extension of the sectoral and occupational collective agreements (or arbitration awards) to non-signatory parties. Over the decades, most of these agreements and compulsory arbitration awards were extended by ministerial decisions in an almost automatic way without any meaningful checking of their coverage, based on representative criteria for the signatory parties.

Although 2010 marked the eruption of the fiscal crisis in Greece and the country's entry into the joint EU-ECB-IMF adjustment programme(s), the collective bargaining structure initially survived during 2010 and 2011 (Ioannou and Papadimitriou 2013). But the routine or "normality" of renewal of the existing bargaining structure was challenged by reforms to both sets of critical rights. First, arbitration rights were initially curtailed in 2011 by changing the role of compulsory arbitration and restricting it to only settling basic wages and salaries.[2] Then, in 2012, the procedures for arbitration were further reformed by requiring mutual agreement of both parties as a precondition to exert the right to access arbitration procedures.[3] Second, the right to extension has been put on hold until the (moving) end of the adjustment programme(s), the latest being for the end of the third adjustment programme on August 20, 2018. The last time ministerial decisions were issued to extend the coverage of collective agreements or arbitration awards beyond the members of the signatory parties was in 2011.

Not surprisingly, significant changes began to occur in 2012, with exponential effects thereafter, as a result of both the worsening economic climate and the successive legislative interventions in the regulatory framework for collective bargaining, culminating in February 2012 with Law 4046/2012. The minimum wage was not negotiated by the EGSSE partners anymore but set by the state. It was cut by 22% and frozen, and automatic progression on the seniority premium ladder was suspended. The extension mechanism of collective agreements and compulsory arbitration awards was already suspended till the end of the adjustment programme(s). The EGSEE and the sectoral and occupational collective agreements became applicable only to the members of the signatory parties. The unilateral recourse to arbitration was abolished.[4] The time extension of collective agreements was reduced to three months, and their after-effect included only the basic wage and four allowances (seniority, children, education, and hazardous work) and not all the terms and conditions of employment set by expired collective agreements and compulsory arbitration awards. Since 2011, firm-level agreements started taking precedence over sectoral or occupational agreements even when the former was less favourable than the latter.[5] In the absence of trade unions, Associations of Persons were given the right to negotiate firm-level agreements[6] and the right to opt out from existing sectoral and occupational agreements (Ioannou 2012a).

The impact of these changes is reflected in the reduced number of sectoral and occupational collective agreements signed during that period. During the crisis and adjustment years, three subperiods of changes in the bargaining structure can be identified (see Table 2.1). Data for the number of collective agreements by type and level in 2012 marks a critical turning point of radical change in the structure of collective bargaining in Greece. It is now clear that from 2012–2016, the longstanding institutional system of collective bargaining, with its 100 sectoral and 90 occupational agreements on average, suffered a landslide and collapsed. Developments that were initiated in 2011–2012 already indicated a transition to both a different structure and an alternative function of collective bargaining in Greece.

To understand the radical and rapid changes in the structure of collective bargaining, it is important to distinguish between stocks and flows. In 2011–2012, most of the 190 sectoral and occupational collective agreements remained in force since they had been concluded either in 2009 or in 2010 with a two- and three-year duration. Nevertheless, the discontinuity in the regular renewal of collective agreements since 2012 is a significant indication of subsequent radical changes in the bargaining structure due to the low flow of renewed sectoral and occupational collective agreements and the rapidly falling stock of collective agreements in force. Out of the 190 sectoral and occupational agreements in 2009–2010, not all of them were renewed in 2010–2011. From the 134 renewed ones, a total of 103 collective agreements expired by February 14, 2013, the date that was set as the milestone for the termination of all pre-existing sectoral and occupational collective agreements that were renewed in 2010–2011 (Ioannou and Papadimitriou 2013: 49–50). During 2012, and after the radical changes in the regulatory framework, only 28 sectoral and occupational collective agreements (at national and regional/local levels) were renewed.[7] At the same time, the number of company collective agreements soared to 976.

These changes in the structure of collective bargaining subsequently became more radical and rapid. The flows of collective agreements lowered and the stocks disappeared. The transition started in 2012 with the increasing failure of parties to renew sectoral and occupational collective agreements and culminated over two years in a relatively low stock of sectoral and occupational collective agreements in force in the Greek labour market in 2013–2014. After their collective agreements had expired, most trade unions initiated formal demands to renew their pre-existing collective agreements mainly with the aim, in a backtracking strategy, to reinstate the terms and conditions of the 2009–2010 collective agreements or arbitration awards. Only a minority of them were able to proceed to collective bargaining processes. The fallback mechanism of unilateral recourse to arbitration was not available any more in 2012–2014.

Among the major national sectoral agreements, only those for the hotel sector (one agreement) and the retail sales sector (two agreements) were renewed in 2012. It is noteworthy that most sectoral and occupational collective agreements signed or renewed in 2012 (16 out of 28) concerned subsectors of the tourism industry.[8] In almost all these agreements, coverage was reduced as some of the parties from the employers' side, which had participated in these collective agreements in previous years, abstained from bargaining and contracting (Ioannou and Papadimitriou 2013: 21) in 2012. In fact, the transformation of the structure of collective bargaining during 2011–2012 has been further consolidated since then by a raft of interrelated factors. A great majority of the existing sectoral and occupation agreements (around 60%) expired automatically in accordance with the law. The remaining 40%, however, was terminated with the initiative of the employers' associations, signifying a new element in the employers' bargaining behaviour. As of February 2013, only 26 sectoral and occupational collective agreements were still active (Ioannou and Papadimitriou 2013: 48).[9] The result was a very low stock of collective agreements in force in the Greek labour market at the end of 2013.

The marginalisation of collective bargaining at the sectoral and occupational level was further consolidated during 2014–2016. Each year, the number of sectoral and occupational collective agreements that were signed (or awarded by compulsory arbitration – [see numbers in parenthesis]) and renewed was lower than in 2012: 22 in 2013, 18(2) in 2014, 18(4) in 2015, 15(10) in 2016. As indicated in Table 2.1, a diminishing number were signed voluntarily, and the total was only influenced in 2014–2016 by the reinstatement of the right to have unilateral recourse to compulsory arbitration and obtaining arbitration awards. In 2014–2016, less than 20 national sectoral and occupational collective agreements "survived."[10]

Another new element in the bargaining behaviour of both employers and employees was the proliferation of company-level collective agreements in 2011–2012. The number of annually concluded company collective agreements increased fivefold in 2012 compared to the average of previous years, with 976 company collective agreements being signed. This figure is largely explained by the conclusion of 705 new agreements by Associations of Persons. Overall, these 976 collective agreements were dispersed across industries: 34% were in manufacturing, 22% in retail, 20% in hotels and restaurants, and the reminder in other sectors (Ioannou and Papadimitriou 2013: 52). These new agreements emerged in both sectors where there was a tradition of company-level bargaining – such as in manufacturing, where numbers of company agreements soared from 79 in 2009 and 145 in 2010 to 336 in 2012 – and in sectors where company-level bargaining was rather marginal, such as in retail (which recorded just six company agreements in 2009 and three in 2010 but 214 in 2012), as well as in the hotels, restaurants, and cafes sector (where 193 new company agreements were concluded in 2012, up from just 13 in 2009 and 10 in 2010 [ibid.:52–53]).

This wave of company agreements occurred well before the termination and expiry dates of sectoral and occupational collective agreements. While there was a tradition of company-level bargaining in manufacturing in addition to the sectoral- and occupational-level bargaining, this was a new phenomenon for most other sectors, such as the retail and hotels, restaurants, and cafes sector. A large share (around one in five) of the company-level agreements in these two sectors was cases of individual employers and Associations of Persons opting out of existing sectoral and occupational collective agreements instead of waiting for their expiry in 2013. The new company agreements largely follow the pattern of sectors where sectoral and occupational collective agreements were in force in 2011–2012 (Ioannou and Papadimitriou 2013: 52–53; see also Giannakopoulos and Laliotis in this volume).

However, the reduced number of company collective agreements signed thereafter in 2013–2016 indicates that the move towards more company-level collective agreements was primarily a one-off move to opt out from pre-existing sectoral and occupation collective agreements, more of a move towards disorganised decentralisation of collective bargaining. Compared to the pre-2010 period, the numbers of company collective agreements signed each year by trade-unions oscillate at low numbers. Associations of Persons are still present in 2013–2016, but their numbers are also much lower than in 2012. Their role is not comparable to the wave of company collective agreements signed during 2012, as the expiry of most sectoral and occupational collective agreements, and the lack of their renewal, created wide room for individual employment contracts.

The collapse of most sectoral and occupational collective agreements in 2013–2016 implied the collapse of bargaining coverage and led to the reduced, if not marginal, role of collective bargaining in wage determination. The increased numbers of company collective agreements signed before and after the 2011–2012 reforms were not able to make up for the losses in bargaining coverage caused by the shrinkage of sectoral and occupational collective agreements. Indeed, the numbers of company collective agreements operating in Greece before and after the crisis, compared to the number of companies where company collective agreements could have been signed, indicate a low starting point of company collective bargaining in the collective bargaining structure in Greece.

Before the 2011 reforms, it was legally possible for company collective agreements to be signed in companies employing more than 50 employees. In 2002, there were 2,857 such companies, but collectively bargained wages at the company level were only present in less than 10% of them. Despite the slight increase in company-level collective agreements in the late 2000s (see Table 2.1), this proportion was not altered significantly. In 2007, there were 3,375 companies employing more than 50 employees, and less than 10% had collectively bargained wages at the company level. The increase of company collective agreements in absolute numbers also indicates that the role of company-level bargaining has changed since the 2011–2012 reforms: company-level bargaining by unions became more autonomous from pre-existing sectoral and occupational collective agreements, and in that sense, company unions and decentralised collective bargaining perpetuated their role. Furthermore, allowing company agreements to be signed by Associations of Persons in companies employing less than 50 employees made a marginal impact on expanding the collective bargaining structure at the decentralised company level.

The low stock of sectoral and occupational collective agreements that remained in force in 2013–2016 in the Greek labour market, and the role of company agreements initially as an opt-out tool, help explain the radical fall in collective bargaining coverage. In the past, there have been few estimates of collective bargaining coverage in Greece, ranging between 65% and 100%. For example, EIRO (Eurofound 2007) estimated the collective bargaining coverage at 100%, while Ioannou (2004) estimated the coverage for 1996 at 65% for the HIVA[11] database. The collective bargaining coverage for Greece at the range of 65% was closer to reality for the period before the crisis, as the 100% coverage rate was based on the assumption that the minimum wage that was set by the National General Collective Agreement until 2012 was applicable to all workers in the Greek labour market. The HIVA database estimate was adopted by the ICTWSS (2007–2011), but in its later versions, it has been revised upwards (Visser 2015). In any case, the change since then is dramatic. ICTWSS reported a drop to 60% in 2011 from 83% in 2009 and a further drop to 42% in 2013. Our estimate for the end of 2013 and the first trimester of 2014 is that bargaining coverage was in the range of 10% (ILO 2014: 16, 162, Cutcher-Gershenfeld et al. 2015: 39).

In 2014, 5% of employees were covered by company collective agreements, while in 2015, this number increased to 7.6% (ERGANI 2014, 2015). The collective bargaining coverage, which seems to have bottomed at around 10% in 2013–2014, appears to be gradually increasing. Our recent estimate for 2014-2016, produced for ILOSTAT, is that the collective bargaining coverage rate increased to 15% at the end of 2014, 16.7% in 2015, and 17.8% in 2016. Coverage by renewed sectoral collective agreements (for banking, hotels, cement industry, and foreign airlines personnel, among others) constitutes the core of the bargaining structure and the bargaining coverage in Greece in 2014–2016. This has been supplemented by some 1,200 company collective agreements, three quarters of which appear to have been a one-off function. Therefore, from 2012–2014, there has been a radical shift from collectively agreed terms and conditions to individualised employment contracts – and the collective bargaining function only gradually recovers its role in wage determination. Overall, the implication of these changes in the bargaining structure and the level of collective bargaining coverage in Greece has been *the rapid and extensive disconnection* of wage determination from the pre-existing collective bargaining institutions and processes (relying largely on the unilateral recourse to arbitration and to ministerial decisions to extend their coverage). This was the procedure through which the macroeconomic objective of internal devaluation has been achieved since 2010, more so since 2012. We will explore this issue in the next section.

3 Wage adjustment for internal devaluation and pay rebalancing

The Greek crisis has mainly been the product of the fundamental asymmetry in the Greek economy between two major sectors: the "internationally tradable" and "internationally non-tradable" goods and services (Ioannou and Ioannou 2017). From 1995–2001, the share of tradables in GDP varied slightly between 24% and 25%. However, from 2001 until 2009, their share decreased, reaching its lowest point (18.7%) in 2009 for the 1995–2017 period. In other words, the roots of the crisis were established before its eruption and originated mainly due to the growing lack of competitiveness. Or, in Tzannatos' (2014: 164) words, "unlike crises in other countries after 2008 ... this (Greek) crisis was homemade." This had severe implications on the allocation of labour, relative prices, and relative wages.

The rise of competitiveness imbalances contributing to national imbalances in total borrowing is a better explanation for the systemic differences in Economic and Monetary Union (EMU) countries' exposure to market speculation. As showed by Johnston et al. (2014), this has an important wage formation dimension as it relates to a country's capacity to limit sheltered wage growth, relative to wage growth in the manufacturing sector, through its collective bargaining institutions, structures, and processes. Although Greece has been lacking a strong manufacturing and export sector, the question of balancing wage formation between the exposed "tradable" sectors and the protected "non-tradable" sectors should have been considered when setting benchmarks in wage determination through collective bargaining. By using these type of benchmarks in wage formation, Greece managed to satisfy the relevant criteria for becoming a member of the EMU (Ioannou 1998). By neglecting these criteria of wage formation during its EMU period in 2002–2009, it moved towards the 2009–2010 crisis and collapse (Ioannou and Ioannou 2013). Therefore, balancing relative wages between these two sectors of the economy to correct the distortions caused as an impact of financialisation in wage formation remained a key challenge (Cutcher-Gershenfeld et al. 2015), which went unnoticed by policy makers and social partners alike for several years.

Internal devaluation through labour and product market reforms became a key objective of Euro Area adjustment programs. The wage adjustment process began in 2010 and has intensified since 2012. Wage determination entered the era of an internal devaluation process, and the collective bargaining processes became part of it, to evolve later in a stage of wage moderation. The basis of accelerating this process was the minimum wage cut by 22% in 2012.

Not surprisingly, downward wage adjustment and internal devaluation were also observed in the pay provisions of the few sectoral and occupational collective agreements that have been renewed since 2012. In 2012, one in two of the sectoral and occupational collective agreements provided for wage cuts. In 2013, wage cuts were agreed upon in one in three sectoral collective agreements. In 2014, this number dropped to one in five. In 2012, one in four agreed to a pay freeze, increasing to one in three in 2013 and one in two in 2014. In 2013, just one in 10 negotiated a wage increase, doubling to one in five in 2014 (Papadimitriou and Ioannou 2015: 109–110). While collective bargaining has shrunk in scale and scope, it has also contributed to the internal devaluation process and rebalancing pay relativities across sectors.

To outline the process of internal devaluation, Table 2.3 presents data on changes in pay provisions in company collective agreements by type of labour organisation during the period 2012–2015 and indicates the scale of the internal devaluation of wages implemented via company collective bargaining. In 2012, two thirds (66.5%) of company agreements that were signed by Associations of Persons downgraded pay to the level of the reduced minimum wage – either the EGSSE or the statutory minimum wage. This remained the main function of this type of company agreements during 2013–2015 as well, although with a decreasing share (55% in 2013, 33% in 2014, and 34% in 2015). The second function of the company collective agreements signed by Associations of Persons in the same period was to facilitate the opting out from sectoral collective agreements and to operationalise a downward wage adjustment, albeit with the base rate somewhere above the national minimum wage (21% of company agreements in 2012, 9% in 2013, 5% in 2014, and 4% in 2015).

Company collective agreements signed by company unions have played a rather different role in wage determination. During 2012–2015, these agreements were more likely to function as a source of pay stability – ranging from one-third of agreements (34%) in 2012 to two-thirds (65.7%) in 2015. Their provisions for downward wage adjustment have been more moderate. Only a very small share of company collective agreements signed by company unions negotiated wages down to minimum wage levels; the highest share was recorded in 2013 at 7%. Similarly, we observe a lower share of the company union collective agreements negotiating large wage adjustments compared to those signed by associations of persons. On the contrary, a greater and increasing share of these company union collective agreements provide pay increases (ranging from 2% in 2012 to 11% in 2015).

Apart from the institutional difference (union versus Association of Persons), this divergence also seems to be related to the sectoral origin/location of the company unions and the company collective agreements ("tradable" sectors – mainly manufacturing – versus "non-tradable" sectors – retail sales, construction, etc). In other words, there have been different trajectories of wage adjustment that can be traced across different sectors. All were subject to concession and adjustment bargaining at the sectoral or the company level, but this probably varied in different sectors

Table 2.3 Pay provisions in company collective agreements by type of labour organisation, 2012–2015

Year	2012			2013			2014			2015		
Change in pay by type of labour organization	Number of CAs	% in total	% of type of union	Number of CAs	% in total	% in type of union	Number of CAs	% in total	% in type of union	Number of CAs	% in total	% in type of union
Association of Persons	**705**	**72,2**	**100,0**	**216**	**52,7**	**100,0**	**135**	**47,2**	**100,0**	**117**	**44,7**	**100,0**
Stable Pay	7	0,7	1,0	54	13,2	25,0	54	18,9	40,0	62	23,7	53,0
Pay Increase	2	0,2	0,3		0,0	0,0	1	0,3	0,7	4	1,5	3,4
Pay Decrease (between 5%-9%)	3	0,3	0,4	3	0,7	1,4	2	0,7	1,5	1	0,4	0,9
Pay Decrease (between 10%-14%)	25	2,6	3,5	8	2,0	3,7	4	1,4	3,0		0,0	0,0
Pay Decrease (between 15%-19%)	33	3,4	4,7	3	0,7	1,4	1	0,3	0,7		0,0	0,0
Pay Decrease (20% +)	84	8,6	11,9	6	1,5	2,8		0,0	0,0	3	1,1	2,6
No reference to pay change		0,0	0,0		0,0	0,0	2	0,7	1,5	4	1,5	3,4
Pay adjusted to the NGCA Minimum Wage (ΕΓΣΣΕ)	461	47,2	65,4	90	22,0	41,7	25	8,7	18,5	27	10,3	23,1
Agreement regulates other than pay issues	82	8,4	11,6	24	5,9	11,1	27	9,4	20,0	3	1,1	2,6
Pay adjusted to Legislated Minimum Wage	8	0,8	1,1	28	6,8	13,0	19	6,6	14,1	13	5,0	11,1
Company Union	**173**	**17,7**	**100,0**	**171**	**41,7**	**100,0**	**136**	**47,6**	**100,0**	**134**	**51,1**	**100,0**
Stable Pay	58	5,9	33,5	62	15,1	36,3	71	24,8	52,2	88	33,6	65,7

(*Continued*)

Table 2.3 (Cont.)

Year	2012			2013			2014			2015		
Change in pay by type of labour organization	*Number of CAs*	*% in total*	*% of type of union*	*Number of CAs*	*% in total*	*% in type of union*	*Number of CAs*	*% in total*	*% in type of union*	*Number of CAs*	*% in total*	*% in type of union*
Pay Increase	4	0,4	2,3	12	2,9	7,0	7	2,4	5,1	15	5,7	11,2
Pay Decrease (between 5%-9%)	7	0,7	4,0		0,0	0,0	5	1,7	3,7		0,0	0,0
Pay Decrease (between 10%-14%)	15	1,5	8,7	5	1,2	2,9	3	1,0	2,2		0,0	0,0
Pay Decrease (between 15%-19%)	5	0,5	2,9	4	1,0	2,3	2	0,7	1,5	1	0,4	0,7
Pay Decrease (20% +)	13	1,3	7,5	2	0,5	1,2	1	0,3	0,7	2	0,8	1,5
No reference to pay change		0,0	0,0	1	0,2	0,6	10	3,5	7,4	11	4,2	8,2
Pay adjusted to the NGCA Minimum Wage (ΕΓΣΣΕ)	6	0,6	3,5	3	0,7	1,8	3	1,0	2,2		0,0	0,0
Agreement regulates other than pay issues	64	6,6	37,0	73	17,8	42,7	33	11,5	24,3	17	6,5	12,7
Pay adjusted to Legislated Minimum Wage	1	0,1	0,6	9	2,2	5,3	1	0,3	0,7		0,0	0,0
Federation	**1**	**0,1**	**100,0**	**10**	**2,4**	**100,0**	**2**	**0,7**	**100,0**	**6**	**2,3**	**100,0**
Stable Pay		0,0	0,0	5	1,2	50,0		0,0	0,0	3	1,1	1,1
No reference to pay change		0,0	0,0	2	0,5	20,0	1	0,3	50,0	1	0,4	0,4
Agreement regulates other than pay issues	1	0,1	100,0	3	0,7	30,0	1	0,3	50,0	2	0,8	0,8
Primary Level Union	**97**	**9,9**	**100,0**	**13**	**3,2**	**100,0**	**13**	**4,5**	**100,0**	**5**	**1,9**	**100,0**

Stable Pay	92	9,4	94,8	4	1,0	30,8	6	2,1	46,2	2	0,8	40,0
Pay Increase	1	0,1	1,0	1	0,2	7,7		0,0	0,0	1	0,4	20,0
Pay Decrease (between 5%-9%)		0,0	0,0	1	0,2	7,7	1	0,3	7,7		0,0	0,0
Pay Decrease (between 10%-14%)		0,0	0,0		0,0	0,0	1	0,3	7,7		0,0	0,0
Pay Decrease (between 15%-19%)		0,0	0,0	1	0,2	7,7	1	0,3	7,7	1	0,4	20,0
Pay Decrease (20% +)	1	0,1	1,0	1	0,2	7,7		0,0	0,0		0,0	0,0
No reference to pay change		0,0	0,0		0,0	0,0	2	0,7	15,4		0,0	0,0
Pay adjusted to the NGCA Minimum Wage (ΕΓΣΣΕ)		0,0	0,0	2	0,5	15,4		0,0	0,0		0,0	0,0
Agreement regulates other than pay issues	3	0,3	3,1	3	0,7	23,1	2	0,7	15,4	1	0,4	20,0
Total	976	100,0		410	100,0		286	100,0		262	100,0	

Source: for 2012: Ioannou and Papadimitriou (2013), for 2013: Papadimitriou and Ioannou (2015), for 2014–2015, own elaboration of data from Ministry of Labour and OMED.

and has also generated a shift in the structure of relative wages across sectors. The evidence from sectoral collective bargaining processes that evolved during the period 2012–2016 suggests the existence of diverging patterns between sectors of "tradables" and "non-tradables". For instance, if we compare collective bargaining outcomes and wage developments in "tradables" (e.g. in the metal industry and the hotel industry) and in "non-tradables" (e.g. the retail trade), there are indications that in the context of the crisis and the adjustment process, the "tradables" sectors have shown more resilience and more continuity of the associational life in the national system of industrial relations than the "non-tradable" ones. On the contrary, in the "non-tradable" retail sector, wage adjustment has been continuous, and the associational life, despite the conclusion of an annual collective agreement in 2012 (for the period 1.8.2012–31.7.2012 providing for wage cuts of 6.7%), failed to preserve any wage floor. Wages continued to fall in 2013–2016 towards the legislated minimum wage, and the social partners in the sector failed successively from 2013–2016 in renewing their collective agreement.

Another relevant and interesting development since 2012 (see Table 2.3) is the occurrence of company collective agreements signed not by company unions but by union Federations or Primary level unions – namely unions that organise employees of a sector or an occupation across many companies. This is explained by the expiry of the umbrella sectoral and occupational collective agreements and highlights some successful trade union efforts to preserve collective bargaining in cases where company trade unions were absent. This development, which was evident most prominently in the hotel sector, aimed to limit the risk of fragmented bargaining that could arise if Associations of Persons were to be included instead and ensured a degree of bargaining coordination at the company level.

Concession and adjustment collective bargaining have been important factors in the internal devaluation process, but they are neither the only factors nor the main ones. Another mechanism has been the provision to management, by the 2012 legal reform, of the right to unilaterally adjust individual wages that had previously been determined by the many sectoral and occupational collective agreements. With a soaring unemployment rate that quadrupled from 7.3% in May 2008 to a peak of 27.9% in July 2013, wage determination in the private sector was under unprecedented pressure for adjustment.

These developments are highlighted by another source of data that refers mainly to private sector employees and overall to employees under private law contracts, namely the register of the Social Security Fund (IKA). In 2009, there were 2.50 million insured employees. This number fell to 2.01 million in 2012 and then recovered partially to 2.21 million by 2014. It is noteworthy that according to the same data from the 2.50 million insured employees in 2009, only around half a million (just 19%) had been continuously employed by the same employer during the 2009–2014 period. The remaining two million employees either had unemployment spells or changed employer, or both. These transitions facilitated the reconfiguration of their pay as their employment contracts were "freed" from the provisions of the pre-existing (sectoral and occupational) collective agreements. The same data suggests that the smaller group of employees in stable employment with the same employer also experienced a cut in average earnings by 6% (IKA 2015: 14). Unpublished data of the ERGANI system confirms this general pattern: from the total number of individual employment contracts registered in 2015, only around 30% were registered with the same employer before 2013.

In a nutshell, all the processes and indicators suggest that wages went through a huge adjustment process for internal devaluation using all available means. It remains an open question whether all these adjustments have moved towards rebalancing wage relativities in the Greek economy. If these wage relativities were in need of adjustment, what is important for rebalancing is not only relative wages and labour costs in the national economy compared to foreign partners, but also relative wages and relative labour costs between the "tradable" and the "non-tradable" sectors of the economy. As an ILO (2014: 8) report argued,

> efforts to restore macroeconomic competitiveness in Greece … focused on unit labour costs – mostly achieved through wage cuts, including the minimum wage … however, this has done little to restore the fundamental sources of external competitiveness. This is due to the fact that wage gains in the pre-crisis period were concentrated in the non-tradable sector.

To assess the impact of internal devaluation on rebalancing wages in the Greek economy throughout this period, a benchmarking exercise is used by estimating relative wages in a two-sector model: "tradables" versus "non-tradables". The analysis is based on estimating the Kaitz index in the "tradable" and "non-tradable" sectors separately. The rationale for the selection of branches to be included in each sector is analysed in Ioannou and Ioannou (2017: 66–67). Wages are from monthly data of the Social Security Fund (IKA) for the average wage of fulltime workers in the period 2003–2015. Changes in employment distribution over this period are accounted for in the Kaitz index for each sector by weighting wages for their changing employment share. The results, presented in Table 2.4 and in Figure 2.1, suggest that in the build-up process to the crisis in 2000–2009, the relative wages in 2003–2009 were higher in the "non-tradables" sector and the gap between the two sectors was rising between 2003 and 2009.

The adjustment process started in 2010, stopped in 2011, and accelerated again in 2012 as part of the process of internal and external rebalancing. The Kaitz index became higher in the "tradables" sector in 2013 and kept rising in 2014–2015. Given that the legislated national minimum wage has

Table 2.4 Relative wages in tradables (T) and non-tradables (N), 2003–2015

	Kaitz index		Relative Wage Gap
Year	T	N	(T-N)
2003	0,558	0,564	-0,006
2004	0,563	0,561	0,002
2005	0,548	0,560	-0,011
2006	0,558	0,569	-0,011
2007	0,554	0,566	-0,012
2008	0,560	0,576	-0,017
2009	0,557	0,569	-0,012
2010	0,557	0,563	-0,006
2011	0,552	0,559	-0,007
2012	0,465	0,471	-0,006
2013	0,487	0,472	0,015
2014	0,516	0,495	0,021
2015	0,527	0,505	0,022

Note: "Tradable" sector (T), T = 1–33, 50, 51, 55–56, 62, 63, 72, Code NACE Rev.2.
Source: Average wage of insured salary and wage earners by sector, Monthly reports, 2003–2015, Social Security Fund (IKA).

been stable in this period, the rising index indicates rising relative wages. Since 2012, pay relativities were also rebalanced within the two sectors. It may be the case that the Kaitz index underestimates relative wages in the "non-tradable" sector because of the source of data from IKA, which covers the great majority of private-sector-dependent employment in Greece, but has not covered fully, over the period 2003–2015, public sector employment that is also part of the "non-tradable" sector. Therefore, the extent to which this rebalancing is taking place and leading to a system of wage formation where the "tradable" sector has guiding role requires further research. Whether this is institutionalised also depends on how the actors of the Greek collective bargaining structure may act towards such a major paradigm shift in wage formation in Greek employment relations.

4 Discussion and conclusions

The evidence suggests that the relationship between collective bargaining and wage determination for the private sector workforce has been radically affected by the new regulatory framework and the changing bargaining behaviour of the parties. The failure to renew sectoral and occupational

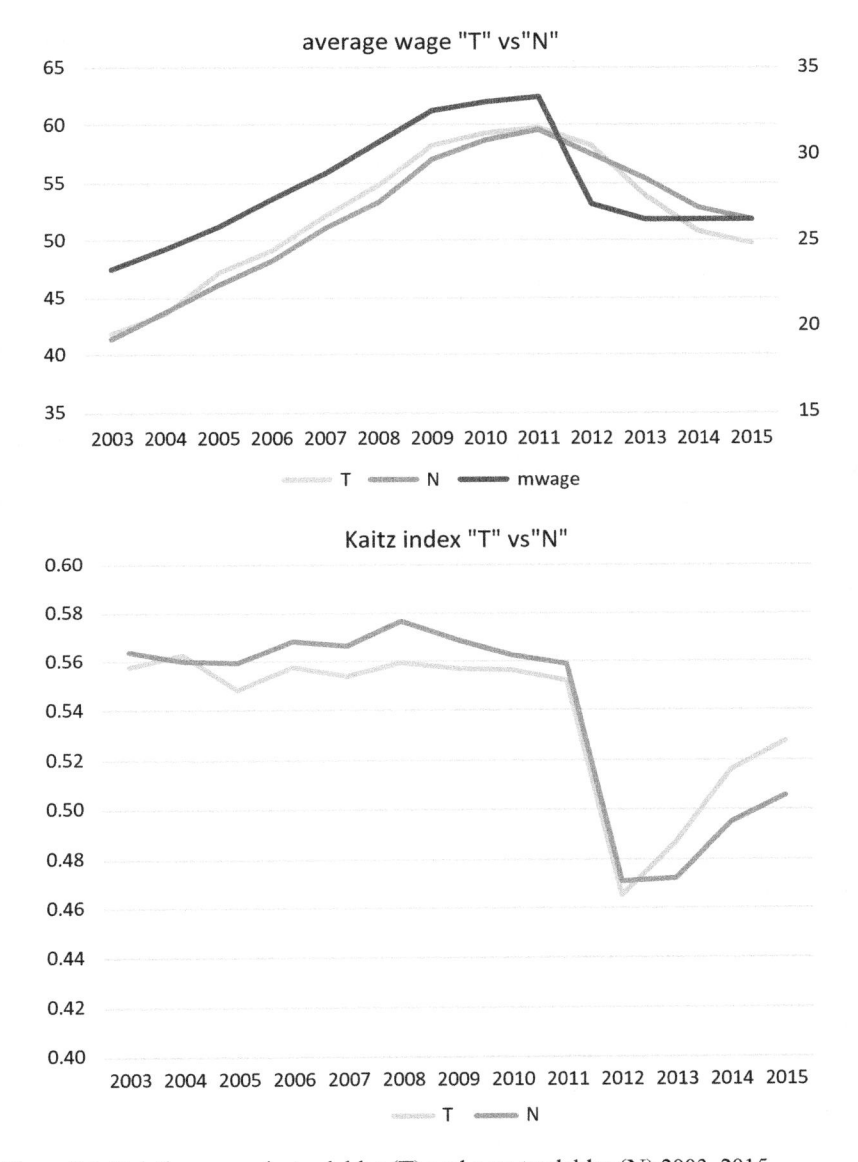

Figure 2.1 Relative wages in tradables (T) and non-tradables (N) 2003–2015

Note: "Tradable" sector (T), T = 1–33, 50, 51, 55–56, 62, 63, 72, Code NACE Rev.2.
Source: Average wage of insured salary and wage earners by sector, Monthly reports,
2003–2015, Social Security Fund (IKA).

collective agreements since 2012 has led to the shrinkage of higher-level collective agreements. The number of sectoral and occupational collective agreements declined from 100 sectoral and 90 occupational agreements before the crisis to less than 20 since 2013. At the same time, there has been an expansion of company collective agreements since 2012, which played a dual role. In most cases, their primary function was to allow the opt-out from existing sectoral and occupational collective agreements; the main mechanism being used here was the Associations of Persons. In many other cases, where company unions were effective, their function has been to co-manage the adjustment and preserve and/or revive collective bargaining coverage at the company level in the absence of the sectoral and occupational collective agreements. The overall outcome of these changes has been the outright collapse of the pre-existing bargaining structure and the collective bargaining coverage – from 65% in 1996 to just 10% in 2013–2014 for private sector employees. In that sense, this has been a case of "disorganised decentralisation" (Traxler 1995), and Greece has been a part of the trend where "the Great Recession and its Aftermath intensified rather than change developments in wage bargaining institutions, such as decreasing bargaining coverage, lower unionisation levels, and decentralisation of wage bargaining" (Visser 2016: 29).

However, even in this context, Greece appears to be an exceptional and unique case. The "disorganised decentralisation" occurred within a period of two years, and to capture the degree of change, the term "collapse" has been used. The reasons for this collapse in collective bargaining structures and coverage should be addressed, which are structural, legal, and behavioural.

The structural reasons are key and refer to the structural collapse of the economy, which lost 25% of GDP, 22% of employment (i.e. 1 million jobs were lost almost entirely in the private sector), and 37% of the total number of enterprises from 2008–2013 (see overview in ILO 2014: 22, 28, 62). That collapse was the result of the collapse of the "non-tradable" sector to a large degree, which in turn was the unavoidable outcome of its previous aberrant growth (Ioannou and Ioannou 2017: 68). As a consequence, many parts of the bargaining structure (levels and units) disappeared before the major regulatory changes in collective bargaining in 2012. In that period, most of the collective bargaining agreements and compulsory arbitration awards (sectoral and occupational) that had been signed or issued in 2009–2010 were typically in force. However, they were quickly outpaced by company agreements or individual contracts. At the time of regulatory changes in 2012, most sectoral and occupational agreements and awards had already become economically and socially irrelevant due to the structural collapse of the economy.

The key regulatory and legal reasons of the collective bargaining structure collapse first refer to the abolition of the right to unilateral recourse to compulsory arbitration, introduced during 2012–2014, and second to the suspension of the extension mechanism until the end of the adjustment programme(s). The

Greek compulsory arbitration[12] and the extension of non-representative collective agreements and compulsory arbitration awards did not contribute in developing collective bargaining institutions and processes.[13] These two cornerstones of the Greek collective bargaining structure were mostly substitutes of free and meaningful collective bargaining, and this is why the collapse of the pre-existing collective bargaining structure is not comparable to any other crisis or "program" country in the EU.

The behavioural reasons for the collapse of the bargaining structure refer to the way the social partners addressed the challenges in the new structural and legal conditions. Both factors have undermined the ability of unions and employers' associations to regulate wages. Indeed, the need for adjustments through collective bargaining was not recognised in the early stages of the crisis, in 2010, not even when it fully developed in 2011–2012 or even later. The dire economic conditions in most sectors and firms and the uncertainty regarding government policies and regulatory changes may have prompted a standstill in bargaining in 2011–2012. Furthermore, the freezing of the extension mechanism since 2011 and the changes in the compulsory arbitration policy since 2012 left most unions aloof. Most union efforts to renew sectoral and occupational collective agreements in 2012–2013 were backtracking attempts.

The lack of understanding even among the national-level social partners regarding what may have gone wrong with the National General Collective Agreement in 2000-2011 did not leave much room for any national-level dialogue on the necessary adjustments. Wage setting and minimum wage setting in Greece in the context of the currency union since 2000 lacked any reasonable benchmarking (for internal and external equilibrium, developments in tradables sector's productivity, and in the Real Effective Exchange Rate (REER), respectively).[14] Strangely enough, the debate about minimum wage setting in Greece has been focused more on the process and less on the outcomes.[15]

Unions have also failed to realise that the Greek compulsory arbitration has been considered incompatible with the aquis communautaire. In an assessment of the legality of the measures taken in the wake of the financial and debt crisis, the measures to abolish compulsory arbitration were assessed in light of the Charter of Fundamental Rights of the European Union, with specific regard to the right of collective bargaining enshrined in Article 28 of the Charter. The conclusion was that "the requirement for compulsory arbitration to be abolished raises no misgivings. In fact, it brings the situation in line with that advocated by the ILO conventions and the ESC" (Rödl and Callsen, 2016: 106).

Under the new regulatory framework, collective bargaining receded, employers' associations initiated the termination of existing sectoral and occupational collective agreements, while their company members initiated decentralised bargaining at the company level. The developments in the use of opt-outs at the company level created problems for bargaining coordination between employers associations and their individual members, on the one hand, and trade unions and their potential members on the other. Against this context, collective bargaining developments at the sectoral level survived in fewer sectors (e.g. in the tourist sector, the tobacco industry, the cement industry), outlining a leaner bargaining structure in Greece, without the critical support of the compulsory arbitration mechanism. However, even after the reinstated right to unilateral recourse to compulsory arbitration in 2014, there was no "resurrection" of most of the pre-existing sectoral and occupational collective agreements that had disappeared from the bargaining structure in 2012–2014. Along the same lines, the lifting of the temporary suspension of the collective agreements' extension mechanism in August 2018 cannot by itself reinstate the pre-existing bargaining structure. Unions (and employers associations to a certain extent) have been victims of the apathetic and ignorant misuse of compulsory arbitration and the abuse of extension mechanisms (for collective agreements signed by parties lacking representation) in the past that buttressed free riders among potential union members. The collective actors need to strengthen their membership base and improve their representation to be able to develop further collective bargaining processes in Greece and expand the current bargaining structure, which is now mainly located in the "tradable" sectors and at the decentralised company level. In this context, both sides and third parties, including dispute resolution institutions, face the challenge of operating as facilitators of good faith collective bargaining and not as bypasses or shortcuts to the outcome of collective bargaining among the parties. Procedural and representational issues apart, the exposed "tradable" sectors and the protected "non-tradable" sectors should be considered for setting benchmarks in wage determination through collective bargaining, and both unions and employers associations should become aware of these.

Notes

1 The ILO Commission of experts on the application of conventions and recommendations (CEACR) had addressed, to the Greek Government, two direct requests on compulsory arbitration – as this functioned under Law 1876/1990 – in 1999 and another in 2000. In its first direct request (87th session of the ILC, 1999), the committee considers that, in general, arbitration imposed at the request of only one of the parties to a dispute is contrary to the principle of voluntary negotiation of collective agreements established under the Convention and, therefore, contrary to the autonomy of joint negotiations (see General Survey of 1994 on freedom of association and collective bargaining, paragraph 257). Given these conditions, the Committee asks the Government to take measures to amend Article 16 (d) so that recourse to compulsory arbitration requires the consent of both parties when the dispute concerns a company agreement or a collective agreement applicable to public services, companies, or authorities, and one of the parties rejects the proposals of the mediator. In general, recourse to compulsory arbitration should only be possible within the context of essential services in the strict sense of the term, or with respect to civil servants. In its direct request of 2000 (88th session of the ILC, 2000) the same Committee, referring to paragraph (e) of article 5 of Convention No. 154, "points out that, in

general, recourse to compulsory arbitration should only be possible within the context of essential services in the strict sense of the term, or civil servants. It once again asks the Government to take measures to bring its legislation into conformity with the provisions of the Convention, and to keep it informed in this regard."

2 "The arbitration is limited to determining the basic wage and/ or basic salary. For other issues, collective bargaining may resume at any time to conclude a collective agreement" (Law 3899/2010, art. 14).

3 Law 4046/2012 art. 1 para. 6 and Ministerial Council Act 6 / 28.2.2012.

4 This provision was reversed in autumn 2014 following decision 2307/2014 of the Council of State, which ruled that unilateral recourse to arbitration procedures were guaranteed by the Constitution. As such, unilateral recourse to arbitration was reinstated by Law 4303/2014 (art. 4, para 1).

5 Law 3899/2010.

6 Law 4024/2011 art.37 para.3.

7 Of the 29 collective agreements registered in 2012 with the Ministry of Labour (see Table 2.1), one referred to the amendment – correction of an already signed and registered in 2012 collective agreement (the local collective agreements for hotel employees at the island of Rodos that was signed in June 2012 and corrected in July 2012). Arbitration awards registered during 2012 are excluded as they concerned cases pending since 2011 and were issued just before the reform of the arbitration procedure. See also note in Table 2.1.

8 The other 12 agreements covered segments of manufacturing (two agreements), health services (1), construction (1), private education (2) and other services (2).

9 Analytical listings of the collective agreements that were terminated and of those still alive are provided in Tables 2 and 3 in Ioannou and Papadimitriou (2013).

10 This comprises fewer than 10 national sectoral collective agreements, found in the hotel sector (coupled with four regional/local ones), banking sector, cement industry, tobacco industry, foreign airlines, and private health sector clinics. This core set of national agreements is supplemented by three sectors in minor segments of manufacturing plus a set of occupational/regional/local collective agreements such as the two local collective agreements for tourist guides, two for employees in travel and shipping agents, and another three in various services (theatre actors and technicians, foreign language teachers, TV and radio stations technicians).

11 HIVA, Research Institute for Work and Society, KU Leuven.

12 On arbitration, the ILO in many occasions, and its Freedom of Association Committee that examined complaints against the Greek government concluded: "As regards the amendments to the law which now only permit recourse to binding arbitration when both parties agree, the Committee recognizes that this measure was taken in an effort to align the law and practice with its principles relating to compulsory arbitration and does not consider this measure to be in violation of freedom of association principles". Case No 2820 (Greece) – Complaint date: October 21, 2010 – Closed, point 1000.

13 On the extension of collective agreements ILO observed: "As regards the suspension of the extension authority of collective agreements more generally, the Committee observes that, while there is no duty to extend agreements from the perspective of freedom of association principles, any extension that might take place should be subject to tripartite analysis of the consequences it would have on the sector to which it is applied" [see Digest, op. cit., para. 1051]. Case No. 2820 (Greece) – Complaint date: October 21, 2010 – Closed, point 999.

14 If the Greek minimum wage in 2000 had followed the Eurozone inflation, it would not end up at 751.39 euros in 2011 but at 575.07 euros. The Greek minimum wage (which started in 2010 without bonuses from 739.56 euros) had not

simply followed domestic inflation. If domestic inflation were to be followed in the form of a yearly indexation increase, it would have been at 639.14 euros in 2010. If it were to be further adjusted in 2011, during – and despite – the crisis, based on the Greek inflation, it would reach 658.95 euros, but it reached 751.39 euros. It is the fallacy of wage convergence in the Eurozone that has driven the Greek minimum wage at levels much higher than e.g. in Portugal and Spain. In 2011 (on a 12-month basis), the Greek nominal minimum wage was (without the additional family and seniority bonuses provided by the minimum wage setting system) 877 euros compared to 566 and 748 euros in Portugal and Spain, respectively. Then, and now, the minimum wage in Greece has been and still is superior than that in Portugal. The 2012 minimum wage correction was necessary and unavoidable (Ioannou and Ioannou 2013).

15 Even in the report of the Expert Group for the Review of the Greek Labour Market Institutions (2016: 32), some members argued with regard to the "Procedures in the determination of minimum wage levels" that "our general conclusion (is) that the traditional Greek model is not exceptional in the EU ... It also worked well in the past. The Greek social partners always found a compromise on minimum wages without going to arbitration and without provoking state intervention." But the social partners were not on a sustainable track compatible with economic fundamentals.

References

Clegg, H. (1976). *Trade Unionism under Collective Bargaining. A Theory Based on Comparisons of Six Countries.* Oxford: Blackwell.

Cordova, E. (1987). 'Collective Bargaining'. In: R. Blanpain (ed.). *Comparative Labour Law and Industrial Relations.* Deventer: Kluwer Law and Taxation Publishers, pp. 307-335.

Cutcher-Gershenfeld, J., Brooks, D., Cowell, N., Ioannou, C., Mulloy, M., Roberts, D., Saunders, T., and Viemose, S. (2015). 'Financialization, Collective Bargaining, and the Public Interest'. In: C. E. Weller (ed.). *Inequality, Uncertainty, and Opportunity, the Varied and Growing Role of Finance in Labor Relations.* Champaign IL: LERA Research Volumes, ILR Press, pp. 31-56.

ERGANI (2014, 2015), *Statistical Report of the Information System.* "ERGANI", Ministry of Labour, (in Greek).

Eurofound. (2007). *Greece: Industrial Relations Profile.* Dublin: Eurofound.

European Commission. (2010). *The Economic Adjustment Programme for Greece,* DG Economic and Financial Affairs, Occasional Paper 61.

European Commission. (2012). *The Second Economic Adjustment Programme for Greece,* DG Economic and Financial Affairs, Occasional Paper 94, March 2012.

Rödl, Fl. and Callsen, R. (2016). *Collective Social Rights under the Strain of Monetary Union, Can Article 28 of the EU Charter of Fundamental Rights Offer Protection?* Brussels: ETUI.

Giannitsis, T. and Zografakis, S. (2015). *Greece: Solidarity and Adjustment in Times of Crisis,* IMK, Macroeconomic Policy Institute, Düsseldorf, Hans-Boeckler-Foundation, Study 38, March 2015.

Guigni, G. (1967). *L' Evoluzione Della Contrattazione Collettiva Nelle Industrie Della Comunita 1953–1963.* Lussemburgo: European Coal & Steel Community.

IKA (2015) *Study of the Economic Employment Data of the Active Insured Employees Members of the IKA –ETAM in Period 2009–2014,* Athens: mimeo (in Greek).

International Labour Organisation (ILO). (2014). *Productive Jobs for Greece.* Geneva: International Labour Office.

International Monetary Fund (IMF). (2012). *Greece: Request for Extended Arrangement under the Extended Fund Facility—Staff Report; Staff Supplement; Press Release on the Executive Board Discussion; and Statement by the Executive Director for Greece.* IMF Country Report No. 12/57. Washington, DC: IMF.

Ioannou, C. (1998). 'EMU and Hellenic Industrial Relations'. In: T. Kauppinen (ed.). *The Impact of EMU on Industrial Relations in European Union.* Helsinki: Finnish Industrial Relations Association Publications.

Ioannou, C. (2004) Indicators Figures and Estimates on Greek Industrial Relations – Report for the Project 'Quality Industrial Relations' (ZKB2327), HIVA - Work and Organisation Sector, Atrecht College, Catholic University of Leuven, March 2004.

Ioannou, C. (2011a). 'The Types of Collective Labour Agreements and the Structure of the System of Collective Bargaining before and after the Law 1876/1990'. *Epitheorisi Ergatikou Dikaiou*, 70(7): 753–786 ([in Greek]).

Ioannou, C. (2011b). 'Tectonic Changes in the Wage Formation System, in Tribute to the Greek Economic Crisis'. *Greek Review of Social Research*, No. 134–135(A–B): 133–164 (in Greek).

Ioannou, C. (2012a). 'Recasting Greek Industrial Relations: Internal Devaluation in Light of the Economic Crisis and European Integration'. *International Journal of Comparative Labour Law and Industrial Relations*, 28(2): 199–222.

Ioannou, C. (2012b). 'How 'Dependent' on Arbitration Were Collective Agreements under Law 1876/1990'. *Epitheorisi Ergatikou Dikaiou*, 71(13): 897–916 (in Greek).

Ioannou, C. (2013). 'Greek Public Service Employment Relations: A Gordian Knot in the Era of Sovereign Default'. *European Journal of Industrial Relations*, 19(4): 295–308.

Ioannou, C. (2016). 'Public Sector Employment Relations in Greece: Adjustment and Reforms'. In: S. Bach and L. Bordogna (eds.). *Public Service Management and Employment Relations in Europe; Emerging from the Crisis?* London: Routledge, pp. 29-56.

Ioannou, C. and Papadimitriou, K. (2013). *Collective Negotiations in Greece during 2011–2012: Trends, Changes and Prospects.* Athens: OMED (in Greek).

Ioannou, C., Zisimopoulos, A., Katrougkalos, G., Fotopoulos, N. and Mpastaki, C. (2011) *Collective Bargaining before and after Law 1876/1990, Organization for Mediation and Arbitration (OMED)*, Athens. January 2011 (in Greek).

Ioannou, D. and Ioannou, C. (2013). 'Wages and the Internal Devaluation in Greece'. *Foreign Affairs The Hellenic Edition*, 21: 96–123 (in Greek).

Ioannou, D. and Ioannou, C. (2017). 'The Fundamental Asymmetry in the Economy of Greece'. *Greek Economic Outlook*, 33: 62–70.

Johnston, A., Hancké, B., and Pant, S. (2014). 'Comparative Institutional Advantage in the European Sovereign Debt Crisis'. *Comparative Political Studies*, 47(13): 1771–1800.

Papadimitriou, K. and Ioannou, C. (2015). Collective Bargaining and Their Results in Practice in the Years 2012-2014 in the Collective Negotiation Today: Findings - Trends - Prospects, EDEKA 14th National Conference Proceedings, Nomiki Bibliothiki Athens 2015 (in Greek).

Rödl, Fl. and Callsen, R. (2016). *Collective Social Rights Under the Strain of Monetary Union, Can Article 28 of the EU Charter of Fundamental Rights Offer Protection?* Brussels: ETUI.

Sciarra, S. (2006). 'The Evolution of Collective Bargaining: Observations on a Comparison in the Countries of the European Union'. *Comparative Labor Law and Policy Journal*, 29(1): 1–27.

Traxler, F. (1995). 'Farewell to Labour Market Associations? Organized versus Disorganized Decentralisation as a Map for Industrial Relations'. In: F. Traxler and C. J. Crouch (eds.). *Organized Industrial Relations in Europe. What Future?* Aldershot: Avebury, pp. 3–19.

Tzannatos, Z. (2014). 'The Greek Adjustment Programme: Fiscal Metrics without Economic Goals?' In: K. Papadakis and Y. Ghellab (eds.). *The Governance of Policy Reforms in Southern Europe and Ireland. Social Dialogue Actors and Institutions in Times of Crisis.* Geneva: International Labour Office, pp. 163–186.

Visser, J. (2015). *Institutional Characteristics of Trade Unions, Wage-Setting, State Intervention and Social Pacts (ICTWSS): An International Database.* Amsterdam: Amsterdam Institute for Advanced Labour Studies (AIAS).

Visser, J. (2016). 'What Happened to Collective Bargaining during the Great Recession?'. *IZA Journal of Labor Policy*, 5: 9.

Windmuller, J. P., et al. (1987). *Collective Bargaining in Industrialised Market Economies: A Reappraisal.* Geneva: International Labour Office.

3 Sectoral returns in the Greek labour market over 2002–2016

Dynamics and determinants

Rebekka Christopoulou and Vassilis Monastiriotis

1 Introduction

When the Great Depression hit Greece in 2009, the country was extremely ill-prepared to deal with the consequences and the new threats that emerged, with much of the burden falling on the labour market. In part, this had to do with the level and depth of knowledge about the workings of the market, for example, the sources of wage disparity across workers and jobs. Before the crisis, a large, albeit mainly descriptive, volume of research focused on issues of wage-setting, collective bargaining, and industrial relations (see Kornelakis and Voskeritsian 2014 for a review). Yet, studies that enlighten policy-makers about the presence of disequilibria, at large and across sectors of the economy, and the extent of inefficiency associated with these were lacking. To a large degree, this remains the case today despite the relative blooming of academic research in the country after the eruption of the crisis. The sources of wage disparities in labour markets and across sectors are generally not easy to track, and even the international literature remains inconclusive. Researchers do not fully understand why similar workers who do similar work in different sectors of the economy often receive different wages. In this chapter, we study how inter-sectoral wage differentials in Greece evolved before and during the recent crisis and try to uncover their sources, also asking the pertinent question of how the crisis has influenced both the level and the drivers of such differentials.

Competitive labour market theories attribute sectoral premia that cannot be explained by observed worker and job characteristics to compensatory differentials; i.e. to working conditions or unobserved abilities that are difficult to measure, such as motivation, perseverance, and commitment (the literature on this is long and longstanding – see Ge and Macieira 2014 for recent evidence). Non-competitive theories link sectoral premia to the presence of market distortions and, more specifically, to efficiency wage mechanisms and monopolistic market power. Efficiency wages are set above market-clearing level to avoid turnover, monitoring costs, adverse selection of workers, and worker dissatisfaction due to wage differentials perceived as unfair (Akerlof and Yellen 1986; Katz 1986; Murphy and Topel 1990). Monopolistic market power allows rents to be created, which will then spill over to workers, at least partly, either due to the presence of strong unions (which can be endogenous to the existence of rents) or due to sector-specific supply-shortages and skill mismatches (Manning 2011 provides a review).

In a dynamic sense, however, for sectoral premia to persist, additional forms of market distortion and imperfection must be present: from asymmetric information and other information costs that may not allow individuals to move across sectors to dampen unaccounted-for sectoral pay differentials to union-based or legal restrictions on sectoral (and occupational) mobility (e.g. closed-shop policies or restricted occupational licensing); to the presence of sector-specific positive externalities on labour productivity so that, for example, workers with a fixed set of productivity-related individual characteristics are more productive in one sector than in another; to capital market imperfections so that investment rates in different sectors do not respond to sectoral differences or changes in productivity and/or profitability (for background literature, see the seminal works by Blanchflower et al. 1996; Dickens and Katz 1987; Katz and Summers 1989, among others).

Given this, it is interesting to examine the size and evolution of sectoral wage premia in the Greek economy during the crisis because Greece has undergone a substantially transformative process, aiming to modernise its economy and remove long-standing distortions and inefficiencies. Indeed, the pervasive programme of fiscal consolidation imposed through the bailout conditionality of the so-called Troika was combined with extensive measures of structural reforms, including liberalisation of closed professions (deregulation of occupational licensing), decentralisation of wage bargaining and broader measures for labour market deregulation, and deregulation of product markets (Ioannou 2016; Katsoulakos et al. 2017; Lyberaki et al. 2017). Therefore, it is pertinent to ask whether this policy effort has led to a measurable decrease in market inefficiencies and distortions, at least as captured by the existence of sectoral wage premia. In addressing this question, we also provide a wider commentary about the sectoral structure of the Greek economy.

To our knowledge, there are three studies that have previously examined inter-industry wage differentials in Greece. Du Caju et al. (2010) included Greece in a sample of eight European countries and estimated sectoral premia for 1995 and 2002. Their results suggest that the premia are inconsistent with sectoral differences in unobserved worker characteristics but reflect variation in rents and industry structure. Nikolitsas (2011) used data for 2006, focusing on Greece alone. This study, too, found a significant role for non-competitive factors as well as provided evidence that competitive factors, namely the risk of accidents at work, contribute to explaining sectoral premia. Lastly, Papapetrou and Tsalaporta (2017) used data for 2010 to more elaborately test whether Greek sectoral premia can be explained by unobserved worker ability. Their results reject this hypothesis. By and large, the findings of these studies are consistent with evidence from other countries that non-competitive factors are the leading determinants of unexplained inter-industry wage differentials (e.g. Du Caju et al. 2011).

Compared to all three, this chapter makes a clear and significant contribution: we describe and attempt to explain Greek sectoral premia in every year over 2002–2016, i.e., we cover the entire period from Greece's entry to the Eurozone to the end of the recent crisis. Our results corroborate the previous findings that unobserved worker characteristics cannot explain sectoral premia, whereas non-competitive factors play a significant role. Provocatively enough, our findings suggest that this role has shifted sizeably during the crisis and has become more important in some way. We show that the least competitive sectors recorded an increase in wage premia during the crisis, and thus, the overall disparity of wages across sectors increased. This happened even though the influence of sectoral rents on premia over the same period decreased and intra-sectoral wage adjustments linked to the public-sector wage cuts pushed premia to fall. Our results imply that market inefficiencies, as manifested by the presence of unaccounted-for sectoral wage differentials, intensified despite all policy efforts in the opposite direction.

2 Empirical strategy

For our analysis, we use data from the Greek Labour Force Survey (LFS), a household survey that collects detailed information on demographic characteristics and labour market outcomes. The LFS reports our main variable of interest – the industry in which workers are employed – at the two-digit level but changes its classification after 2008. To end up with harmonised industry categories over the entire period of study, we create 19 aggregate sectors that resemble the one-digit sectors of NACE Rev. 2 quite closely.

All previous studies on Greece (Du Caju et al. 2010; Nikolitsas 2011; Papapetrou and Tsalaporta 2017) have used the Structure of Earnings Survey (SES), which in some ways is superior as it collects information from employers instead of households, thus providing more information (e.g. the SES reports firm IDs, the principal market for each firm's products, and the level at which bargaining takes place) and more precise information (e.g. employer reports on wages and their components are more accurate compared to those reported by individuals, which is especially true for the LFS, which reports wages in bundles for most years of study[1]). In some respects, however, the SES is unsuited for studying the case of Greece as it surveys only large firms (those with ten or more workers), thus covering a small share of Greek employers, and does not report worker citizenship and marital status, both of which are important determinants of Greek wages. The LFS covers firms of all sizes and includes richer demographics (place of birth, marital status, number of children). More importantly, the SES is collected every four years and is therefore inferior to the LFS when studying dynamics.

With the data at hand, we proceed to analyse annual sectoral wage premia in two forms: (a) gross, i.e., as observed in the data; and (b) net, i.e., as derived from a Mincer wage regression of the following form:

$$\ln W_i = \beta X_i + \varepsilon_i \tag{1}$$

Here, W_i is the monthly wage of individual i, X is a vector of control variables (see Table 3A.1 in the Appendix for a list of the variables used and summary statistics), β the respective returns, and ε is a random error. In both cases, we calculate premia as deviations of log mean sectoral wages from the grand mean (i.e., the premia sum up to zero over all sectors).

We then attempt to test whether net premia can be attributed to unobserved productive characteristics of workers. To do this, we follow Martins (2004), who argues that if unobserved worker heterogeneity is indeed the driving source of sectoral premia, then these should be higher at the top tail of the wage distribution compared to the bottom.[2] We test this by applying interquantile regressions to differences in log wages at the 25th versus the 75th percentile and at the 10th versus the 90th percentile of the wage distribution. Formally, we estimate:

$$Q_{0.75}(\ln W_i) - Q_{0.25}(\ln W_i) = (\beta_{0.75} - \beta_{0.25})X_i + v_i \tag{2}$$

$$Q_{0.90}(\ln W_i) - Q_{0.10}(\ln W_i) = (\beta_{0.90} - \beta_{0.10})X_i + v_i \tag{3}$$

Finally, we test the degree to which premia net of worker and job characteristics can be attributed to non-competitive factors. To do that, we pool together all net sectoral premia over the period of study and compile a panel database that varies by sector and year. We then estimate fixed effects panel data models of the following form:

$$\hat{\beta}_{st} = \gamma Y_{st} + \eta_s + \varphi_{st} \tag{4}$$

Here, $\hat{\beta}_{st}$ represents the estimated premia of sector s in year t from Equation (1), Y is a vector of explanatory variables that vary by sector and year, η_s represents the unobserved time-invariant sector-effect, and φ_{st} is the error term. In Y we include factors linked to the employers' ability to pay rents (sectoral profitability and a relatively oligopolistic market structure) and workers' potential for extracting rents (as proxied by the concentration of public-sector jobs). Specifically, we use lagged (ln) gross operating surplus as a direct measure of the availability of rents[3] (derived from the OECD-Stan database, available over 2002–2015); the share of workers who work in small firms (with less than 10 employees) as the (inverse of) potential for rents (calculated from the LFS data); and the share of workers who work in publicly owned firms as a measure of the potential of workers in the sector to extract rents (also calculated from the LFS data). The rationale behind the latter variable is that higher concentration of public sector jobs implies generally a higher unionisation rate in the sector and greater "outside opportunities" and thus bargaining power for workers employed in the private part of the sector. Both create a wage-push potential for the sector as a whole, especially as wages in public-sector jobs, net of individual characteristics, are typically higher (Christopoulou and Monastiriotis 2014, 2016).

As a last exercise, we test whether the relationship between the sectoral premia and the explanatory variables changes after the onset of the crisis. We do this in two ways. First, we allow the constant term and the coefficients of the explanatory variables to differ between the crisis (2009–2016) and the pre-crisis periods (2002–2008), and subsequently, we test whether the difference between the two coefficients is statistically significant.

3 The evolution of raw and net wage premia across sectors

We present raw and net sectoral premia for the entire period of study in Figure 3.1. As can be seen, raw premia are substantial, ranging in most years between –50% and 50% of average wages. They are generally higher in sectors with higher minimum efficient scales of production (high fixed costs), such as mining and quarrying; energy; water, sewerage, waste; and transportation and storage; as well as in the public (public administration, defence, and social security) and business services sectors (finance and insurance; real estate; and ICT). Premia net of worker and job characteristics are much lower in value but still sizeable, now ranging between –20% and 20% of average wages in most years. Net premia are higher in the same sectors with high raw premia, though in the sectors where public-sector jobs are dominant, they appear to fall over time. This pattern is intuitive: sectoral premia are higher in high value-added sectors, such as banking/finance and ICT; they are also high in monopolistic sectors and in sectors where market competition pressures are low, such as the cases of utilities (energy and water) and public administration. For the public sectors, the decline in net premia over time is consistent with the deregulation efforts that took place during the crisis and, as we discuss later, they may also signal a labour-supply adjustment process.

One particular pattern in Figure 3.1 stands out. Both gross and net premia appear to diverge during the crisis. This is even more apparent in Figure 3.2, where we plot the standard deviation of sectoral premia over time. In all the years before the crisis, the standard deviation remains more or less constant, but after the beginning of the crisis, it increases considerably. Over 2009–2016, the standard deviation of raw premia increases by 42%, whereas the standard deviation of net premia increases by 25%.

In practice, this means that as the crisis hit, premia decreased in some sectors and increased in others; i.e., whilst wages were falling on average,

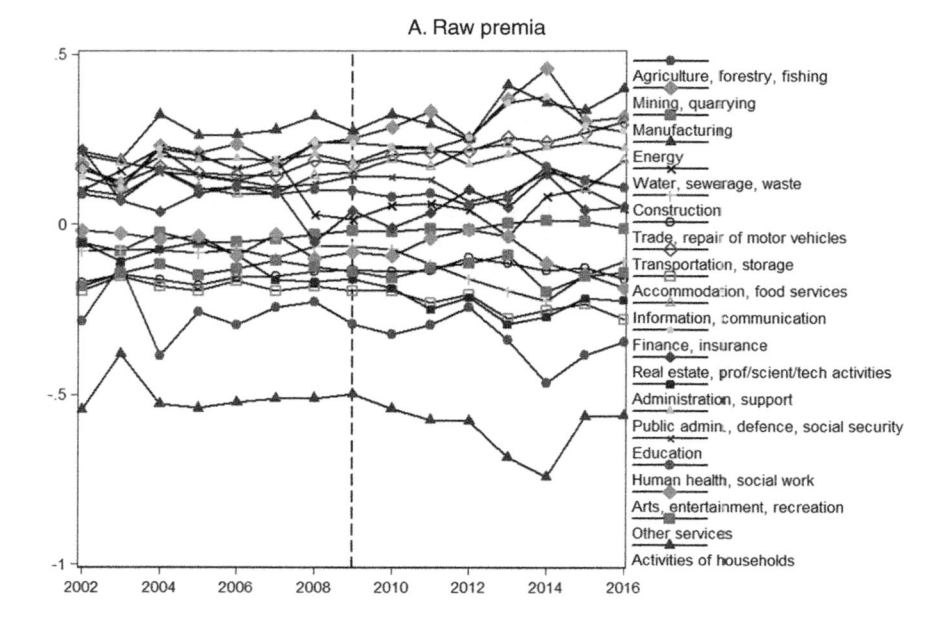

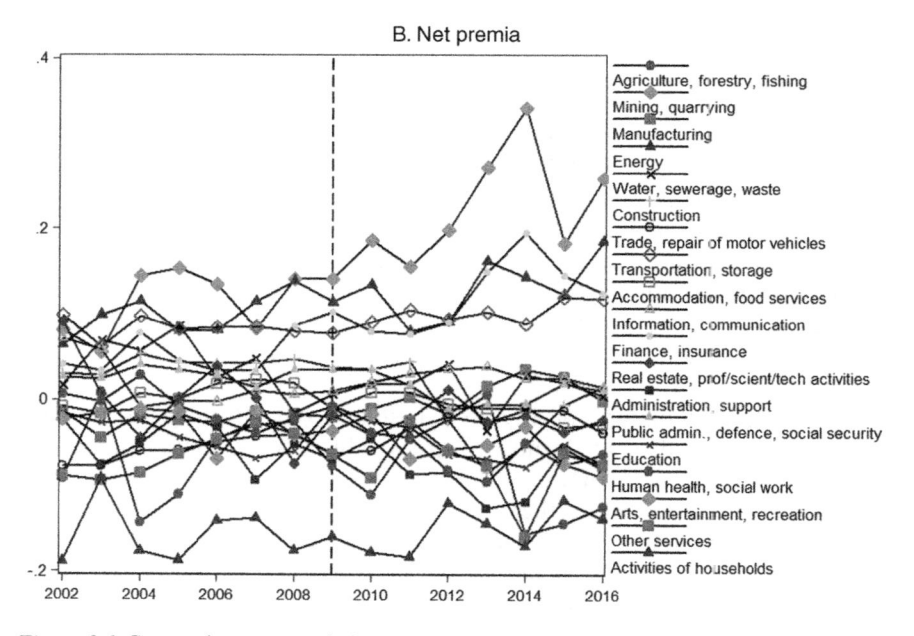

Figure 3.1 Sectoral wage premia by year, 2002–2016

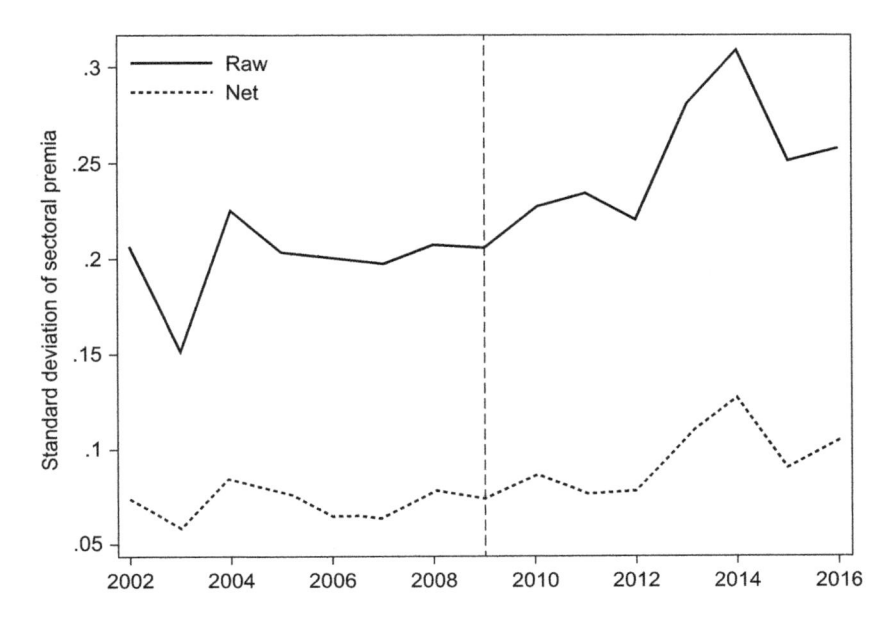

Figure 3.2 Standard deviation of sectoral premia by year, 2002–2016

they endured in some sectors. To demonstrate this, we plot mean pre-crisis premia against the change in premia during the crisis in Figure 3.3. For both gross and net premia, there is a clear positive association between premia levels and changes, suggesting that on the whole, premia increased in sectors in which they were already high. Focusing on the net premia in particular, which are of more interest to our analysis, this seems to be the case with the high fixed costs and high value-added sectors identified earlier (B: Mining, quarrying; D: Energy; E: Water, sewerage, waste; H: Transportation, storage; and K: Finance and insurance), although exceptions to this general pattern exist: both in the sense of high-premia sectors experiencing relative decline in their premia (F: Construction; and O: Public administration, defence and social security) and in the sense of low-premia sectors experiencing a rise in their relative premia (mainly L: Real estate; M: Professional, scientific and technical activities; and T: Activities of households). The case of the Construction and Public administration sectors is telling, as it reflects the market (for construction) and non-market (for public administration) pressures that were applied during the crisis, pushing wages in these sectors down disproportionately. For the case of sector T (activities of households), which is by far the biggest outlier, the result presented in Figure 3.3 indicates a significant compositional shift in the sector, presumably with a significant worsening of worker quality.

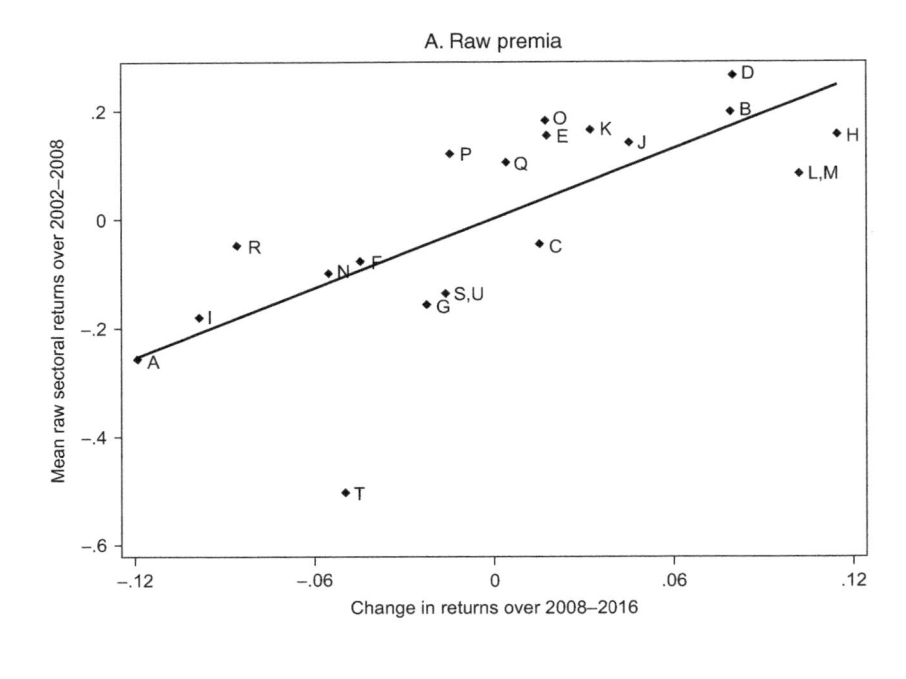

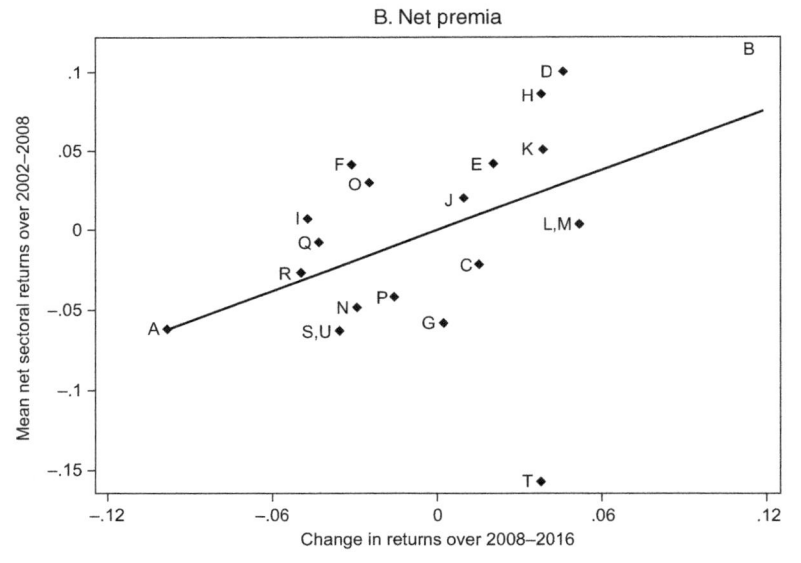

Figure 3.3 Correlation between pre-crisis premia and change in premia during the crisis

Note: Labels correspond to one-digit NACE Rev.2 codes (A: Agriculture, forestry, fishing; B: Mining, quarrying; C: Manufacturing; D: Energy; E: Water, sewerage, waste; F: Construction; G: Trade, repair of motor vehicles; H: Transportation, storage; I: Accommodation, food services; J: Information, communication; K: Finance, insurance, L: Real estate, M: Prof/sci/tech activities; N: Administration, support; O: Public adm., defence, social sec.; P: Education; Q: Human health, social work; R: Arts, entertainment, recreation; S: Other services; T: Activities of households; U: Extraterritorial organizations.) Grey lines represent linear fits.

Another insight into these changes can be obtained by jointly plotting the gross and net premia, but separately for the crisis and pre-crisis periods (Figure 3.4). Plausibly, workers whose observed characteristics beget higher than average wages (i.e. the high-skilled) are concentrated in high-paying sectors, while workers whose characteristics result in lower than average wages (i.e. the low-skilled) are in low-paying sectors. In general, explained

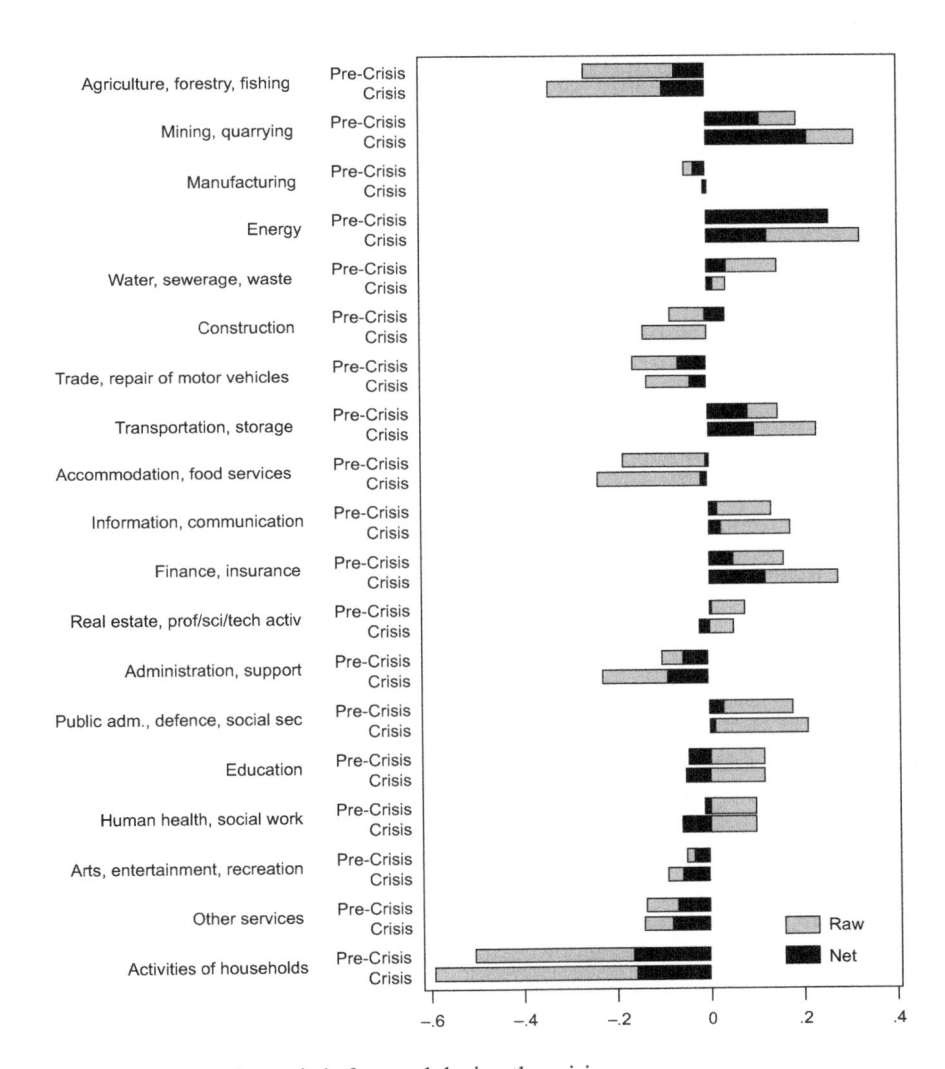

Figure 3.4 Sectoral premia before and during the crisis

Note: When raw and net premia have the same sign, raw premia are represented by the sum of the grey and black bar, i.e. the black bar demonstrates the portion of the raw premia that cannot be explained by observed characteristics. When raw and net premia have opposite signs, the sum of the black and grey bars demonstrates premia explained by observed characteristics which, in these cases, exceed raw premia in (absolute) value.

and unexplained premia are in the same direction and only in a few cases do they appear with opposite signs. In Education, Health, and Real estate (crisis only) gross premia are positive and sizeable, whereas net premia are negative, suggesting that these sectors employ high-skilled workers whose wage premia are dampened by unobserved factors. In Manufacturing (crisis only) and Accommodation and Food services (pre-crisis only), raw premia are negative and sizeable, while net premia are positive and small, suggesting that in these cases, the two sectors employ low-skilled workers whose wages are somehow boosted by unobserved factors.

Regarding the differences between the pre-crisis and crisis periods, we see again that premia increased in most of the sectors in which they were already high, while they declined further in virtually all sectors that had below-average premia pre-crisis. More instructive here, however, is the sectoral heterogeneity in the difference between the "net" and "raw" premia. In some sectors (Agriculture, Energy, Water, and ICT), the ratio of net-to-raw premia, and thus the share of the sectoral premium that remains unaccounted for after controlling for worker and job characteristics, remained rather stable despite some, sometimes large, shifts in the size of these premia. In some others (Mining, Finance, Arts/entertainment and Other services), this ratio increased, showing that sectoral, rather than compositional, drivers became more important over the crisis. The inverse is true for a host of other sectors (Trade, Transport, Administration, Public administration, and Household activities), where, presumably, compositional shifts during the crisis played a bigger role in maintaining or shifting the observed raw wage premia.

The natural question to ask at this point is what drives the unexplained premia. In the next section, we assume the task to illuminate the determinants and their evolution over time.

4 Exploring the factors that have shaped net (unexplained) wage premia across sectors

Despite their sizeable heterogeneity, net premia do not pose efficiency concerns if they are created by differences in unobserved characteristics of workers and jobs and by the way these differences change over time. As we explained in Section 2, we examine whether this is indeed the case by employing an interquantile regression analysis to test whether sectoral premia are higher at the upper tail of the wage distribution, i.e., whether the difference in the coefficients $\beta_{0.75}$ and $\beta_{0.25}$ in Equation 2 (or in $\beta_{0.90}$ and $\beta_{0.10}$ in Equation 3) is positive and statistically significant. If that is the case, it indicates that sectoral premia reflect worker ability for which we have not controlled (as this is expected to be higher for the high-pay earners). Table 3.1 summarises the results from this analysis.

The results are generally unsupportive for the unobserved heterogeneity hypothesis. Out of a total 285 coefficients (19 sectors × 15 years) that we estimated for each model, less than 16% appear positive and statistically

Table 3.1 Years in which coefficients of interquantile regressions are positive and statistically significant

Sector	$Q_{0.75}-Q_{0.25}$	$Q_{0.90}-Q_{0.10}$
Agriculture, forestry, fishing		2004, 2006, 2014
Mining, quarrying	2006, 2010–2011, 2013–2014	2010–2012, 2014–2015
Manufacturing		
Energy	2002, 2009, 2013, 2016	2009–2010, 2012–2013, 2016
Water, sewerage, waste	2009	2009
Construction	2013	2002, 2013
Trade, repair of motor vehicles	2002	2003
Transportation, storage	2002–2005, 2007, 2010–2011, 2013–2016	2002–2005, 2007–2011, 2015–2016
Accommodation, food services		
Information, communication	2010	2008
Finance, insurance		
Real estate, prof/sci/tech activities		2002
Administration, support		
Public adm., defence, social security	2009–2010, 2015	2009–2011
Education		
Human health, social work	2012	
Arts, entertainment, recreation	2013	2009
Other services	2012, 2015–2016	2002–2003, 2016
Activities of households	2003–2005	2004–2008, 2012
Positive coefficients as a share of total estimated coefficients	12.3	15.4

significant, and in most cases, these are scattered across sectors and years. A result we do not report in Table 3.1 is that in over one-fifth of the cases, the estimated coefficients are negative, thus going against the argument that premia may be reflecting unobserved differences in worker quality across sectors. Transportation and storage is the only sector for which we find positive and significant coefficients relatively consistently for the entire period of study; while we also find a few positive and significant coefficients for the energy and mining sectors, mostly after the crisis and mostly when comparing the 10th and 90th quantiles. These results suggest that unobserved worker ability may play a role in these special cases but definitely not across the board. We thus conclude that one should look for the main determinants of net premia elsewhere – i.e., on non-competitive factors. As we mentioned earlier, a similar result in the case of Greece (using 2010 data from the SES dataset) has been found by Papapetrou and Tsalaporta (2017).

We test the role of non-competitive factors in Table 3.2. As described earlier, we pool together all net premia estimates to create a sector-year panel, which we use to estimate the impact of variables proxying for the availability of rents and the potential for these to be extracted by workers in the form of sectoral premia. We present estimates of three specifications: in column 1, we test the significance of the explanatory variables over the whole sample period, assuming that the relationships under investigation remain constant between the pre-crisis and crisis years; in columns 2 and 3, we let the effect of all regressors change after the beginning of the crisis to allow for a shift in the relationships under investigation between the pre-crisis and crisis periods; and in columns 4 and 5, we run the same models as in columns 2 and 3, replacing the crisis dummy with a full set of year-specific fixed effects, which allow us to examine further the evolution of sectoral premia (net of their econometric determinants) over time. In all cases, the models are estimated using the fixed-effects estimator with robust standard errors. The inclusion of sectoral fixed effects, although econometrically warranted (the Hausman test for fixed versus random effects returns an X^2 value for the first of our models of 21.06, p-value=0.0001), removes the time-invariant cross-sectoral variation in our dependent variable, thus forcing estimation on the basis of inter-temporal ("within" sectors) variations. To examine whether, by so doing, we are missing out on some important sector-specific influences, which are important in the cross-sectional dimension, we re-estimated the regressions presented in Table 3.1 using the GLS random-effects estimator and a simple OLS estimation instead. The results remained highly consistent across alternative specifications.

Starting from the first specification, which looks at the total period under investigation as a whole, we find some very instructive results. Our proxy for profitability (gross operating surplus) returns a positive and statistically significant coefficient (at the 5% level), showing that sectors with higher profitability offer higher wage premia. This result is highly intuitive: sectoral premia appear larger in high-profitability sectors where employers' ability to pay rents is higher. In turn, our second and third variables, measuring the extent of intra-sectoral competition (share of workers in small firms) and workers' ability to extract rents (the weight of public sector jobs in the sector), return coefficients that are statistically indistinguishable from zero. This is a very interesting finding, which suggests that sectoral wage premia are linked more directly with the *availability* of rents in the sector than with the sector's *potential* for rents or the *ability* of workers to extract such rents.[4] Importantly, this also means that despite the known tendency of the public sector to offer sizeable wage premia, the presence of public sector jobs per se in not responsible for the presence of high wage premia in particular sectors.

The results from specifications (2)-(5) examine how these relationships have been altered with the crisis. As can be seen, we find strong evidence that sectoral premia went up during the crisis. In columns 2 and 3, the

Table 3.2 Fixed effects regressions of net sectoral premia

	(1)	*(2)*	*(3)*	*(4)*	*(5)*
Lagged ln (gross operating surplus)	1.2589 [0.5549]**				
Pre-crisis		2.4978 [0.8088]***	2.4978 [0.8088]***	3.2405 [0.9663]***	3.2405 [0.9663]***
Crisis		0.8739 [0.5634]		1.4516 [0.7117]**	
Difference			−1.6240 [0.5118]***		−1.7889 [0.5311]***
Share of workers in small firms	−0.0282 [0.0444]				
Pre-crisis		0.0553 [0.0629]	0.0553 [0.0629]	0.0281 [0.0702]	0.0281 [0.0702]
Crisis		−0.0570 [0.0471]		−0.0821 [0.0593]	
Difference			−0.1123 [0.0334]***		−0.1103 [0.0341]***
Share of workers in public firms	−0.0358 [0.0340]				
Pre-crisis		0.0228 [0.0417]	0.0228 [0.0417]	0.0219 [0.0417]	0.0219 [0.0417]
Crisis		−0.0571 [0.0352]		−0.0608 [0.0360]*	
Difference			−0.0799 [0.0209]***		−0.0827 [0.0206]***
Crisis period (years 2009–2016)		0.1348 [0.0361]***	0.1348 [0.0361]***		
Year 2003				−0.0023 [0.0136]	−0.0023 [0.0136]
Year 2004				−0.0063 [0.0124]	−0.0063 [0.0124
Year 2005				−0.0100 [0.0126]	−0.0100 [0.0126]
Year 2006				−0.0102 [0.0120]	−0.0102 [0.0120]

(*Continued*)

Table 3.2 (Cont.)

	(1)	(2)	(3)	(4)	(5)
Year 2007				−0.0126 [0.0121]	−0.0126 [0.0121]
Year 2008				−0.0140 [0.0122]	−0.0140 [0.0122]
Year 2009				0.1303 [0.0382]***	0.1303 [0.0382]***
Year 2010				0.1306 [0.0377]***	0.1306 [0.0377]***
Year 2011				0.1350 [0.0379]***	0.1350 [0.0379]***
Year 2012				0.1303 [0.0381]***	0.1303 [0.0381]***
Year 2013				0.1303 [0.0392]***	0.1303 [0.0392]***
Year 2014				0.1402 [0.0423]***	0.1402 [0.0423]***
Year 2015				0.1400 [0.0386]***	0.1400 [0.0386]***
Year 2016				0.1389 [0.0387]***	0.1389 [0.0387]***
Constant	−0.0165 [0.0366]	−0.1177 [0.0569]**	−0.1177 [0.0569]**	−0.1232 [0.0583]**	−0.1232 [0.0583]**
R-squared	0.828	0.845	0.845	0.848	0.848

Note: Robust standard errors in brackets, ***p < 0.01, **p < 0.05, *p < 0.1. Observations: 285.

crisis-specific constant term is statistically significant and positive, showing directly that the crisis is associated with a substantial increase in wage premia,[5] while in columns 4 and 5, the year dummies show a similar effect, which appears to be largely non-trended. From this, it follows that the estimated crisis effect can be rather safely attributed to the qualitative changes brought about by the crisis than to any underlying trend pre-dating the crisis (see Figure 3.5 for a visual illustration of this). The crisis effect emerges after we control the (period-varying) effects of the level of profitability, the share of small firms, and the presence of public sector jobs in each sector, and in that sense, it appears to be a horizontal, economy-wide effect. Following Nikolitsas (2011), one could attribute this to competitive factors that our analysis does not account for, such as relative changes in pure compensating wage differentials related to job quality (e.g. the risk of work accidents and the associated wage compensation may have increased in the Mining or Energy sectors relative to the Construction sector, given that nearly all activity there came to a halt during the crisis). However, our view is that such effects cannot be far-reaching (if present at all), as job quality during the crisis has likely worsened to a similar degree throughout the economy (also in terms of pace of work, insecurity, etc.). We are more inclined to attribute the year fixed effects to non-competitive factors for which we have no direct control.

The remainder of Table 3.2 also points to significant non-competitive factors. For the public-sector variable, we find an effect that is not different from zero pre-crisis but statistically significant and negative during the crisis period, showing that sectoral premia fell during the crisis in public-sector

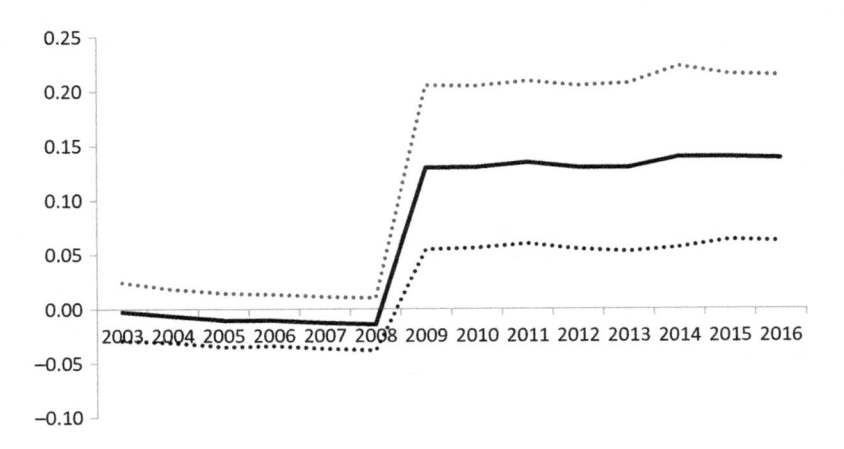

Figure 3.5 Estimated year fixed-effects for the net sectoral wage premia

Note: Estimates as reported in columns 4 and 5 of Table 2. Dotted lines show 95% confidence intervals.

dominated sectors. This effect is statistically significant both when measured in terms of differences from the pre-crisis period (cols. 3 and 5) and, marginally, when measured as a total period-specific effect (col.4). Given that the pre-crisis effect for this variable is not statistically positive (and noting that private-sector wages declined with the crisis in parallel with public-sector wages – Christopoulou and Monastiriotis 2016), it is unlikely that the crisis estimate captures a purely compositional effect (reflecting the decline in public sector wages per se).[6] Instead, it appears that the obtained result reflects a labour-market effect whereby public sector wage cuts and downsizing trigger downward wage pressures in private firms as well, especially when the proportion of public sector jobs in the sector is large. This interpretation is consistent with the sizeable literature that argues for, and empirically demonstrates, wage interactions and feedback effects between the public and private sector, with Greece categorised among the countries where the public sector operates as the wage leader (e.g. Camarero et al. 2014).

To conceptualise this, think of the education sector: as hiring of teachers in state schools essentially froze with the crisis and wages declined, an excess supply of teachers must have been directed to the private part of the sector, pushing down wages there as a result. This would show as an absolute reduction in net wage premia in the sector to the extent that this downward pressure was horizontal (i.e., not fully mediated by sorting on the basis of productive characteristics). It should be noted, however, that in the specific example of the education sector, the link between public and private wages arises not only through the forces of demand and supply, but also through the collective agreement of private sector teachers. The teachers' wages in private schools are historically linked to the ones in the public sector so that any changes in public sector wages automatically apply to the private sector as well. Thus, when wages in the public sector started to decline because of the memoranda, the same happened in the private sector as a consequence of the institutional framework in which wages in the private sector are determined.

Moving on to the profitability variable, we find that the crisis dampened the influence of this on wage premia: gross operating surplus continues to have a strong positive association with sectoral premia before the crisis, but this association diminishes both in size and in statistical significance during the crisis (the difference is always statistically significant at 1%, but the overall effect in the post-crisis period, reported in columns 2 and 4, is reduced by between half and two-thirds and is statistically different from zero only in column 4). This is a novel but broadly intuitive result: as employers have become more resource-constrained and perhaps also more prudent with the crisis – and as the crisis has significantly weakened the bargaining power of organised labour and individual workers – we would expect to see a lower increase in wage premia for any extra percentage point of profitability postcrisis compared to the increase in wage premia for a similar percentage increase in profitability pre-crisis.

In contrast, in the case of the small firms' variable, we find that it returns an effect that is again not different from zero pre-crisis (nor during the crisis), but its crisis value is negative and statistically different from the pre-crisis value. Thus, it is only with the advent of the crisis that we see wage premia become lower in sectors with larger proportions of small-firm employment and presumably with a more competitive market structure. Taken literally, this indicates that, controlling for actual sectoral rents, the sectors' potential for rents as captured by market structure did not explain the distribution of wage premia across sectors throughout the study period in any way; however, the crisis allowed for such wage premia to emerge in sectors overrepresented by large firms even if the overall effect has remained statistically not different from zero. This is again a novel but rather intuitive result: as the crisis progressed, small firms suffered more by the fall in domestic demand and struggled more with costs and liquidity, whereas larger firms may have found it easier to tip into export markets and external borrowing in a way that allowed them to maintain higher wages overall.

On the whole, these results provide a very interesting – and intimate – picture of the nature of wage premia in Greece. On the one hand, they tell us that generally, such premia are not driven by unobservables and worker sorting across sectors (Table 3.1), nor are they driven by the ability of workers to "extract" rents (see our discussion around column 1 of Table 3.2) or the employers' potential for rents. Rather, the drivers of sectoral rents appear to be related to the availability of rents/ability to pay rents as captured by the extent of profitability in each sector. On the other hand, they show that the crisis had a variable effect on these premia. It suppressed the wage premia afforded by high profitability (i.e., it reduced the elasticity of these premia to the gross operating surplus), but it also led to a wage disadvantage in sectors dominated by smaller firms and sectors dominated by public-sector jobs – neither of which had high premia, in a statistical sense, and thus evidence of pre-crisis inefficiency. The end result of these influences was a divergence of sectoral wage premia for the economy as a whole, as is corroborated both by our descriptive evidence (Figure 3.2) and our econometric results (Table 3.2). In other words, the crisis did not lead to an overall decline in cross-sectoral wage differentials, either on the whole or in the part that was due to non-competitive attributes – despite the fact that rents (profits) as a driver of wage differentials became less significant and deregulation played its part as well. In this token, the crisis does not seem to have led to a more efficient labour market equilibrium.

5 Conclusion

In this study, we examined the extent, sources, and temporal change of inter-sectoral wage differentials in Greece over a 15-year period, which coincided with dramatic changes – and challenges – for the Greek economy. We were motivated to do this by the general perception that sectoral wage premia reflect market distortions and inefficiencies and the lack of systematic evidence about sectoral wage premia in the country, especially post-crisis. Specifically, our interest was to explore the extent to which the crisis may have worked to dampen sectoral premia, i.e., unaccounted-for sectoral wage differentials. This could be for two reasons. First, because the crisis should naturally have compressed "excess" (non-competitive) wages and put pressure for more market-based (competitive) practices in wage-setting by removing the scope/space for non-competitive premia. Second, because the crisis was followed by an extensive programme of labour and product market reforms that were meant to rationalise the Greek economy and improve competitive conditions across all sectors.

Our analysis followed previous research, both in Greece and in the international literature. To measure sectoral wage premia, we relied on data derived from the Greek Labour Force Survey, which is an imperfect but by far the best source of relevant information, especially in its historical temporal dimension. We calculated raw sectoral wage differentials directly from the data and estimated net wage differentials (sectoral premia) using a Mincerian wage equation as is standard in the literature – controlling for various individual and job characteristics. Our descriptive evidence presented a rather unexpected picture of widening differentials – both in their "raw" and their "net" form. While such differentials have remained rather stable in the pre-crisis period, they increased rather substantially post-crisis by 42% and 25%, respectively (measured in terms of standard deviations).

In trying to explain this temporal pattern as well as the very existence of these premia, we implemented two pieces of analysis. First, we employed an interquantile regression approach, seeking to examine whether differentials at the top end of the distribution are systematically higher compared to the bottom end of the distribution. As is standard in the literature, evidence in favour of this could be interpreted as suggesting that sectoral premia are, to some extent at least, driven by sectoral differences in unobservable characteristics of workers, thus reflecting equilibrium processes of sorting (across sectors, on the basis of unobservable skills). Second, we employed a panel-data analysis, treating the estimated sectoral net premia as our dependent variable and examining their drivers by introducing a number of controls associated with the availability and appropriation potential of rents. Our results showed that sectoral wage premia are associated more strongly with "rent availability" factors (sectoral profits) on the whole than with "rent potential," "appropriation," or "competitive" factors. They also showed, rather unequivocally, that the heterogeneity of sectoral premia – and, in this token, market inefficiency – increased with the crisis. Indeed, while the crisis seems to have coincided with a decline in the extent to which premia may be attributable to the availability of rents (as proxied by sectoral profits), it also led to a widening of gross and net sectoral wage differentials, which is only in part accounted for by the suppression of wages in sectors dominated by small firms and public sector jobs.

We find these results particularly instructive. They indicate that economic efficiency has not increased in the post-2009 period: in the sense that unaccounted-for sectoral wage differentials have not declined, despite the dramatic economic pressures that were applied to the Greek economy and the significant reform effort undertaken by successive governments – even if imperfectly and not fully whole-heartedly. We believe that by and large, this has to do with more structural characteristics of the Greek economy. As the evidence for the pre-crisis period shows, sectoral premia and penalties were almost exclusively linked to profitability ("appropriated rents"), with practically no influence from factors linked to asymmetric worker (or union) power. In this sense, sectoral premia were of a "supply-side" nature: where firms could afford to do so, they would offer higher wages horizontally (i.e., not rationed in relation to any individual or job characteristics), but this would be independent of characteristics that afford workers more power, such as the presence of a large public-sector employer or of large employers more generally (both of which are linked, for example, to higher rates of unionisation). The crisis reduced the intensity of the relationship between profits and premia, but it also led to new sectoral cleavages – with sectors dominated by public sector jobs now offering lower wages ceteris paribus. The end result was not an overall reduction in sectoral wage differentials, i.e., a tendency towards cross-sectoral equalisation of net wages, but rather an amplification of these. Thus, on the whole, the reforms and economic pressures that came with the crisis did not lead to a more competitive market environment. Firms continue to offer wage premia when they can (when they have higher profits), and they offer lower wages horizontally when they are exposed to more competitive pressures. But equilibration mechanisms, which would dampen the existing sectoral differentials (for example, sectoral mobility or capital shifts), do not seem to have been strengthened with the crisis – if anything, they have become more subdued.

Of course, the amount and type of evidence presented here is not sufficient to categorically support such a conclusion. For this, one would need to utilise good-quality matched employee-employer data from administrative sources (which, however, Greek authorities do not make available to researchers), which would allow the implementation of advanced counterfactual methods of analysis. Nevertheless, our evidence points undoubtedly to this direction. To us, this indicates the importance of further examining the workings of the Greek labour market, both prior and after the eruption of the crisis. The continuing study of this is a necessary condition for obtaining a deeper understanding of the problems of the Greek economy in general and of its labour market in particular, and thus for devising policies that can help with the sustainable recovery of the economy and the enhancement of its competitiveness.

Appendix

Table 3A.1 Weighted means and frequencies of variables used in the analysis

Year	2002	2003	2004	2005	2006	2007	2008	2009	2010	2011	2012	2013	2014	2015	2016
Ln(monthly wage)	6.56	6.65	6.74	6.76	6.78	6.81	6.85	6.90	6.90	6.90	6.79	6.70	6.62	6.67	6.66
Weekly hours of work	40.2	40.2	39.9	40.0	39.7	39.6	39.9	39.5	39.3	39.0	38.9	38.7	38.6	38.7	38.8
Female	0.40	0.40	0.41	0.41	0.42	0.42	0.42	0.43	0.44	0.44	0.45	0.44	0.46	0.47	0.46
Years of education	12.6	12.8	13.0	13.0	13.1	13.2	13.2	13.3	13.4	13.6	13.9	14.0	14.5	14.5	14.7
Years of experience	18.9	19.0	18.8	19.2	19.3	19.6	19.6	19.7	20.0	20.3	20.3	20.5	19.5	19.7	19.8
Married	0.61	0.60	0.63	0.61	0.60	0.61	0.60	0.60	0.61	0.62	0.62	0.64	0.60	0.61	0.60
Has child(ren)	0.39	0.38	0.40	0.39	0.39	0.38	0.37	0.38	0.39	0.40	0.39	0.41	0.40	0.38	0.38
Foreign-born	0.08	0.09	0.09	0.09	0.09	0.10	0.12	0.13	0.13	0.13	0.11	0.11	0.10	0.10	0.09
Public job	0.35	0.35	0.37	0.35	0.36	0.36	0.35	0.35	0.35	0.36	0.36	0.37	0.36	0.34	0.33
Part-time job	0.04	0.03	0.04	0.04	0.05	0.05	0.04	0.05	0.06	0.06	0.08	0.10	0.11	0.11	0.11
Temporary job	0.12	0.11	0.12	0.12	0.11	0.11	0.11	0.12	0.13	0.12	0.10	0.10	0.12	0.12	0.12
Small firm worker	0.41	0.43	0.42	0.43	0.42	0.43	0.43	0.44	0.44	0.43	0.39	0.38	0.51	0.53	0.50
Agriculture, forestry, fishing	0.01	0.01	0.01	0.01	0.01	0.01	0.01	0.02	0.02	0.02	0.02	0.02	0.02	0.02	0.02
Mining, quarrying	0.01	0.00	0.01	0.01	0.01	0.01	0.01	0.00	0.00	0.00	0.00	0.01	0.00	0.00	0.00
Manufacturing	0.17	0.16	0.15	0.15	0.15	0.14	0.14	0.13	0.13	0.12	0.11	0.11	0.10	0.11	0.11
Energy	0.01	0.01	0.01	0.01	0.01	0.01	0.01	0.01	0.01	0.01	0.01	0.01	0.01	0.01	0.01
Water, sewerage, waste	0.00	0.00	0.00	0.00	0.00	0.00	0.01	0.01	0.01	0.01	0.01	0.01	0.01	0.01	0.01
Construction	0.08	0.09	0.08	0.09	0.08	0.09	0.09	0.08	0.07	0.06	0.05	0.04	0.04	0.04	0.04

Trade, repair of motor vehicles	0.14	0.14	0.14	0.15	0.14	0.14	0.15	0.15	0.16	0.16	0.16	0.17	0.16	0.17	0.16
Transportation, storage	0.05	0.05	0.05	0.05	0.05	0.05	0.05	0.05	0.05	0.05	0.05	0.05	0.05	0.05	0.05
Accommodation, food services	0.07	0.06	0.06	0.06	0.06	0.06	0.06	0.06	0.06	0.07	0.07	0.07	0.09	0.10	0.09
Information, communication	0.02	0.02	0.02	0.02	0.02	0.02	0.02	0.02	0.03	0.03	0.03	0.03	0.03	0.03	0.03
Finance, insurance	0.03	0.04	0.04	0.04	0.04	0.03	0.04	0.03	0.04	0.04	0.04	0.04	0.03	0.03	0.03
Real estate, prof/sci/tech activities	0.01	0.01	0.01	0.01	0.01	0.01	0.03	0.04	0.03	0.03	0.03	0.04	0.03	0.04	0.04
Administration, support	0.04	0.04	0.04	0.05	0.04	0.04	0.02	0.02	0.02	0.02	0.03	0.02	0.03	0.03	0.03
Public adm., defence, social security	0.12	0.12	0.13	0.12	0.14	0.14	0.13	0.13	0.14	0.14	0.14	0.15	0.14	0.13	0.14
Education	0.10	0.10	0.11	0.11	0.11	0.11	0.10	0.11	0.11	0.11	0.12	0.12	0.12	0.12	0.12
Human health, social work	0.06	0.06	0.07	0.07	0.07	0.07	0.06	0.07	0.07	0.08	0.08	0.08	0.07	0.07	0.07
Arts, entertainment, recreation	0.02	0.02	0.02	0.02	0.02	0.02	0.01	0.01	0.01	0.01	0.01	0.01	0.01	0.01	0.01
Other services	0.03	0.02	0.02	0.02	0.02	0.02	0.02	0.02	0.02	0.02	0.02	0.02	0.02	0.02	0.02
Activities of households	0.02	0.02	0.02	0.02	0.02	0.02	0.02	0.03	0.03	0.03	0.02	0.02	0.02	0.02	0.02
Central Macedonia	0.17	0.17	0.17	0.18	0.18	0.17	0.18	0.17	0.17	0.17	0.17	0.17	0.17	0.17	0.17
Western Macedonia	0.02	0.02	0.02	0.02	0.02	0.02	0.02	0.02	0.02	0.02	0.02	0.02	0.02	0.02	0.02
Epirus	0.02	0.02	0.02	0.02	0.03	0.03	0.03	0.02	0.03	0.02	0.02	0.02	0.02	0.03	0.03
Thessaly	0.06	0.05	0.06	0.06	0.06	0.06	0.06	0.06	0.06	0.05	0.06	0.06	0.06	0.06	0.06
Ionian Islands	0.02	0.02	0.02	0.02	0.02	0.02	0.02	0.02	0.02	0.02	0.02	0.02	0.02	0.02	0.02
Western Greece	0.05	0.05	0.05	0.05	0.05	0.05	0.05	0.05	0.05	0.05	0.04	0.04	0.03	0.05	0.05
Central Greece	0.05	0.04	0.04	0.05	0.04	0.05	0.05	0.04	0.04	0.05	0.05	0.05	0.05	0.04	0.04
Attica	0.45	0.45	0.43	0.42	0.42	0.42	0.42	0.44	0.44	0.45	0.45	0.44	0.45	0.41	0.41
Peloponnese	0.04	0.04	0.04	0.04	0.04	0.04	0.04	0.04	0.04	0.04	0.04	0.04	0.03	0.04	0.04
North Aegean	0.01	0.01	0.01	0.01	0.01	0.01	0.02	0.02	0.01	0.01	0.01	0.01	0.02	0.02	0.02

(*Continued*)

Table 3A.1 (Cont.)

Year	2002	2003	2004	2005	2006	2007	2008	2009	2010	2011	2012	2013	2014	2015	2016
South Aegean	0.03	0.03	0.02	0.03	0.02	0.02	0.02	0.02	0.02	0.02	0.02	0.02	0.04	0.04	0.03
Crete	0.04	0.05	0.06	0.06	0.05	0.06	0.05	0.05	0.05	0.05	0.05	0.05	0.06	0.06	0.06
Managers	0.02	0.02	0.02	0.02	0.02	0.02	0.02	0.02	0.02	0.02	0.02	0.02	0.02	0.01	0.01
Professionals	0.15	0.15	0.17	0.16	0.16	0.16	0.16	0.17	0.17	0.20	0.22	0.22	0.21	0.21	0.21
Technicians and associates	0.10	0.10	0.10	0.10	0.11	0.11	0.11	0.11	0.11	0.11	0.11	0.10	0.10	0.10	0.11
Clerical support workers	0.17	0.16	0.17	0.17	0.18	0.17	0.17	0.16	0.16	0.15	0.15	0.14	0.14	0.15	0.15
Service and sales workers	0.17	0.17	0.17	0.18	0.17	0.17	0.17	0.18	0.18	0.20	0.21	0.21	0.22	0.24	0.24
Skilled primary sector workers	0.01	0.01	0.01	0.01	0.01	0.01	0.01	0.01	0.01	0.01	0.01	0.01	0.01	0.01	0.01
Craft and related trades workers	0.18	0.18	0.16	0.16	0.15	0.16	0.15	0.14	0.13	0.11	0.10	0.10	0.09	0.09	0.09
Plant/machinery operators/ assemblers	0.09	0.09	0.09	0.09	0.09	0.09	0.09	0.09	0.08	0.07	0.07	0.07	0.08	0.06	0.06
Elementary occupations	0.10	0.10	0.09	0.10	0.10	0.09	0.10	0.10	0.11	0.11	0.10	0.10	0.10	0.11	0.10
Observations	15142	14722	16301	15998	15292	14851	14749	15379	15186	12520	9182	8277	8543	9328	10571

Notes

1 Prior to 2015, the LFS collected wage data in bundles that differ from year to year and cannot be fully harmonised for the period of study. Although this clearly prohibits comparisons of wage levels over time, it poses fewer challenges to comparisons of relative wages, as is the case here. Following common practice, we take the mean value of the bundles as a proxy for each individual's monthly wage. In previous work, we have shown that this measure produces robust estimates of Mincer equations when using alternative methods of estimation, namely OLS and interval regressions (Christopoulou and Monastiriotis 2014). From 2015 onward, the LFS reports actual values of wages rather than wage bundles.

2 Other researchers have applied alternative tests for this hypothesis based on workers moving across sectors (Krueger and Summers 1988; Murphy and Topel 1987) and on differences in sectoral premia across occupations (Dickens and Katz 1987; Krueger and Summers 1988). The former test runs the risk of selectivity bias and it is impossible to do with the LFS data as they lack the necessary longitudinal dimension. The latter test is unsuitable for Greece as differences of sectoral premia across occupations may reflect the prevalence of occupational-level bargaining instead of differences in unobserved worker heterogeneity.

3 We use the lagged value of this variable to sidestep potential endogeneity with wage premia. Endogeneity is plausible because high wages may attract highly productive employees in a particular sector, which will then increase the sector's profits.

4 Note that in the random effects and OLS specifications, we find the coefficient of the share of small-firm employment to also be statistically significant (negative), suggesting that in the cross-sectional dimension, the potential for rents, or the degree of inter-firm competition, matters as well.

5 With an expected mean value at zero (by construction) and a range, for the full period, between –19% and +34% (from the data), the inclusion of the crisis dummy returns a fixed effect for the post-crisis period of 13.5% (significant at 5%), which naturally renders the derived constant significantly negative.

6 The result is also inconsistent with a market share interpretation, where we would expect the decline in public sector jobs to lead to market share gains for private firms with subsequent positive effects on their profitability and thus potentially also their sectoral wage premia.

References

Akerlof, G. and Yellen, J. (1986). *Efficiency Wage Models of the Labor Market*. Cambridge, UK: Cambridge University Press.

Blanchflower, D. G., Oswald, A. J. and Sanfey, P. (1996). 'Wages, Profits, and Rent-Sharing'. *The Quarterly Journal of Economics*, 111(1): 227–251.

Camarero, M., D'Adamo, G. and Tamarit, C. (2014). 'Wage Leadership Models: A Country-by-Country Analysis of the EMU'. *Economic Modelling*, 44(S1): 2–11.

Christopoulou, R. and Monastiriotis, V. (2014). 'The Greek Public Sector Wage Premium before the Crisis: Size, Selection and Relative Valuation of Characteristics'. *British Journal of Industrial Relations*, 52(3): 579–602.

Christopoulou, R. and Monastiriotis, V. (2016). 'Public-Private Wage Duality during the Greek Crisis'. *Oxford Economic Papers*, 68(1): 174–196.

Dickens, W. T. and Katz, L. (1987). *Inter-Industry Wage Differences and Theories of Wage Determination*. NBER Working Paper 2271. Cambridge, MA: National Bureau of Economic Research.

Du Caju, P., Katay, G., Lamo, A., Nikolitsas, D. and Poelhekke, S. (2010). 'Inter-Industry Wage Differentials in EU Countries: What Do Cross-Country Time Varying Data Add to the Picture?'. *Journal of the European Economic Association*, 8 (2–3): 478–486.

Du Caju, P., Rycx, F. and Tojerow, I. (2011). 'Inter-Industry Wage Differentials: How Much Does Rent Sharing Matter?' *The Manchester School*, 79(4): 691–717.

Ge, Suqin and Macieira, Joao, Unobserved Worker Quality and Inter-Industry Wage Differentials (February 15, 2014). Available at SSRN: https://ssrn.com/abstract= 2396656 or http://dx.doi.org/10.2139/ssrn.2396656.

Ioannou, C. N. (2016). 'Public Sector Employment Relations in Greece: Adjustment and Reforms, in Public Service Management and Employment Relations in Europe'. In: S. Bach and L. Bordogna (eds.). *Emerging from the Crisis?* London: Routledge, pp. 29–55.

Katsoulakos, Y., Genakos, C. and Houpis, G. (2017). 'Product Market Regulation and Competitiveness: Towards a National Competition and Competitiveness Policy for Greece'. In: C. Meghir, C. Pissarides, D. Vayanos, and N. Vettas (eds.). *Beyond Austerity: Reforming the Greek Economy*. Cambridge, MA: MIT Press, pp. 139-178.

Katz, L. F. (1986). 'Efficiency Wage Theories: A Partial Evaluation'. In: S. Fischer (ed.). *NBER Macroeconomics Annual*. Vol. 1, Cambridge, MA: MIT Press, pp. 235–290.

Katz, L. F. and Summers, L. H. (1989). 'Industry Rents: Evidence and Implications'. In: Brookings Institution (ed.). *Brookings Papers on Economic Activity: Microeconomics* Washington, DC: Brookings Institution Press, pp. 209–290.

Kornelakis, A. and Voskeritsian, H. (2014). 'The Transformation of Employment Regulation in Greece: Towards a Dysfunctional Liberal Market Economy?' *Industrial Relations/Relations Industrielles*, 69(2): 344–365.

Krueger, A. B. and Summers, L. H. (1988). 'Efficiency Wages and the Industry Wage Structure'. *Econometrica*, 56: 259–294.

Lyberaki, A., Meghir, C. and Nicolitsas, D. (2017). 'Labor Market Regulation and Reform in Greece'. In: C. Meghir, C. Pissarides D. Vayanos and N. Vettas (eds.). *Beyond Austerity: Reforming the Greek Economy*. Cambridge, MA: MIT Press, pp. 211-250.

Manning, A. (2011). 'Imperfect Competition in the Labor Market'. *Handbook of Labor Economics*, 4: 973–1041.

Martins, P. S. (2004). 'Industry Wage Premiums: Evidence from the Wage Distribution'. *Economics Letters*, 83: 157–163.

Murphy, K. M. and Topel, R. (1987). 'Unemployment Risk and Earnings: Testing for Equalizing Wage Differences in the Labor Market'. In: K. Lang and J. Leonard (eds.). *Unemployment and the Structure of Labor Markets*. London: Basil Blackwell, pp. 103-140.

Murphy, K. M. and Topel, R. (1990). 'Efficiency Wages Reconsidered: Theory and Evidence'. In: Y. Yoram Weiss and G. Fishelson (eds.). *Advances in the Theory and Measurement of Unemployment*. London: Macmillan, pp. 204–242.

Nikolitsas, D. (2011). 'Evidence on Inter-Industry Wage Differentials in Greece'. In: S. Balfousias P. Hatzipanagiotou and K. Kanellopoulos (eds.). *Essays in Economics: Applied Studies in the Greek Economy*. Athens: Centre of Planning and Economic Research, pp. 285–397.

Papapetrou, E. and Tsalaporta, P. (2017). 'Inter-Industry Wage Differentials in Greece: Evidence from Quantile Regression Analysis'. *International Economic Journal*, 31(1): 51–67.

4 Firm-level bargaining and wage adjustments before and during the crisis

Evidence from the 2011 industrial relations reform

Nicholas Giannakopoulos and Ioannis Laliotis

1 Introduction

The institutional aspects of the collective bargaining system play a central role in the determination of nominal wage rigidities. Through collective negotiations, firms and their employees agree upon wage levels that reflect productivity and other characteristics of the firm and the market into which it operates. It is well established that under normal economic circumstances, nominal wage floors rarely adjust downwards. However, Daouli et al. (2016) show that during deep and prolonged recessions, such in the case of Greece, most wage floors defined in firm-level collective agreements downgraded due to firm-specific attributes and specific institutional factors.

Despite the policy relevance and the increasing interest in the process and future of decentralised collective bargaining in Greece (e.g. van Ours et al. 2016), little is known about the actual effects of the 2011 reform on nominal wage floors. In this chapter, we extend the analysis of Daouli et al. (2016) using a much larger dataset of firm-level contracts, which covers a longer period (2002–2016) capturing adequately the decentralised bargaining landscape before and after the reform. A suitably chosen comparison group of firms not engaged in decentralised negotiations is appended to the original dataset to estimate the determinants of firm-level contracting before and after the reform of the industrial relations framework. Finally, we analyse the wage adjustment process at the firm level by exploring how bargain outcomes were affected by the reform, the role of Associations of Persons, and the subsequent decrease of the National Minimum Wage (NMW) imposed by the government in early 2012.

The contribution of this study is threefold. First, it uses contractual data to offer a first formal assessment of the impact of firm-level collective bargaining on wage adjustments in a European economy with considerable downward wage rigidities. We should note that while relevant research focuses on the determinants of firm-level contracting in Canada, the United States, and some European counties (Avouyi-Dovi et al. 2013; Card and de la Rica, 2006; Christofides and Stengos 2003; Daouli et al. 2013, 2016), none of them examine wage floor adjustments for a long time period during which a reform has been implemented with a sharp reduction in the NMW. The importance of nation-wide base wage floor for the investigation of the determinants of wage floor adjustments has recently been highlighted by Fougere et al. (2016) but in the context of industry-level agreements in France. Second, it provides detailed evidence on negotiated base wage adjustments associated with a reformed collective bargaining regime in a recessionary period. Third, it explores the impact of a new form of workers' representation (the association of persons) on collectively bargained wage outcomes.

2 Institutional framework

In October 2011, a major restructuring of the Greek labour relations framework was implemented (Law 4024/2011). The new legislation redefined the limits within which firm-specific nominal base wages can oscillate and allowed workers in small-sized firms to engage in decentralised negotiations over wage issues with their employers. The objective of Law 4024/2011 was to confront the longstanding wage rigidities and bring labour costs in line with firm-specific productivity and the prevailing labour market conditions. More specifically, the reform allowed workers in firms employing less than 50 employees to participate in firm-level negotiations over wage issues. This was facilitated by introducing a new type of worker representation, the association of persons, with the only prerequisite being that they represent at least the 60% of the total number of employees. Given the right-skewed firm-size distribution of the Greek economy, the reform targeted on expanding the institution of firm-level bargaining and facilitating the wage adjustment process for the largest part of the private sector of the economy. In addition, it allowed contractual base wages to deviate below thresholds set at higher levels of collective bargaining (i.e. sectoral, occupational, and regional) but not below the national minimum wage (NMW) one.

Shortly after the reform of the collective bargaining framework, a dramatic increase in the number of firm-level contracts was observed. A detailed description of the structure of decentralised bargaining before and after the reform is provided in Daouli et al. (2013, 2016) and Voskeritsian and Kornelakis (2014). According to the Ministry of Labour, Social Security, and Welfare, the number of firm-level agreements spiked to 976 in 2012, while this number ranged between 63 and 242 in the period 1991–2011 and between 263 and 409 between 2013 and 2016. Moreover, the number of nation-wide sectoral and occupational agreements and region-specific occupational agreements was considerably lower in the post-reform period. In addition, the coverage by collective agreements fell sharply from 83% in 2009 to 42% in 2013 with a clear further downward trend (van Ours et al. 2016; Ioannou, this volume). With respect to the wage settlements in decentralised bargaining, using a unique dataset with firm-level contracts for the period 2010–2013, Daouli et al. (2016) show that the direction of base wage changes in the post-reform period became negative due to the intention of firms to adopt massive reductions following the reduction of the NMW set by the government (it was cut by 22% for workers above 25 years old and 32% for workers under 25 years old). Furthermore, they found that nominal base wages were reduced after the reform, especially in firms in which workers were represented by an association of persons.

3 Theoretical underpinnings and empirical strategy

Despite the ample evidence regarding the determinants of firm-level contracting in the related empirical literature (e.g. Card and de la Rica 2006), the lack of comprehensive data has limited our knowledge regarding the Greek labour market (Daouli et al. 2013, 2016). To obtain a better understanding of the structure and outcomes in decentralised collective bargaining, we have developed a unique dataset that contains every official firm-level collective agreement signed in Greece during the period 2002–2016. The appropriateness and superiority of contract data compared to the survey data for examining wage rigidities has been highlighted in several studies (Christofides and Stengos 2003; Druant et al. 2012; Le Bihan et al. 2012). The data used here is drawn from firm-level contracts that are publicly available in a raw format (i.e. scanned documents uploaded as PDF files) by the Ministry of Labour, Social Security, and Welfare and the Greek Organisation for Mediation and Arbitration (OMED). They contain detailed information for 3,893 contracts regarding the type of representation, timing, and duration of each contract; wage settlements; place of the agreement; as well as the business name and tax identification number of each firm. Using the latter, we matched each firm engaged in decentralised negotiations to additional characteristics, such as the number of employees, sectoral affiliation, and ownership. This information is drawn from iMentor, an online database that covers all firms operating in Greece and provides information on business demographics and balance sheet data. Moreover, using iMentor, we appended an appropriately selected sample of firms that did not engage in firm-level bargaining in the period under study. This will enable us to estimate the probability of a firm to engage in decentralised collective bargaining. Hence, in the first step of our empirical strategy, we estimate a simple logistic regression model (Model 1) that conditions the incidence of a firm-level collective agreement on a range of firm-specific characteristics, time, and region fixed effects. Moreover, we include a Herfindahl-Hirschman index and indicators for the asset turnover ratio (sales and assets are CPI deflated, 2015=100), both calculated at the 4-digit level of economic activity (NACE Rev. 1.1.). In this way, we control the level of concentration in the market each firm is operating in and its ability to make rent payments (Breda 2015; Guertzgen 2009).

However, such a model specification, although controlling for several determinants of firm-level contracting, is not informative about any possible differentiation of the decentralised collective bargaining structure before and after the reform. There was a massive increase of firm-level contracts after the reform, and firms with different characteristics could participate in decentralised wage negotiations. Therefore, we specify a second, more flexible model (Model 2), where instead of year fixed effects, we introduce a binary period control indicating the post-reform years and include interactions of that period variable with the observed characteristics, alongside those characteristics themselves. This will be indicative of whether the likelihood of firm-level contracting has changed during the post-reform period and whether its relationship with observable characteristics remained unaffected or changed (and in what way) under the new industrial relations regime.

Finally, we model bargained nominal wage changes at the firm level (Model 3). These changes are not observed for the total sample of firms used so far but only for those engaged in decentralised negotiations at some point before or after the industrial relations reform. To correct possible non-random selection of firms into decentralised negotiations, we adopt the two-step Heckman estimator (Heckman 1979). In the first stage, a selection equation for the probability of a firm to engage in firm-level negotiations is estimated, i.e. as in Model 1. In the second stage, the observed nominal bargained wage changes (for firms engaged in decentralised negotiations) are regressed upon a series of observable characteristics, time, and location fixed effects. Furthermore, the model specification also includes a binary indicator on whether the contract was negotiated by an association of persons or a TU, a binary indicator on whether the bargained outcomes were explicitly linked to the terms and provisions set by the NMW agreement and interactions between these two variables and year indicators. These interactions will be informative of how nominal wage changes bargained by an association of persons and how nominal wage changes specified in contracts linked to the NMW have evolved over time. It should be noted that alongside the control variables, all these regressions of bargained nominal wage changes also include the estimated non-selection hazard rate (the inverse Mill's ratio) derived from the selection equation, estimated in the first stage.

Using this two-step modelling procedure, we attempt to avoid any biases due to the non-random selection of firms in this level of bargaining. In this way, sample selection bias is corrected by taking into consideration whether a firm belongs to the non-random sample of contracts with base wage provisions. We expect that contracts signed by an association of persons (as compared to TUs) will be associated with much greater reductions in the years 2011–2013 than during the period 2014–2015, implying a greater downward adjustment in base wages due to the reform. Moreover, downward adjustments in contracts signed either by Associations of Persons or trade unions but linked to the NMW should be higher after 2012, given the NMW cut imposed by the government in early 2012.

4 Data sources

We use information from the universe of the official contracts signed after firm-level collective negotiations during the period 2002–2016 to examine the variation of bargained nominal base wages. We call this Firm-Level Contracts Greek Database (FLCGDB hereafter). It has been developed by using (a) information extracted from the registry maintained by the Ministry of Labour, Social Security, and Welfare for the period 2002–2008, (b) the publicly available agreements from the website of the Ministry of Labour, Social Security, and Welfare covering the period 2010–2016, and (c) the publicly available agreements from the website of the Greek Organisation for Mediation and Arbitration (OMED) covering the period 2006–2016. To ensure that each contract is a unique entry in the dataset, we match all contracts using the name of the firm and the signing date.

The database contains 3,893 contracts with information on the business name, the place of agreement, and the signing and effective dates. For contracts signed during the period 2002–2005, we are not able to identify specific provisions on base wage outcomes since we have access only to the registry maintained by the Ministry of Labour, Social Security, and Welfare (we do not handle the core document of the contract). However, for the period 2006–2016, we can extract detailed additional information on the type of representation (TU or association of persons) and base wage settlements (nominal base wage level, wage change, adoption of NMW) since these contracts are publicly available by two official websites (Ministry of Labour, Social Security, and Welfare and OMED). For this period, the number of contracts is 3,364, and base wage provisions are included in more than 85% of them (2,912 contracts). Regarding the period 2002–2016, we were unable to identify the tax identification number (based on the company name) for 220 contracts corresponding to 5.6% of the total sample. For contracts with a valid tax identification number, we could find the sector of economic activity for each firm (4-digit NACE Rev 1.1.), the number of employees, the year of establishment, the legal form, and the ownership status. The matching of this information using the tax identification number has been made possible due to the access granted from Infobank Hellastat S.A. (IBHS) to its iMentor online search engine. IBHS is a major business information provider, and iMentor covers all firms that operate in Greece and provides information on their basic characteristics, balance sheet data, contact details, etc. Given the increased incidence of decentralised agreements in the post-reform period, the constructed database enables us to investigate the structure of firm-level collective bargaining in the post reform period. We use iMentor to construct a sample of firms not engaged in firm-level bargaining, so they can be collated to those in the FLCGDB group and used a means of a comparison group.

This will allow us to study the determinants of firm-level contracting before and during the industrial relations reform.

5 Empirical analysis

5.1 Descriptive evidence

Figure 4.1 displays the evolution of firm-level contracting in the Greek labour market from 1990, when decentralised negotiations were originally introduced to the Greek industrial relations system, until 2016, which is the latest year available in our data. The grey bars represent the annual number of signed firm-level agreements as those are provided by the registry maintained by YPAKP. The red bars represent the number of signed contracts according to the online OMED resources, and the black bars represent the subset of those contracts containing nominal base wage provisions as there is a small number of agreements each year referring to organisational issues, internal regulations, insurance schemes, etc. The total number of contracts was stable during the pre-reform period; about 160 contracts were signed each year. It is apparent that firm-level contracting was not very popular in

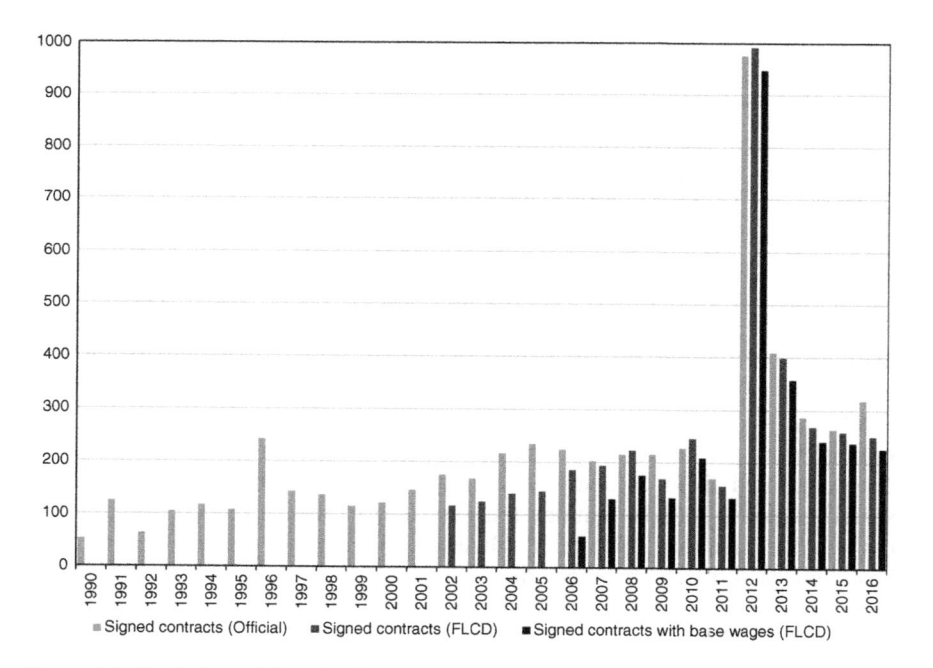

Signed contracts (Official) ▪ Signed contracts (FLCD) ▪ Signed contracts with base wages (FLCD)

Figure 4.1 Evolution of firm-level contracting

Source: Ministry of Labour, Social Security, and Welfare; OMED.

Greece, mostly due to the firm-size restriction imposed by industrial relations framework in the early 1990s (Law 1876/1990). However, their number rapidly increased in 2012, which was the first year of the reform (Law 4024/2011), and then decreased again during later years but to a much higher level, i.e., around 270 contracts per year.

Table 4.1 provides evidence on the structure of firm-level bargaining using information from the FLCGDB for contracts containing base wage provisions. We define three sub-periods in order to demonstrate the changing structure of collective bargaining in Greece across periods of significant events that affected the economic activity in Greece. During the first period (2006m1-2010m4), there were no policy interventions in the wage formation process. The second one (2010m5-2011m10) is the pre-reform period during which a fiscal consolidation agenda started being implemented (First Memorandum of Understanding between the Greek government and the Troika), and the third one is the post-reform period (2011m11–2016m12). For the last period, descriptive statistics are estimated by the type of workers' representation (TU or association of persons) since the association of persons is the new wage bargaining entity introduced by the reform.

Regarding the duration of firm-level contracts before the reform, most of them were one-year agreements, with their frequency being increased during the second pre-reform sub-period. However, during the post-reform period, Associations of Persons signed contracts with longer duration (more than two years), and many of them were open-ended. This may indicate that firms used decentralised negotiation as a tool to minimise pressure within the workplace during a period of increased uncertainty. The firm-size distribution of decentralised agreements has changed considerably between the two pre-reform sub-periods. During the first one, firm-level contracting was more prevalent across large firms. However, during the second sub-period, smaller firms that were facing severe financial problems were also allowed to sign special firm-level agreements with their base wages set below the sectoral/occupational thresholds (Law 3899/2010). As a result, nearly half of the signed labour contracts come from the smaller size category, while the frequency of firm-level contracting became smaller in the upper firm-size categories. However, during the post-reform period, we observe that the majority (79.5%) of small firms (1–49 employees) negotiated base wages through an association of persons, while the distribution of firm-level contracting with a TU is more dispersed across the firm-size distribution. The firm-age distribution has not changed much between the two pre-reform sub-periods, but in the post-reform period, contracts signed by an association of persons correspond to younger firms. In addition, most firms engaged in decentralised bargaining operate in the private sector, and the incidence of firm-level contracting in firms affiliated with the government or local authorities is considerably smaller in the post-reform period. Also, contracts signed by Associations of Persons seem to concentrate exclusively on the private sector. Regarding the legal type of the firm, we observe that

Table 4.1 Frequencies of firm-level contracts by period, worker representation type, and firm-level characteristics

	Pre-reform sub-periods		Post-reform period	
	2006m1–2010m4	*2010m5–2011m10*	*2011m11–2016m12*	
		TU[1]	TU	AP[1]
Contract duration				
1 year or less	57.7	69.8	48.8	35.3
More than 1 year – 2 years or less	32.1	14.3	28.2	21.0
More than 2 years – 3 years or less	3.4	7.2	11.6	27.1
More than 3 years – 4 years or less	1.6	1.1	0.9	5.5
More than 4 years	5.1	7.6	10.5	11.3
Firm size				
1–49 employees	4.9	45.7	22.5	79.5
50–249 employees	36.9	23.0	30.7	12.0
≥250 employees	48.0	29.8	41.7	1.4
Unknown	10.2	1.5	5.2	7.0
Firm age				
0–5 years	4.7	5.6	2.7	8.5
6–10 years	19.9	10.9	4.6	17.3
≥11 years	73.4	72.4	85.8	59.3
Unknown	2.0	10.9	6.9	14.9
Ownership status				
Private	58.5	83.0	71.9	94.7
Government/State control	22.6	5.6	10.9	0.2
Local authority	12.6	7.2	4.4	0.9
Other	6.3	4.1	12.7	4.2
Legal form				
Sole proprietorship	0.0	10.6	4.9	9.4
Sector				
Mining and quarrying	.08	1.1	2.2	0.4
Manufacturing	32.8	61.2	43.9	24.4
Electricity, gas, and water supply	10.7	6.0	5.6	0.1
Constructions	0.8	0.7	1.0	2.6
Wholesale and retail trade	5.9	4.6	9.5	27.5
Hotels and restaurants	2.6	1.4	5.9	29.1
Transportations	16.2	7.1	9.7	4.0

(Continued)

Table 4.1 (Cont.)

	Pre-reform sub-periods		Post-reform period	
	2006m1–2010m4	*2010m5–2011m10*	*2011m11–2016m12*	
Financial institutions	6.5	2.5	4.7	0.7
Real estate	5.3	4.6	7.5	5.7
Public administration	2.2	1.4	1.2	0.0
Education	3.0	1.8	1.5	0.6
Health	4.1	3.2	4.1	3.4
Other community services	8.9	4.3	3.0	1.3
Region				
East Macedonia and Thrace	4.7	5.3	5.4	6.4
Central Macedonia	15.2	8.9	15.0	29.6
West Macedonia	0.0	0.4	0.7	0.2
Thessaly	2.8	2.5	5.0	6.9
Epirus	1.2	0.4	1.7	5.2
Ionian Islands	0.4	0.7	0.7	0.3
West Greece	6.5	4.6	5.9	2.9
Central Greece	5.5	2.5	4.5	1.9
Peloponnese	4.9	3.2	3.4	1.3
Attica	51.7	67.8	48.4	27.4
North Aegean	0.4	0.0	1.4	0.5
South Aegean	2.2	1.1	0.6	9.4
Crete	4.5	2.5	7.2	8.0

Source: Ministry of Labour, Social Security, and Welfare; OMED (authors' calculations).
Notes: Raw frequencies (%) calculated using the unweighted sample of firm-level contracts. [1] AP: Association of persons, TU: Trade union.

nearly 11% of contracts refer to sole proprietorships in the second sub-period, while no contracts exist for those firms in the first sub-period.

With respect to the sectoral distribution of firm-level contracting, we observe that in the pre-reform period, it was more evident in manufacturing firms, representing 30% of the total agreements. Together with the transportations sector, they cover nearly half of the firm-level agreements signed in the first period. A notable difference appears in the second period (2010m5-2011m10), where there is a sharp increase of firm-level contracting in the manufacturing sector. This is mostly due to the reduced contracting incidence in transportations and nearly all other economic activity sectors. During the third period, the sectoral distribution of firm-level contracting became more dispersed. Apart from manufacturing, labour contracts were signed in wholesale and retail trade firms as well as in hotels and restaurants. It should be noted that in the case of the Associations of Persons, the majority of contracts are to be found in hotels and restaurants and wholesale and retail trade and manufacturing firms. On the other hand, most contracts signed by TUs come from manufacturing firms. This indicates that the changing distribution of contracts across sectors of economic activity is due to the introduction of the association of persons in wage negotiations. Lastly, decentralised agreements appeared to be concentrated in highly urbanised areas (Attica and Central Macedonia) in the pre-reform years. In the post-reform period, firm-level agreements signed by association of persons are much more dispersed across the country. Regarding the timing of firm-level contracting, it should be noted that during the pre-reform period, most contracts were signed in May or June. However, the introduction of Law 4024/2011 was followed by a post-reform peak observed in December 2011, and most of the firm-level contracting seemed to occur in spring ever since. The peak observed in December 2011 is mainly due to firm-level contracts signed by Associations of Persons, while firm-level agreements established by trade unions peaked in July 2010.

Table 4.2 displays descriptive statistics regarding the bargained base wage outcomes (changes and levels) by period and type of worker representation. During the first period, none of the contracts signed by trade unions included downward adjustments, and nearly all of them (98%) were associated with base wage increases. This resulted in an average base wage increase of 6.6%. In the second period, 6% of the contracts signed by trade unions set lower base wages, but most of them (69.3%) kept establishing base wage increases. The percentage of contracts with unchanged wages increased to 25%. This led to an average base wage change of 2.1%, considerably lower then the mean increase observed in the first period. An inversed picture emerged soon after the collective bargaining framework reform, when reductions in nominal base wages became more frequent. More specifically, 36.3% of the total agreements led to reductions and 56.3% left base wages unchanged. The average nominal base wage reduction was 5.2%. Separating between trade unions and Associations of Persons reveals that this evolution was mostly driven by bargaining in firms in which workers formed an association of persons. Only 4.7% of these contracts led to higher base wages, and nearly half of them led to reductions (8.3% on average). The wage adjustment process was more moderate in firms where workers were represented by a trade union. Nearly 67% of these contracts left wages unaltered, and 9.9% of them led to wage increases (the mean base wage reduction was 2.7%). These differences are also found to be sound in terms of statistical significance, according to the reported t-statistics in the last column. Table 4.2 also presents descriptive information regarding the bargained nominal base wage level. There is a statistically significant difference between trade unions and Associations of Persons possibly reflecting, among other things, productivity differences and changing wage bargaining structures across firms (see also Daouli et al. 2016). According to the data

Table 4.2 Firm-level negotiated nominal base wage adjustments: summary statistics by worker representation type before and after the reform

	Pre-reform sub-periods		Post-reform period				
	2006m1–2010m4	2010m5–2011m10	2011m11–2016m1				
	TU^1		All contracts	TU	AP^1	Diff: AP-TU	t-stat
Extensive Margin (%)							
Downward adjustment	0.0	6.0	36.3	23.2	50.3	27.1***	11.3
Unchanged	1.8	24.7	56.3	67.0	45.0	−21.9***	−8.7
Upward adjustment	98.2	69.3	7.4	9.9	4.7	−5.1***	−3.8
Number of contracts	498	251	1,480	760	720	-	-
Intensive Margin (%)							
Mean	6.6	2.1	−5.2	−2.7	−8.3	−5.5***	−10.3
Median	5.7	2.7	0.0	0.0	0.0	-	-
Standard deviation	4.4	4.7	10.2	7.6	11.9	-	-
Number of contracts	454	244	1,349	748	601	-	-
Monthly nominal base wage (€)							
Mean	894.0	1149.2	696.1	894.3	605.4	−288.9***	−24.9
Median	585.6	1339.8	568.1	820.0	586.1	-	-
Standard deviation	230.3	243.8	205.1	262.6	62.7	-	-
Number of contracts	239	201	1,679	527	1,152	-	-

Source: Ministry of Labour, Social Security, and Welfare; OMED (authors' calculations)
Notes: Raw estimates calculated using the unweighted sample of firm-level contracts with base wage provisions. [1] AP: Association of persons, TU: Trade union.

used here, nominal base wages bargained by Associations of Persons were almost 25% lower than those signed by trade unions.

5.2 *Estimation results*

Table 4.3 displays the results from estimating Model 1, where the probability of a firm to sign a firm-level agreement is conditioned upon a vector of observable characteristics. This includes indicators for firm size, as measured by the number of employees, region where the firm is located (NUTS-II), sector of economic activity (2-digit NACE Rev.1.1.), legal form, a Herfindahl-Hirschman index, and indicators for the asset turnover ratio. To control common variance components across firms, we correct standard errors for heteroskedasticity and clustering by region and two-digit sector of economic activity. We estimate model 1 using alternative samples and empirical specifications, and the regressions are weighted by the total number of firms in the respective four-digit sector of economic activity (NACE Rev.1.1.). In column 1, we use the total matched sample of the firms that are not participating in decentralised bargaining. Regarding the evolution of firm-level contracting over time, the probability is significantly higher in 2012, significantly lower and without a clear trend before the reform, and not statistically different in 2013–2014 compared to 2015 (the reference year). Regarding firm size, the probability of firm-level contracting is steadily increasing with the number of employees. It is much smaller for firms for which information on the number of employees is not available; however, these are mainly very small firms that do not publish information about their size.

Next, we examine how the contracting probability varies for firms located in different geographical regions compared to those observed in Attica. For example, it is more likely for a firm located in Macedonia to sign a firm-level agreement, while this is not statistically different for firms located in Peloponnese, West Greece, and the Ionian Islands. Regarding the sectoral distribution, the incidence of decentralised agreements is particularly high in electricity, gas and water supply, hotels and restaurants, and financial institutions (compared to the constructions sector). A firm-level contract is more likely to be in effect in sole proprietorships compared to all other legal forms. Finally, firms operating in sectors with a higher degree of market power are more likely to sign firm-level contracts, while this probability is significantly lower for firms operating in low performance sectors (according to the asset turnover ratio).

In column 2, the sample is restricted to exclude firms that have not published any balance sheet data regarding sales over a three-year period. This criterion has been imposed during estimations to exclude firms that may have exited from the market. The deleted observations refer to firms that did not participate in decentralised bargaining since we assume that the firms that signed a firm-level contract during a specific year are alive. This leaves us with a sample of 458,267 firms instead of the original one containing 1,412,052 observations. However, the estimated results lead to the same conclusions regarding the association between firm-level contracting and observable characteristics. The only notable change is that the estimated parameter for sole proprietorships is much higher, confirming the fact that these are very small firms and do not publish data on their size. In column 3, we exclude those firms for which the number of employees is not available, leading to a further reduction of the utilised sample to 253,340 observations. However, the estimated coefficients and standard errors are remarkably similar to those of the previous column, providing reassurance that our results are not sensitive to the lack of this information or the omission of those firms from the estimation sample. Finally, in column 4, we specify the model of the previous column but including an additional indicator on whether the firm was under a decentralised collective agreement during the previous year. As expected, it takes some bias out from nearly all the other estimated coefficients that still indicate towards the results already discussed. Moreover, the estimated coefficient of the lagged dependent variable indicates that the probability of firm-level contracting exhibits some degree of persistence since is largely determined from the existence of an agreement during the previous year.

Table 4.4 presents the estimated results of Model 2 using the adopted specification presented in the last column of Table 4.3. This will allow us to see whether the observable characteristics of firms affect the probability of a firm-level collective agreement in a differentiated way during the post-reform period. According to the results, the probability of firm-level contracting becomes much higher after the reform, and it still affected by the existence of an agreement in the last year, although to a lesser extend in the second period. This implies that persistence in firm-level bargaining is smaller in the post-reform period due to the inclusion of firms without any prior experience in firm-level negotiations. Larger firms are less likely to sign a contract during the second period. However, smaller firms appear more likely to participate in decentralised negotiations given that Law 4024/2011 offered them this opportunity. For firms operating in certain regions, e.g. Central Greece, Thessaly, Ionian Islands, and West Greece, the contracting probability did not change after the reform. However, it has considerably increased for firms in other regions, e.g. Epirus and Aegean Islands, and it appears to have reduced for firms located in Peloponnese. After the implementation of Law 4024/2011, the contracting probability is lower in sectors such as transportation, real estate, health, education, and other community services. This is mostly due to the fact that under the new regime, more firms from other sectors (and located in regions with a low incidence of firm-level contracts) tend to sign collective agreements, e.g. hotels and restaurants. With respect to characteristics referring to the legal status of the firm or the market power and the profitability of the sector, statistically, there is no differentiation in the contracting probability during the post-reform period.

With respect to wage floor adjustments, Table 4.5 presents the results obtained from the estimation of Model 3 using the same empirical specifications as those presented in Table 4.3. More specifically, the results are obtained from a two-step Heckman selection model that corrects the probability of a firm to engage in decentralised bargaining. Since we are interested in the

Table 4.3 Determinants of firm-level contracting

Independent variable	[1]	[2]	[3]	[4]
Sign year: 2002	−1.942***(0.326)	−2.200***(0.329)	−2.199***(0.331)	−
Sign year: 2003	−2.052***(0.232)	−2.310***(0.232)	−2.332***(0.233)	−2.348***(0.230)
Sign year: 2004	−1.850***(0.358)	−2.106***(0.349)	−2.131***(0.352)	−1.829***(0.382)
Sign year: 2005	−2.033***(0.447)	−2.348***(0.438)	−2.341***(0.440)	−2.168***(0.481)
Sign year: 2006	−1.810***(0.393)	−2.126***(0.386)	−2.131***(0.389)	−1.956***(0.404)
Sign year: 2007	−1.907***(0.360)	−2.222***(0.357)	−2.218***(0.360)	−2.056***(0.369)
Sign year: 2008	−1.751***(0.391)	−2.120***(0.376)	−2.111***(0.378)	−1.913***(0.395)
Sign year: 2009	−2.079***(0.409)	−2.449***(0.393)	−2.440***(0.395)	−2.356***(0.409)
Sign year: 2010	−1.911***(0.579)	−2.280***(0.565)	−2.272***(0.567)	−2.321***(0.465)
Sign year: 2011	−1.520***(0.394)	−1.878***(0.384)	−1.879***(0.387)	−1.584***(0.427)
Sign year: 2012	1.212***(0.254)	0.852***(0.243)	0.862***(0.246)	1.079***(0.311)
Sign year: 2013	0.259(0.257)	−0.101(0.256)	−0.0910(0.257)	−0.789***(0.260)
Sign year: 2014	−0.127(0.216)	−0.141(0.220)	−0.137(0.222)	−0.336(0.321)
Firm size: 1–9 employees	−5.115***(0.587)	−4.690***(0.613)	−4.694***(0.610)	−3.764***(0.455)
Firm size: 10–19 employees	−3.660***(0.580)	−3.501***(0.605)	−3.506***(0.601)	−2.839***(0.450)
Firm size: 20–49 employees	−3.735***(0.612)	−3.483***(0.631)	−3.487***(0.628)	−2.808***(0.486)
Firm size: 50–99 employees	−2.958***(0.688)	−2.704***(0.685)	−2.706***(0.683)	−2.008***(0.528)
Firm size: 100–249 employees	−2.354***(0.638)	−2.106***(0.659)	−2.107***(0 657)	−1.621***(0.534)
Firm size: 250–499 employees	−2.419***(0.763)	−1.894***(0.698)	−1.894***(0.697)	−1.525**(0.630)
Firm size: 500–999 employees	−0.564(0.793)	−0.370(0.819)	−0.366(0.819)	−0.327(0.649)
Firm size: Unknown	−10.85***(0.706)	−9.800***(0.734)	−	−
Region: East Macedonia and Thrace	1.690***(0.285)	1.603***(0.255)	1.612***(0.255)	1.419***(0.195)
Region: Central and West Macedonia	1.224***(0.201)	1.200***(0.181)	1.204***(0.181)	1.132***(0.160)
Region: Thessaly	0.758**(0.378)	0.865**(0.344)	0.873**(0.345)	0.832***(0.306)

Region: Epirus	1.468***(0.270)	1.427***(0.293)	1.431***(0.293)	1.336***(0.185)
Region: West Greece and Ionian Islands	−0.201(0.609)	−0.199(0.595)	−0.191(0.596)	−0.251(0.587)
Region: Central Greece	0.963**(0.397)	0.876**(0.341)	0.882***(0.342)	1.050***(0.332)
Region: Peloponnese	0.477(0.346)	0.435(0.329)	0.444(0.328)	0.536(0.326)
Region: Aegean Islands	1.035***(0.206)	0.923***(0.191)	0.927***(0.191)	0.819***(0.177)
Region: Crete	0.409*(0.214)	0.318(0.197)	0.322(0.197)	0.561***(0.177)
Sector: Manufacturing	1.356***(0.279)	1.414***(0.278)	1.412***(0.279)	0.988***(0.211)
Sector: Electricity, gas, and water supply	2.253***(0.395)	2.271***(0.467)	2.337***(0.474)	1.666***(0.472)
Sector: Wholesale and retail trade	0.322*(0.169)	0.542***(0.156)	0.543***(0.156)	0.467***(0.152)
Sector: Hotels and restaurants	2.115***(0.208)	2.199***(0.206)	2.229***(0.206)	1.642***(0.201)
Sector: Transportation	1.017***(0.271)	1.218***(0.284)	1.234***(0.284)	0.932***(0.267)
Sector: Financial institutions	2.010***(0.495)	2.270***(0.508)	2.305***(0.507)	1.572***(0.422)
Sector: Real estate	1.347***(0.297)	1.324***(0.315)	1.311***(0.317)	1.023***(0.262)
Sector: Health, education	1.722***(0.240)	1.601***(0.246)	1.578***(0.250)	1.095***(0.253)
Sector: Other community services	1.674***(0.349)	1.925***(0.360)	1.937***(0.360)	1.314***(0.323)
Legal form: Sole proprietorship	0.647**(0.253)	2.520***(0.255)	2.503***(0.257)	0.986**(0.414)
Herfindahl-Hirschman index	0.567**(0.232)	0.689**(0.335)	0.683**(0.333)	0.615***(0.214)
Asset Turnover Ratio <25%	−0.487**(0.227)	−0.802***(0.215)	−0.834***(0.215)	−0.535***(0.182)
Asset Turnover Ratio >75%	−0.0351(0.156)	−0.221(0.151)	−0.241(0.152)	−0.191(0.132)
Firm-level contract in previous year	–	–	–	4.000***(0.276)
Constant	−2.169***(0.630)	−1.624**(0.649)	−1.625**(0.647)	−2.583***(0.557)
Observations	1,412,052	458,267	253,340	236,216

Source: OMED; iMentor
Notes: Parameter estimates from weighted logit regressions are done using the number of firms by four-digit sector of economic activity as weights. Standard errors in parentheses are corrected for heteroskedasticity and clustering by region (NUTS-II) and two-digit sector of economic activity (NACE Rev.1). ***, **, and * denote statistical significance at the 1%, 5%, and 10% level, respectively. For groups of variables, the base categories are as follows: 2005, more than 1,000 employees, Attica, Constructions, ≥25% Asset Turnover Ratio <75% (sales and assets are CPI deflated, 2015=100).

Table 4.4 Determinants of firm-level contracting after the reform: estimates from an interacted model

Independent variable	Estimated coefficient	Standard error
Law 4024/2011	2.640**	(1.196)
Firm-level contract in the previous year	4.692***	(0.363)
Law4024/11 × Firm-level contract in the previous year	−1.717***	(0.425)
Law4024/11 × Firm size: 1–9 employees	0.400	(0.751)
Law4024/11 × Firm size: 10–19 employees	0.430	(0.748)
Law4024/11 × Firm size: 20–49 employees	−1.086	(0.710)
Law4024/11 × Firm size: 50–99 employees	−2.186***	(0.681)
Law4024/11 × Firm size: 100–249 employees	−1.431*	(0.801)
Law4024/11 × Firm size: 250–499 employees	−1.282*	(0.733)
Law4024/11 × Firm size: 500–999 employees	−1.202	(0.735)
Law4024/11 × Region: East Macedonia and Thrace	1.662***	(0.600)
Law4024/11 × Region: Central and West Macedonia	1.109***	(0.351)
Law4024/11 × Region: Thessaly	1.046	(0.666)
Law4024/11 × Region: Epirus	2.092**	(0.932)
Law4024/11 × Region: West Greece and Ionian Islands	−0.360	(0.366)
Law4024/11 × Region: Central Greece	0.592	(0.692)
Law4024/11 × Region: Peloponnese	−1.775***	(0.382)
Law4024/11 × Region: Aegean Islands	3.210***	(0.909)
Law4024/11 × Region: Crete	0.850***	(0.322)
Law4024/11 × Sector: Manufacturing	−1.117	(0.684)
Law4024/11 × Sector: Electricity, gas, and water supply	−0.886	(0.959)
Law4024/11 × Sector: Wholesale and retail trade	−0.560	(0.700)
Law4024/11 × Sector: Hotels and restaurants	0.594	(0.729)
Law4024/11 × Sector: Transportation	−1.710**	(0.687)
Law4024/11 × Sector: Financial institutions	−0.642	(0.984)
Law4024/11 × Sector: Real estate	−1.579**	(0.656)
Law4024/11 × Sector: Health, education	−1.300**	(0.643)
Law4024/11 × Sector: Other community services	−1.925***	(0.661)
Law4024/11 × Legal form: Sole proprietorship	−0.665	(0.934)
Law4024/11 × Herfindahl−Hirschman index	−0.201	(0.123)
Law4024/11 × Asset Turnover Ratio <25%	−0.581	(0.444)
Law4024/11 × Asset Turnover Ratio >75%	0.323	(0.397)

(Continued)

Table 4.4 (Cont.)

Independent variable	Estimated coefficient	Standard error
Law4024/11 × Time trend	0.053	(0.089)
Constant	−5.244***	(0.772)
Observations		236,216

Source: OMED; iMentor
Notes: Parameter estimates from weighted logit regressions are done using the number of firms by four-digit sector of economic activity as weights. The model includes the same set of independent variables as in Column 4 of Table 3 (except year dummies). Standard errors in parentheses are corrected for heteroskedasticity and clustering by region (NUTS-II) and two-digit sector of economic activity (NACE Rev.1). ***, **, and * denote statistical significance at the 1%, 5%, and 10% level, respectively.

impact of the interaction terms, we do not present estimates for the rest of the independent variables.

Focusing on the estimated effects of the interaction between the association of persons indicator and the year indicators, we see that there is a reduction of 6.1% (last column) in nominal base wages originating in 2012, which was the first post-reform year. However, no further wage adjustment is evident during later years. This result is stable across different model specifications and sub-samples. With regard to the interaction effects between the indicator denoting adoption of the NMW and the year indicators, it seems that contracts linking base wages to the NMW terms and conditions experience a further reduction of approximately 11% in base wages during 2011 and 2012. This finding is confirmed across all models reported in Table 4.5, and there is no evidence for further nominal base wage changes in recent years. Base wage adjustments in firms where workers are represented by Associations of Persons follow closely the evolution of the NMW. Moreover, the major adjustment process in those firms occurred in 2012, and no significant changes were observed since then. At the same time, a sizeable base wage premium is observed for workers in firms where workers have formed typical trade unions instead of an association of persons (around 22%). This premium seems to be quite stable before and after the reform, although a much smaller adjustment process has taken place in these firms after 2010.

6 Discussion and conclusion

In this chapter, we attempted an empirical investigation of how the 2011 industrial relations reform (Law 4024/2011) affected firm-level bargaining and nominal contractual base wage adjustments in Greece. The reform redefined the limits within which nominal base wages can oscillate and

Table 4.5 Nominal base wage adjustments in firm-level collective bargaining

Independent variable	[1]		[2]		[3]		[4]	
	Association of persons (interaction with year effects)							
Sign year: 2011	−2.632	(3.394)	−2.498	(2.395)	−2.945	(2.430)	−2.849	(2.710)
Sign year: 2012	−7.518***	(2.724)	−7.120***	(1.690)	−7.541***	(1.707)	−6.091***	(1.834)
Sign year: 2013	0.269	(2.998)	0.517	(1.853)	0.109	(1.871)	0.081	(1.999)
Sign year: 2014	1.360	(3.097)	1.397	(1.945)	0.955	(1.953)	0.673	(2.054)
	Adoption of National Minimum Wage (interaction with year effects)							
Sign year: 2011	−5.729	(4.137)	−5.845**	(2.512)	-5.206**	(2.538)	-5.069*	(2.761)
Sign year: 2012	−5.800**	(2.713)	−5.855***	(1.693)	-5.187***	(1.709)	-5.980***	(1.857)
Sign year: 2013	−1.775	(3.027)	−1.824	(1.872)	−1.186	(1.891)	−1.740	(2.021)
Sign year: 2014	−0.672	(3.103)	−0.665	(1.951)	−0.178	(1.958)	0.311	(2.073)
Mills' ratio (lambda)	−33.117	(25.739)	−19.145	(12.330)	−17.942	(11.929)	−0.742***	(0.272)
Wald chi-squared	432.86***		1140.43***		1193.78***		1444.25***	
Total observations	1,007,665		337,697		184,803		184,493	
Censored observations	1,005,942		335,974		183,085		183,085	
Uncensored observations	1,723		1,723		1,718		1,408	

Source: OMED; iMentor.
Notes: Estimations are based on a two-step Heckman selection model. Specifications [1]-[4] correspond to those of Table 3. Robust standard errors are in parentheses.

allowed Association of Persons to negotiate wages in workplaces where a typical trade union did not exist. Our assessment covered the period 2002–2016, and it relied on information extracted from the universe of firm-level contracts signed during that period. According to the results, the number of firm-level contracts sharply increased right after the reform, covering a larger pool of workers and firms, especially small-sized ones. In order to examine the determinants of firm-level contracting, we matched firms engaged in decentralised negotiations with firms that did not and provided empirical evidence on the factors shaping the incidence of a firm-level agreement. Furthermore, we showed that this probability increased substantially after the introduction of the new industrial relations framework. The determinants of this probability appear to be differentiated between the pre-and the post-reform period. More specifically, smaller firms appear more likely to participate in decentralised negotiations, taking advantage of the fact that the reform allowed Associations of Persons to bargain over wages in firms where trade unions did not exist. Moreover, firm-level contracting became more prevalent in specific sectors, e.g. hotels and restaurants and NUTS-2 regions.

With respect to the nominal base wage adjustments, we provided evidence regarding two very important features of the post-reform period, i.e. the ability of workers in small firms to form Associations of Persons and negotiate over wage issues as well as the sharp decrease in the National Minimum Wage in 2012. Taking the possible non-random selection of firms in decentralised wage negotiations into consideration, we presented evidence that contractual base wage reductions were higher in firms where workers were represented by Associations of Persons rather than typical trade unions. Moreover, our results indicate that reductions related to the type of worker representation as well as the explicit adoption of the terms and conditions of the national collective agreement occurred shortly after the reform, with no significant changes being observed in more recent years. These results indicate that after the reform, and given an already deteriorating economic environment, workers in small firms, without any prior experience in wage bargaining, were organised in Associations of Persons with limited bargaining power and agreed upon substantial wage reductions, even adopting the national minimum wage floor. Moreover, the relatively longer duration of these contracts indicates that the rationale behind this behaviour was to secure the employment level and reduce uncertainty. Bargained wage outcomes were more favourable in firms where workers were organised around a typical trade union. This can be attributed to several factors; e.g. it is well known that larger firms can pay higher wages, typical trade unions have greater bargaining power, and prior experience of both employers and employees in decentralised negotiations can lead to bargained wage outcomes that are better linked to productivity and firm-specific and market characteristics.

References

Avouyi-Dovi, S., Fougère, D. and Gautier, E. (2013). 'Wage Rigidity, Collective Bargaining, and the Minimum Wage: Evidence from French Agreement Data'. *Review of Economics and Statistics*, 95(4): 1337–1351.

Breda, T. (2015). 'Firms' Rents, Workers' Bargaining Power and the Union Wage Premium'. *Economic Journal*, 125(589): 1616–1652.

Card, D. and de la Rica, S. (2006). 'Firm-Level Contracting and the Structure of Wages in Spain'. *Industrial and Labor Relations Review*, 59(4): 573–592.

Christofides, N. L. and Stengos, T. (2003). 'Wage Rigidity in Canadian Collective Bargaining Agreements'. *Industrial and Labor Relations Review*, 56(3): 429–448.

Daouli, J. J., Demoussis, M., Giannakopoulos, N. and Laliotis, I. (2013). 'Firm-Level Collective Bargaining and Wages in Greece: A Quantile Decomposition Analysis'. *British Journal of Industrial Relations*, 51(1): 80–103.

Daouli, J. J., Demoussis, M., Giannakopoulos, N. and Laliotis, I. (2016). 'The 2011 Industrial Relations Reform and Nominal Wage Adjustments in Greece'. *Journal of Labor Research*, 37(4): 460–483.

Druant, M., Fabiani, S., Kezdi, G., Lamo, A., Martins, F. and Sabbatini, R. (2012). 'Firms' Price and Wage Adjustment in Europe: Survey Evidence on Nominal Stickiness.' *Labour Economics*, 19: 772–782.

Fougere, D., Gautier, E. and Roux, S. (2016). 'Understanding Wage Floor Setting in Industry-Level Agreements: Evidence from France', IZA Discussion Paper No. 10290.

Guertzgen, N. (2009). 'Rent-Sharing and Collective Bargaining Coverage: Evidence from Linked Employer-Employee Data'. *Scandinavian Journal of Economics*, 111(2): 323–349.

Heckman, J. J. (1979). 'Sample Selection Bias as a Specification Error'. *Econometrica*, 47(1): 153–161.

Le Bihan, H., Montornès, J. and Heckel, T. (2012). 'Sticky Wages: Evidence from Quarterly Microeconomic Data'. *American Economic Journal: Macroeconomics*, 4(3): 1–32.

van Ours, J. et al. (2016). 'Recommendations Expert Group for the Review of the Greek Labour Market', Review of Greek Labour Market Institutions, Ministry of Labour, Social Security, and Welfare, September 2016, Athens.

Voskeritsian, H. and Kornelakis, A. (2014). 'The Transformation of Employment Regulation in Greece: Towards and Dysfunctional Liberal Market Economy?' *Relation Industrielles/Industrial Relations*, 69(2): 344–365.

5 Mind the (twin) gap

Job quality in Greece in comparative perspective

Michail Veliziotis and Andreas Kornelakis

1 Introduction

The nature and level of job quality in the Greek labour market has been an underexplored issue in academic and policy debates for several years. Before the deep and persistent crisis of the Greek economy in the post-2009 period, the discourse on job quality among political and policy circles (e.g. trade unions, employers, the government, and political parties) was, more often than not, based on anecdotal evidence. The debate also focused on crude indicators of quality, drawing on macro-level data related to the average level of wages, the minimum wage increases, or the average number of working hours. Perhaps this omission can be attributed to a cyclical effect: in a fast-growing economy, with rising wage levels and – to a lesser extent – rising employment levels, the qualitative aspects of everyday working life can be obscured by increasing relative affluence, rising household incomes, and increased spending and consumption (Clark 2005; Green 2006).

A detailed account and discussion of job quality is also largely missing from contemporary academic and policy debates concerning the dire state of the Greek labour market (see e.g. Dedoussopoulos et al. 2013; ILO 2014; Kornelakis et al. 2017). The question of the quality of jobs is often reduced to an issue of secondary importance. In the context of a severe and persistent recession and a sharp increase in unemployment and under-employment, the focus of the successive Greek governments and their international creditors (the "Troika", or the "Institutions") since 2010 has been on creating more jobs and putting more people back to work. In this respect, the proclaimed aim of the extensive labour market deregulation that Greece experienced was to render the labour market more flexible, lower labour costs and, as a result, boost competitiveness and reduce unemployment (i.e. the "internal devaluation" policy strategy; see Kornelakis et al. 2017; Theodoropoulou 2016). Therefore, the centrality of the issue of "quantity" on the jobs front can hardly go unnoticed.

This chapter aims to address this gap in our knowledge and provide a detailed account of the overall quality of jobs in the Greek labour market during the last two decades, adopting a comparative European perspective.

For this exercise, the analysis will exploit microdata from the successive European Working Conditions Surveys (1995, 2000/01, 2005, 2010, and 2015). Job quality is defined here by adopting an objective, "worker-centred" approach (Eurofound 2012, 2017; Green 2006; Green et al. 2013). As per this conceptualisation, the quality of a job is measured through the presence of job aspects and characteristics that lead to a fulfilling and meaningful work experience that satisfies human needs and enhances employee well-being (Felstead et al. 2015; Green 2006; Spencer 2015). Such aspects include, but are in no way limited to, the following: skill use and development, job autonomy/task discretion, the physical working environment, work intensity, working time quality, job prospects, and the social environment at work. In short, in this chapter, we move beyond wages and other material benefits (which are the focus of other chapters in this volume) and concentrate on job attributes that are related to the intrinsic quality, the physical and social environment, working time quality, and the prospects of the job that the individual employees hold (Eurofound 2012; Felstead et al. 2015).

The following research questions are the main focus of the present chapter: How does Greece compare relative to other EU countries in terms of the quality of its jobs? How has the average quality of jobs in Greece evolved in the last two decades and, particularly, during the current economic crisis? What are the possible explanations for the patterns revealed by the examination of the above two questions? The first two questions seek to document, with a focus on Greece, the cross-country patterns and over-time trends in job quality, while the third question aims to explain these patterns and trends.

Overall, these questions will help us test one main hypothesis. This hypothesis concerns the apparent existence of a "twin disadvantage" or "twin gap" in the labour market experience of the working population in Greece relative to the working population of other European Union (EU) countries (Kornelakis et al. 2017: 21–28): on the one hand, the well-known gap is the relatively worse performance of the Greek labour market in terms of "quantity", manifested through a relatively higher and persistent unemployment rate. On the other hand, the relatively unknown gap is the job "quality" gap. The expectation is that, during the crisis period, this "twin gap" has grown, reflecting the combined effects of the economic slump, the implemented policy measures, and the strengthening of the managerial prerogative due to labour market deregulation.

The structure of this chapter is as follows. The second section outlines the conceptual framework we follow in our thinking about job quality, describes the data we use, and presents the job quality indicators we construct using this data. The third section, after briefly documenting the "quantity" gap, tries to answer two of the questions we posed earlier: how Greece compares in terms of its job quality relative to other European countries and how this comparison and relative standing have changed in recent years. Then, the fourth section proposes and discusses possible explanations for our results. The final section discusses the implications of our findings and concludes.

2 Concepts, data, and the measurement of job quality

2.1 The concept of job quality

One of the longstanding arguments in relation to job quality among academics from various disciplines is that the quality of a job held by an individual employee cannot be judged only by reference to the wage and fringe benefits associated with this job (Green 2006; Rosenthal 1989). Not surprisingly, policy makers and international organisations have also adopted a broader agenda for job quality. For example, the International Labour Organisation (ILO) launched its Decent Work agenda in 1999, and the resulting indicators used to measure Decent Work across countries cover a broad array of items, some of them related to various intrinsic job aspects that are considered indicative of a job of high quality (see ILO 2013). Related to this, the stated aim of the EU's Lisbon Strategy, launched in 2000, was to promote the capacity of Europe to produce "more and better jobs" (see Burchell et al. 2014; Eurofound 2012; Kornelakis and Veliziotis 2018). To this aim, the European Commission has dopted a concept of "Quality in Work", which includes elements pertaining to the broader labour market context as well as job characteristics related to intrinsic job quality, skills, and career development (see Green 2006: 19–22). More recently, the European Pillar of Social Rights, announced by the European Commission in November 2017, builds upon three categories of principles, one of which is named "fair working conditions" and enshrines principles related to secure employment, wages, information, social dialogue, work–life balance, and safe working environments. The Organisation for Economic Cooperation and Development (OECD) also recognised that job quality is an important driver of increased labour force participation, productivity, and economic performance and developed a framework to measure and assess the quality of jobs in its member countries (see Cazes et al. 2015).

Departing from these (quite broad in their scope) policy frameworks and building from the relevant academic contributions (Eurofound 2012; Felstead et al. 2015; Green 2006), in this chapter, we adopt a "worker-centred" view on the quality of a job, and we define job quality as an all-encompassing concept that includes aspects and characteristics of a job that satisfy certain human needs and lead to a meaningful and fulfilling working experience for the individual employee. We focus specifically on the non-wage working experience of individual employees. Although wages are surely an important dimension of job quality, mainly because they enable the fulfilment of basic, material needs, many recent investigations of the Greek labour market have focused on the analysis of wage developments and inequalities (see the relevant chapters in this volume; see also Christopoulou and Monastiriotis 2014; Daouli et al. 2016; Kornelakis et al. 2017). On the other hand, non-wage aspects have been relatively ignored (for exceptions to this, see ILO 2014; Kornelakis et al. 2017). The non-wage dimensions of job quality we focus on (skill use and development, autonomy, the physical environment, work intensity, working time quality, job prospects, and social environment) are widely considered as indicative of a fulfilling work experience that is directly related to workers' well-being.

Thus, our measurement of job quality is based on a set of objective indicators (reported by workers themselves), not on subjective evaluations of overall feelings or satisfaction with a job. The latter indicators (e.g. job satisfaction) have been shown to be reflecting not only the objective reality of a job, but also workers' (and societal) norms and expectations (Brown et al. 2012; Muñoz de Bustillo Llorente and Fernández Macías 2005). For example, some earlier studies have found that women report higher job satisfaction than observationally similar men, although the former admittedly hold worse jobs than the latter. An explanation for this is that women also have lower expectations from their jobs than men (Clark 1997), making them appreciate the same objective characteristics of a job more. However, another long-standing finding is that objective aspects are strongly related to subjective evaluations (Eurofound 2012; Green 2006), and this fact adds credibility and validity to the used objective indicators of job quality.

2.2 Data source and sample selection

We use the microdata from the successive waves of the European Working Conditions Survey (EWCS), administered by the European Foundation for the Improvement of Living and Working Conditions (Eurofound). The EWCS is a nationally representative survey of all residents in the participating countries aged 15 or older that were in employment at the time of the (face-to-face) interviews. The representativeness of each country's sample is additionally ensured if the relevant weights that are included in the publicly available data files are applied to the analyses (all results that are reported here are based on weighted data). The EWCS was first conducted in 1990/91, and since then, it has been organised every five years: 1995, 2000/01, 2005, 2010, and 2015. It has been extensively used in recent studies of job quality (e.g. Eurofound 2012, 2017; Green et al. 2013; Holman 2013) and is the most authoritative source of information for European comparative analyses of working conditions. In this chapter, we make use of the EWCS Integrated Data File 1991–2015 and focus on the five waves since 1995, since the great majority of the variables we use in the following analysis are only available in a consistent way since that year.

The 1995 wave of the EWCS samples data from the EU-15 countries. From 2000/2001, data from the rest of the EU-27 countries is added in the survey, while Croatia participates for the first time in 2005. From that year on, data from EU candidate or associated countries is also added successively. Therefore, in 2015, the survey covers all 28 EU countries, plus FYROM, Turkey, Norway, Albania, Montenegro, Switzerland, and Serbia (Kosovo also participated in the survey in 2010 only). In the analysis that follows, we utilise data from Greece and the rest of the EU-28 countries and focus only on employees, excluding the self-employed people. In total, there are around 122,000 employee observations in 1995–2010, ranging from 392 sampled employees in Cyprus in 2000/2001 to 3,343 in Belgium in 2010.

2.3 The job quality indicators

Following closely the work by Eurofound [2012, 2017]), we construct seven indices of job quality dimensions. These are detailed in Table 5.1, along with the survey items used to construct them.

Each quality dimension's value is calculated by taking, for each individual worker, the mean of the respective items, which have first been normalised to the 0–1 scale (with 0 indicating the lowest and 1 the highest quality for

Table 5.1 Survey items included in the job quality indicators.

Skill use and development	Training provided by employer over the past 12 months, job involves solving unforeseen problems, complex tasks, and learning new things
Autonomy/discretion	Be able to choose or change order of tasks, methods of work, and speed/rate of work
Physical environment	Exposed to vibrations, noise, high/low temperatures, smoke/fumes, and chemicals; job involves tiring positions, carrying heavy loads, repetitive hand/arm moves
Work intensity	Job involves working at very high speed, working under tight deadlines, having enough time to get the job done, pace of work dependent on work done by colleagues, direct demands from customers, numerical production or performance targets, automatic speed of a machine, direct control of boss
Working time quality	Working at nights, Sundays, Saturdays, working more than 48 hours per week (usual hours)
Prospects (available 2005–2015)	Might lose job in the next 6 months, job offers good prospects for career advancement
Social environment (available 2005–2015)	Colleagues help and support, manager helps and supports, have been subjected to unwanted sexual attention, have been subjected to physical violence
Overall job quality index	All the above items that are consistently available since 1995, i.e., items for skill use and development, autonomy, the physical environment, work intensity, and working time quality

Source: Author's own definitions, based on EWCS data and following the work by Eurofound (2012, 2017) to a certain degree. As detailed in the text, items that indicate "negative" quality have been reversed in order for the value of 0 to indicate the lowest (and the value of 1 the highest) quality for each specific item. The specific survey questions and the computer code used to construct the indicators are available from the authors on request.

each specific item; items indicating "negative" attributes are reversed). Hence, our resulting quality indicators also range in value between 0 and 1. As already mentioned in the previous sections, the job quality dimensions include skill use and development, discretion/autonomy, the physical work environment, work intensity, working time quality, the job prospects, and the social environment at work. The first five of these are available throughout the period of our investigation, i.e., from 1995 to 2015. In contrast, prospects and the social environment dimensions are calculated only for the 2005–2015 period due to the availability of the relevant survey items. As Table 5.1 indicates, we also calculate an overall index of job quality, which is simply the individual mean of all items used to construct all different job quality dimensions' indices (apart from those comprising prospects and social environment). In parts of the analysis that follows, we will make use of this overall index to paint a comparative picture of the overall job quality in Greece and the rest of Europe.

3 The "twin gap" in Greece before and during the crisis

As mentioned earlier, the well-known gap between Greece and the rest of the EU concerns the poor performance of the Greek labour market in terms of its "quantity" side. This is depicted in Figure 5.1. Apart from 1995, Greece has been a relatively high unemployment country in the EU. It should also be noted that the relative position of Greece in terms of unemployment *vis-à-vis* the rest of the EU deteriorated up until the beginning of the global financial crisis in 2008. This gradual decline gave way to a dramatic deterioration in unemployment following the eruption of the economic crisis and the implementation of the measures included in the Memoranda of Understanding (MoUs) signed by the successive Greek governments and the Troika of its creditors. Thus, by 2015, unemployment in Greece reached unprecedented levels of around 25%.

But how has Greece fared comparatively on the "quality" front? In other words, can we identify a "twin gap" with the rest of Europe? To answer this question, we start our analysis of the EWCS data with the plotting of the relative ranking of Greece on the various job quality dimensions we defined in the previous section. To keep our presentation simple, we select 11 EU countries for this comparison (these countries were also used in Figure 5.1 earlier): Bulgaria, Denmark, France, Germany, Hungary, Ireland, Poland, Portugal, Spain, Sweden, and the UK. This selection covers a representative set of EU countries, spanning the whole diversity of development, wealth, and labour market regulations observed in the EU.[1] Figures 5.2–5.9 present the average country scores (also ranging between 0–1 and calculated as the country-year means) for the various job quality dimensions for all the EWCS years we investigate.

Starting from *skill use and development*, Figure 5.2 presents the comparative European picture. Greece is consistently ranked in one of the last

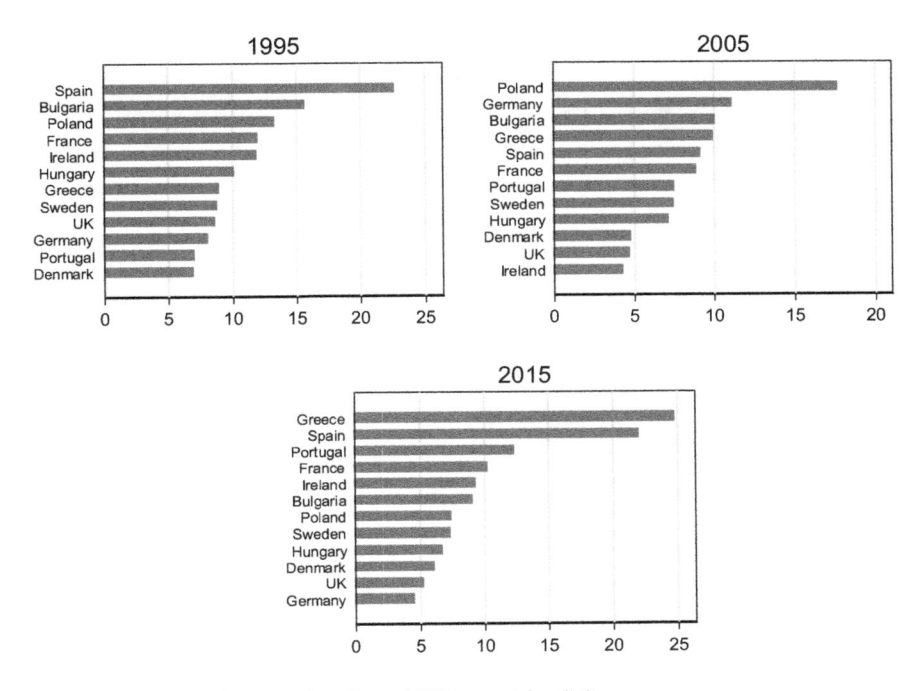

Figure 5.1 Unemployment in selected EU countries (%)
Source: The World Bank, World Development Indicators.

positions, along with Bulgaria. Also note that countries relatively poorer than Greece, as measured by their GDP *per capita* (Hungary, Poland, and Portugal), perform much better on this indicator. Another important finding is that when the differences in average scores are checked in terms of their statistical significance in all years, they reveal an interesting pattern: in the years that Greece occupies the last position in the ranking (1995 and 2015), all other countries record a significantly higher score. On the other hand, Greece's score is not statistically different from that of Portugal in 2000–2001, Bulgaria and Spain in 2005, and Bulgaria in 2010. In other words, Greece is the *only* among the 12 countries that are compared here that consistently occupies the last position in skill use and development ranking across all years. Moreover, a large decline in Greece's score can be observed during the crisis. Between 2010 and 2015, Greece's skill use and development score reduced by about 0.06 points (in a 0–1 range; $p < 0.01$), possibly reflecting the economic crisis and the cutback on expenses related to training and overall skill development to a certain extent. Further calculations revealed that in 2015, no country in the whole EU-28 exhibited worse job quality in terms of skill use and development than Greece.

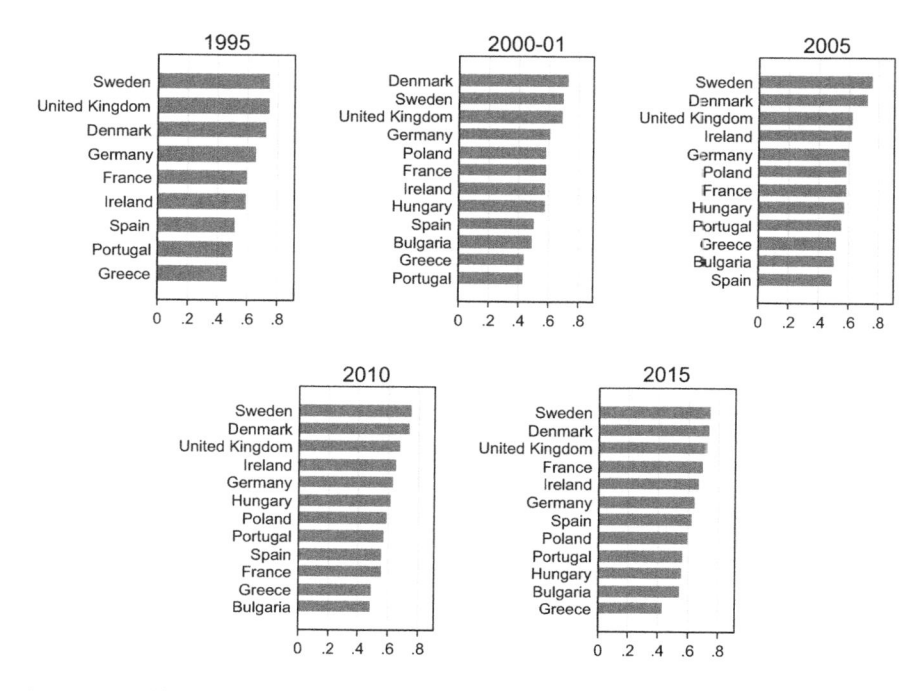

Figure 5.2 Skill use and development index in selected EU countries
Source: EWCS 1995–2015 and authors' calculations.

A similar picture emerges from the analysis of *job autonomy*. Figure 5.3 presents the relevant country averages over these 20 years. Greece occupies the bottom position in all years, sometimes (in 2005 and 2010) sharing it with countries such as Bulgaria, Portugal, or Spain. Again, poorer and less regulated (at least up to 2010) countries such as Portugal and the Eastern European ones reveal a pattern of work organisation that affords more autonomy and task discretion to individual employees. Job autonomy also declined markedly during the crisis (around 0.07 points, $p < 0.01$), and by 2015, Greece had the worst job autonomy score in the whole EU-28.

A somewhat better picture for Greece emerges if we look at the *physical environment* component of job quality. Figure 5.4 presents the relevant estimates. The physical environment index seems to have slightly improved over the years in Greece. While Greece occupied the last position among the countries presented in the figure in 2005, its relative ranking improved in 2010 and 2015. However, Greece is still among the countries with the worst quality in this aspect, again below poorer and less regulated member states. No significant change in the average value of the physical environment index occurred in Greece during the crisis years.

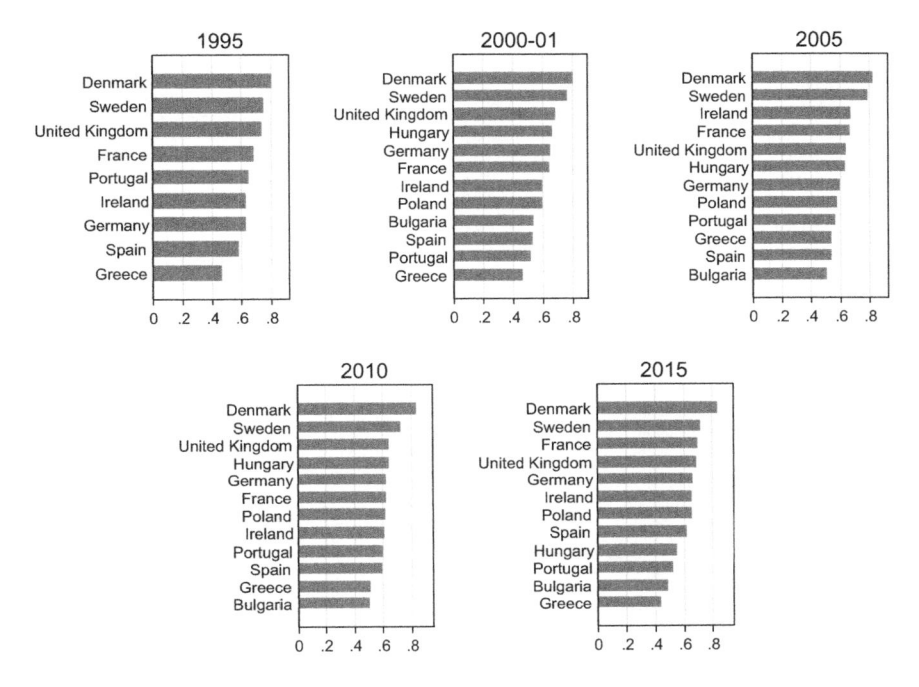

Figure 5.3 Job autonomy index in selected EU countries
Source: EWCS 1995–2015 and authors' calculations.

A process of *work intensification* (Green 2004) in Greece is revealed by the average scores for the work intensity index depicted in Figure 5.5. While countries such as Sweden and the UK scored worse than Greece on this aspect in 1995, 2000, and 2001, by 2005, Greece was the country occupying the bottom position, with all other countries scoring a significantly higher score in all subsequent years. Indeed, the work intensity index declined in Greece in both 2000–2001 and 2005, and significantly so. In contrast, the severe crisis taking place between 2010 and 2015 in the country did not cause any significant change in its average value. If we compare Greece with all EU-28 countries in 2015, only Cyprus and (to a lesser extent) Romania fared worse than Greece on work intensity in that year.

Greece also shows a particularly poor performance on *working time quality*. In all EWCS years, Greece occupies the last position on this aspect relative to all other comparator countries (see Figure 5.6). The only exception to this pattern is 2010, when working time quality in the UK and Bulgaria is equally poor (the differences between the three countries' scores are not statistically significant). Again, no change is observed during the crisis years

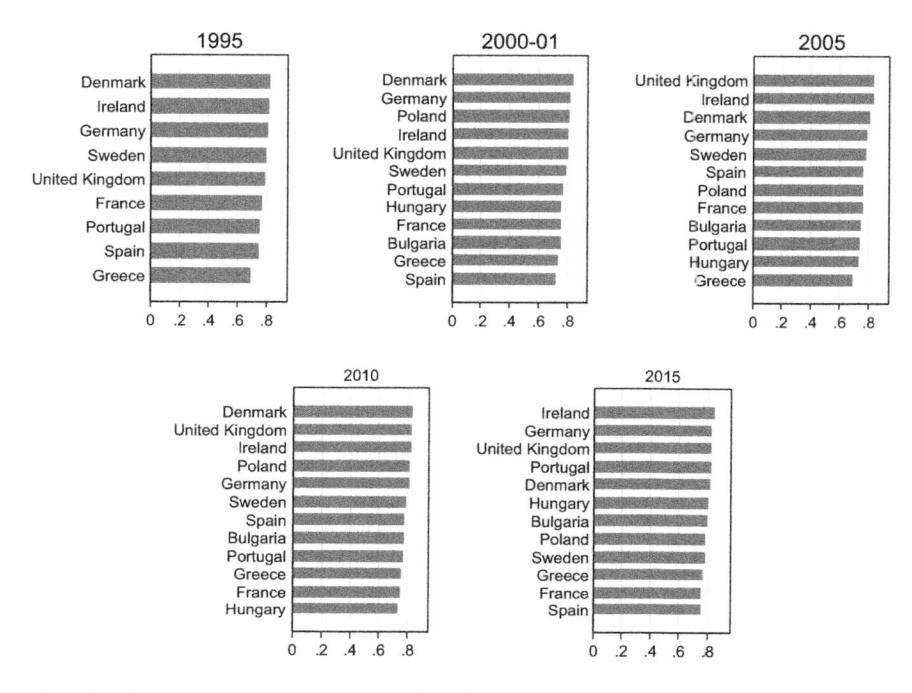

Figure 5.4 Physical environment index in selected EU countries
Source: EWCS 1995–2015 and authors' calculations.

for Greece. Finally, compared to the whole EU-28, only Croatia and Malta scored an equally poor performance on working time quality in 2015.

We now turn to the two job quality dimensions for which we have data only since 2005: job prospects and the social environment of work. Figure 5.7 shows that *job prospects* became particularly poor for employees in Greece during the crisis. This is something that should be expected, since the drastic increase in unemployment and the extensive labour market deregulation (which also entailed a weakening in the strictness of employment protection legislation; see Kornelakis et al. 2017) led to a relative decrease in feelings of job security and a more negative assessment of career prospects among employees in Greece. Together with Spain and Portugal, which have also experienced severe crises and far-reaching labour market reforms during the same period (see Molina 2014), Greece scores the lowest value on the prospects index in 2015 relative to all other comparator countries. In contrast, Hungary and Bulgaria were faring worse than Greece in the job prospects index in both 2005 and 2010.

The only exception to this painted picture is the *social environment* of work indicator. Indeed, Figure 5.8 shows a steady improvement in the

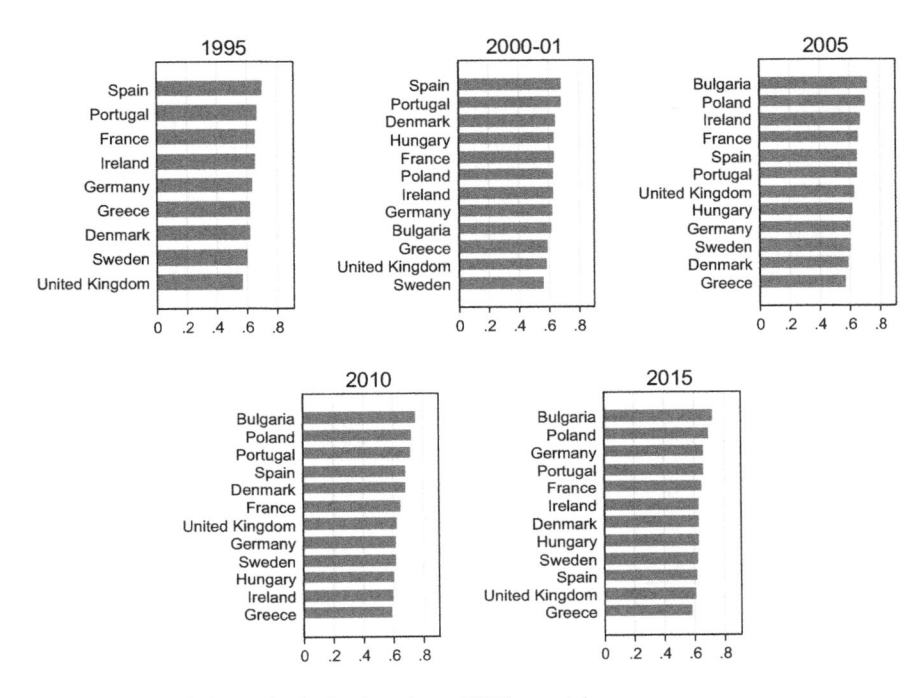

Figure 5.5 Work intensity index in selected EU countries
Source: EWCS 1995–2015 and authors' calculations.

relative ranking of Greece in this respect throughout the years. Greece never occupies the last position in the ranking, and it is actually among the top performers in 2015, i.e. in a year when most of the other job quality aspects fared particularly poorly. This picture does not change if we compare Greece with all the countries in the EU-28. It would not be far-fetched to conclude that Greek employees hold particularly bad jobs, but at least they hold them in a socially supportive work environment.

It does not come as a surprise, thus, that overall job quality in Greece is particularly poor throughout the EWCS years. The average scores for our overall summary index of job quality are shown in Figure 5.9, and they vividly depict what we should expect from the above findings: overall job quality in Greece is poorer than in any other comparator country, while it also significantly declined during the crisis years (by about 0.016 points, $p < 0.10$). Moreover, in 2015, all other countries in EU-28 fared much better than Greece in overall job quality. This finding holds even if the (relatively favourable for Greece) social environment of work and the job prospects indices are included in the construction of the overall index.

Figure 5.6 Working time quality index in selected EU countries
Source: EWCS 1995–2015 and authors' calculations

An apparent conclusion from the above analysis is that a "job quality gap" exists (and persists) between Greece and the rest of the EU-28 countries. Apart from the social environment of work, Greece occupies the last position in the EU in almost all other quality dimensions throughout the EWCS years that cover the most recent 20-year period. This gap also increased during the present crisis that the Greek economy and labour market face: two of the individual dimensions of quality (skill use and development and job autonomy), as well as the overall job quality index, declined in value between 2010 and 2015. A further important finding is that the "twin gap" in quantity and quality with the rest of Europe increased dramatically during the recent years, mirroring both the large increase in unemployment and the (relatively more contained) decrease in job quality relative to the rest of the EU member states.

To a certain extent, the job quality gap presents an interesting puzzle. Whereas unemployment levels are determined by the level of economic activity to a large extent, and Greece documents cyclical improvements and deteriorations in its relative unemployment rate, poor job quality appears as a permanent and structural characteristic of the Greek labour market.

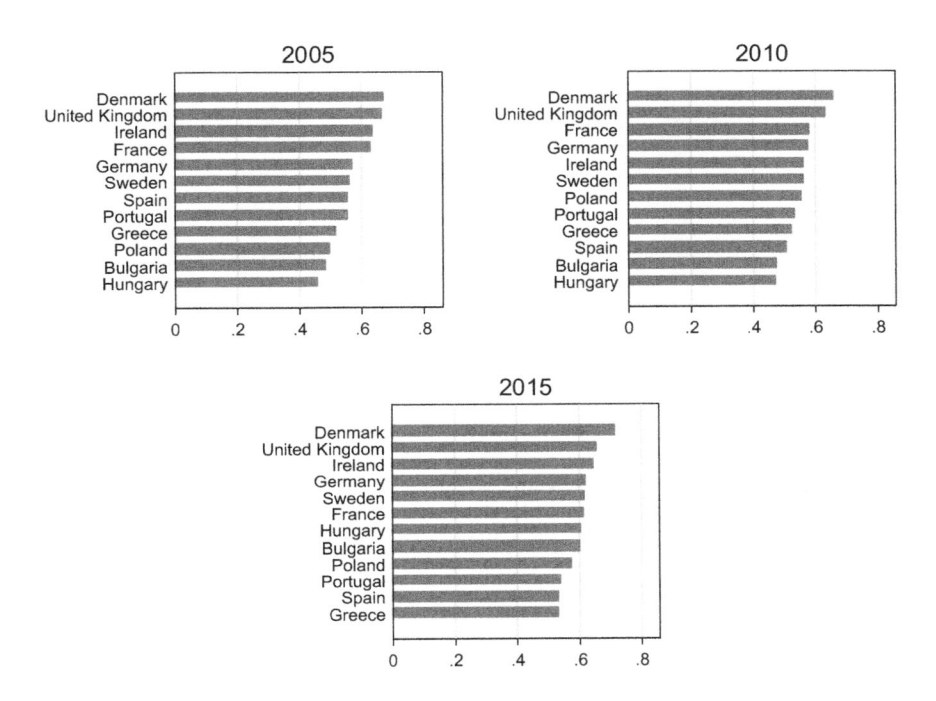

Figure 5.7 Job prospects index in selected EU countries
Source: EWCS 2005–2015 and authors' calculations.

Indeed, no other country in the EU-28 is so consistently present at the bottom of the job quality ranking in nearly all relevant quality dimensions. This cannot be explained by the relative level of economic development, since the jobs that the Greek labour market creates are apparently worse than those in countries with lower *per capita* GDP. This is quite convincingly shown in Figure 5.10. The left-hand panel of the figure confirms the position of Greece as an "outlier" in the overall job quality ranking among the EU-28 countries: in 2010, its average score on overall job quality cannot be explained by its relative level of economic development, the latter being measured by GDP *per capita*. This finding becomes even more puzzling if we contrast it with the relationship between average earnings and GDP *per capita*, which is depicted in the right-hand panel of Figure 5.10: the average level of earnings in Greece closely follows the country's relative ranking in terms of GDP per capita in the same year.[2]

Finally, we also calculated the overall job quality index for the non-EU countries that are available in the EWCS 2005–2015 waves. Figure 5.11 presents their scores along with those for Greece, Bulgaria, Romania, and Croatia. Again, Greece occupies a low position relative to all these relatively

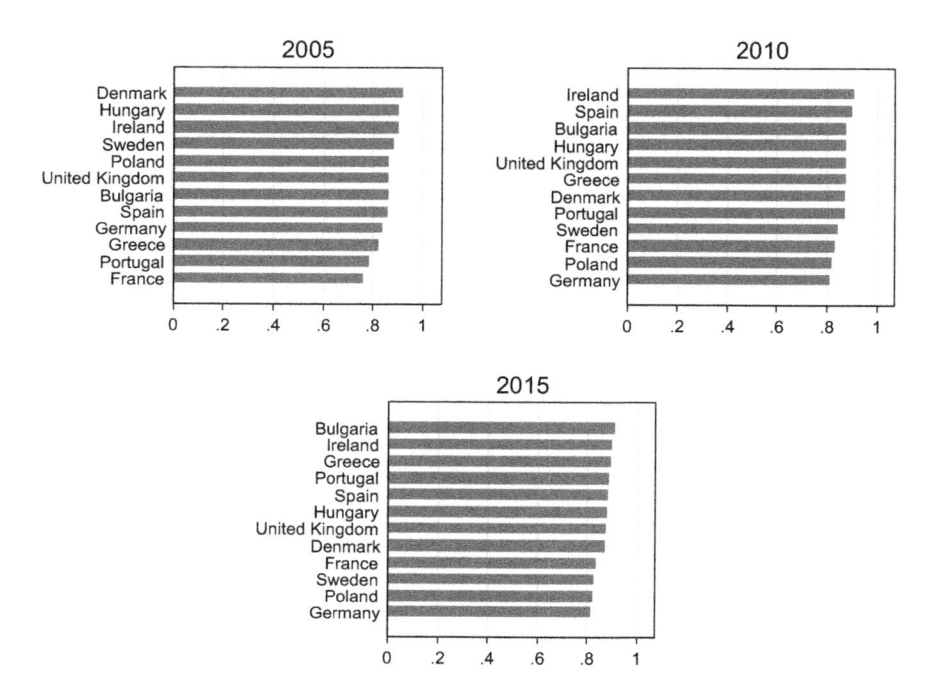

Figure 5.8 Social environment of work index in selected EU countries
Source: EWCS 2005–2015 and authors' calculations.

poorer countries, particularly in 2015. Only Turkey performs worse than Greece in all years – note, however, that in 2015, the difference in the average values of Greece and Turkey is not statistically significant. Thus, it is obvious that some further exploration of this particularly poor job quality performance of Greece is required.

4 Explanations for the cross-national patterns and trends

The purpose of this section is to try to provide some possible explanations for the puzzle identified in the previous section. Admittedly, the analysis here is exploratory, and its main aim is to guide further research on the subject. Specifically, through the use of suitable explanatory variables, regression analysis can help us test some possible explanations for this puzzling job quality gap between Greece and the rest of the EU-28 member states. To this end, we aggregate and average the EWCS 1995–2015 data by country and year, and we use the overall job quality score presented above as the dependent variable in a linear multiple regression model where the unit of the observation is the country/year.[3] This leaves us with around 130 country/year

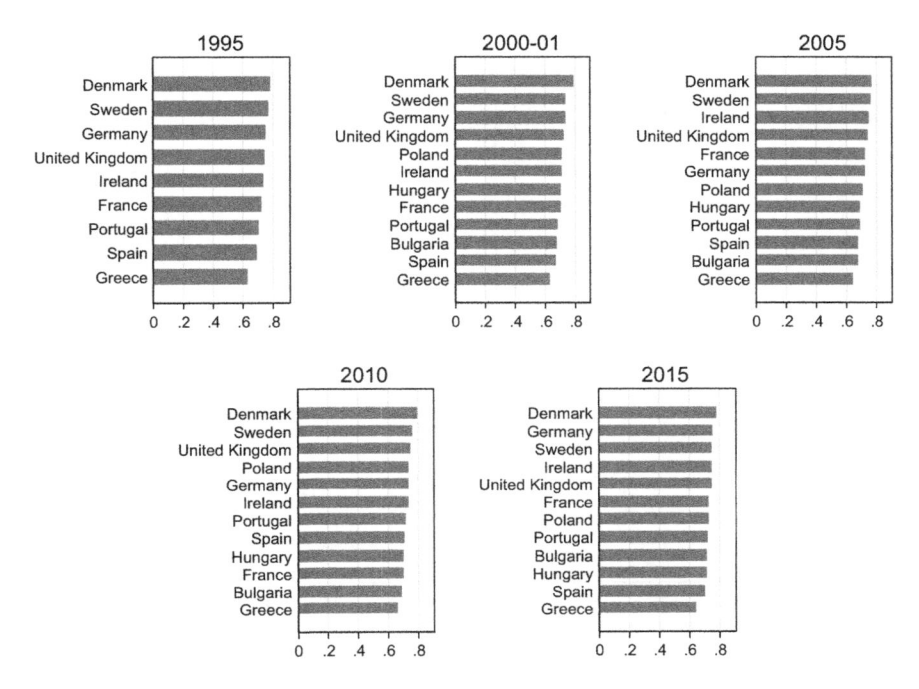

Figure 5.9 Overall job quality index in selected EU countries
Source: EWCS 1995–2015 and authors' calculations.

observations for the EU-28 countries.[4] The next step is to try to explain the job quality gap between Greece and the rest of the EU-28 by referencing some of the observable differences between Greece and the other member states (see Table 5.2, Columns 1–7).

Column 1 of Table 5.2 regresses overall job quality on the dummy variable for Greece. This shows the raw gap in the overall job quality between Greece and the "average" EU-28 country in an "average" year. As documented above, a large, negative, and statistically significant gap of about 0.09 points is estimated for the whole 1995–2015 period. Controlling for EWCS year (Column 2) leaves the gap unchanged. This is something to be expected, since we have seen that poor overall job quality performance of the Greek labour market is a permanent and structural characteristic, not associated with a specific year in our sample (see Figure 5.9). This is true even if we account for the different gender and age composition of employees in Greece relative to the rest of the EU (Column 3). Gender and age can be considered demographic proxies for employee labour market power and should be associated with the quality of jobs that employers design and offer (see the various chapters in Felstead et al. 2015). However, the difference between Greece

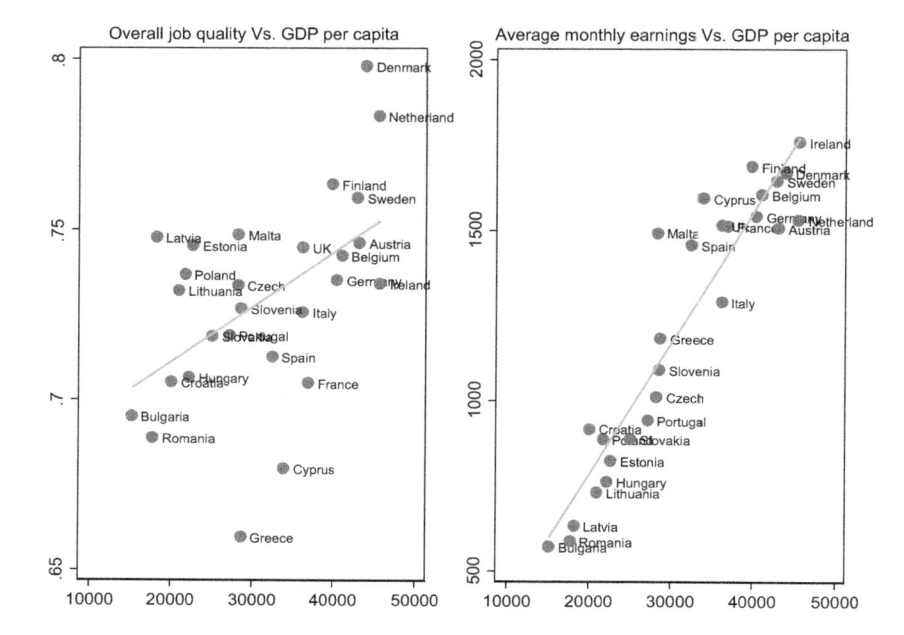

Figure 5.10 Overall job quality, average earnings, and GDP per capita in the EU in 2010

Source: EWCS 2010, World Development Indicators, and authors' calculations. Figure excludes Luxembourg due to its outlier status concerning GDP per capita.

and the average EU-28 country is not too big in these respects, and hence the gap remains unaffected by the introduction of these controls.

A more promising explanation (as we have already seen, however, that it cannot fully explain our puzzling raw result) concerns the level of economic development and the business cycle of the countries in our sample. To this end, Column 4 controls GDP per capita and the unemployment rate.[5] A reduction of less than 0.02 points in the coefficient of the Greek dummy is observed. This is in line with what we mentioned earlier: Greece appears as an outlier in the job quality ranking of the EU-28 countries if the relationship between job quality and the level of economic development is examined. Moreover, cross-country differences in the unemployment rate do not seem to explain much of the job quality gap we have identified.[6]

Column 5 proceeds with an even more promising explanation of Greece's exceptionally bad overall quality of its jobs: the different occupational and industrial composition of the country relative to those of the average EU-28 member state. Some of the structural characteristics of the Greek economy relative to the average EU-28 country, such as the lower shares of managerial and associate professional employees and the higher shares of clerical and

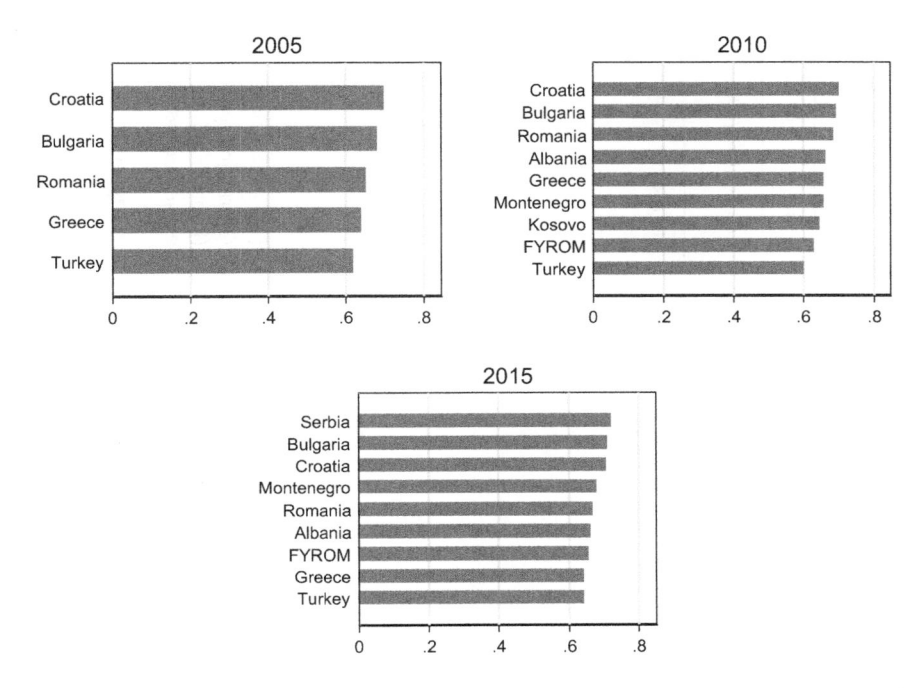

Figure 5.11 Overall job quality index in Greece, the newest EU member states, and EU candidate countries

Source: EWCS 2005–2015 and authors' calculations.

service and sales workers or the higher shares of employees in hotels and restaurants, are expected to explain part of the gap between Greece and the EU-28, considering the average job quality levels for these occupations and industries presented in the disaggregated analysis of Eurofound (2012). Indeed, when the relevant occupational and industrial shares are entered in the model as controls, the coefficient of the Greece dummy is halved (Column 5). Still, though, a sizable and significant gap remains unexplained.

The next step is to try to offer some institutional explanation for our puzzle. Employee collective power should be associated with higher quality jobs in theory. Empirically, this association is also well documented. Gallie (2003) stresses the important role of Scandinavian unions and their involvement in "quality of working life" programmes and work organisation in contributing to the exceptional quality of work observed in these countries (a finding also apparent in the ranking of these countries for almost all job quality indicators presented in Figures 5.2–5.9). Ollo-López et al. (2011) and Esser and Olsen (2012) also report a positive association between union strength and the level of job autonomy observed across European countries.

Table 5.2 The job quality gap between Greece and Europe.

	(1)	(2)	(3)	(4)	(5)	(6)	(7)
	Overall job quality	*Overall job quality*	*Overall job quality*	*Overall job quality*	*Overall job quality*	*Overall job quality*	*Overall job quality*
Greece	-0.087***	-0.088***	-0.086***	-0.068***	-0.034***	-0.035***	-0.043***
Year dummies	-	√	√	√	√	√	√
Female share, average age	-	-	√	√	√	√	√
GDP per capita, Unemployment rate	-	-	-	√	√	√	√
Occupational and industrial structure	-	-	-	-	√	√	√
Union density	-	-	-	-	-	√	√
EPL	-	-	-	-	-	-	√
Observations	126	126	126	126	126	125	95
R-squared	0.24	0.30	0.31	0.60	0.83	0.84	0.89
	(8)	(9)	(10)	(11)	(12)	(13)	(14)
	Skill use and development	Job autonomy	Physical environment	Work intensity	Working time quality	Overall job quality (Poorer EWCS countries, density excluded)	Overall job quality (Poorer EWCS countries, density included)
Greece	-0.007	-0.075***	-0.039***	-0.016	-0.044***	-0.091***	-0.078***

Year dummies	√	√	√	√	√	√	√
Female share, average age	√	√	√	√	√	√	√
GDP per capita, Unemployment rate	√	√	√	√	√	√	√
Occupational and industrial structure	√	√	√	√	√	√	√
Union density	√	√	√	√	√	-	√
Observations	125	125	125	125	125	67	59
R-squared	0.77	0.72	0.66	0.57	0.72	0.91	0.95

Notes: OLS regressions; standard errors clustered by country are used for statistical significances; *** $p < 0.01$; ** $p < 0.05$; * $p < 0.10$; poorer countries in Columns 13 and 14 are those in the EWCS that had a lower GDP per capita than Greece in 2010, namely Bulgaria, the Czech Republic, Estonia, Latvia, Lithuania, Hungary, Malta, Poland, Portugal, Romania, Slovakia, Slovenia, Croatia, FYROM, Turkey, Albania, Montenegro, and Serbia; in Column 14, FYROM, Albania, Montenegro, and Serbia are excluded due to missing union density data.
Source: EWCS 1995–2015, World Development Indicators and authors' calculations.

Considering that Greece is a relatively low unionisation country with limited workplace employee representation (Forth et al. 2017), coupled with a union movement mostly focused on wage bargaining, distribution, and government policy, one may expect this fact to explain part of our puzzling result. However, Column 6 in Table 5.2 shows that this is not the case. Controlling union density leaves the coefficient of interest unaffected.[7] Moreover, while the strictness of employment protection legislation (EPL) is not too straightforwardly related to the quality of jobs available in a specific country (Esser and Olsen 2012), apart from a possible link resulting from increased employee power in countries with a stricter EPL, the OECD's EPL index does not affect the coefficient for Greece when entered into the model (Column 7).[8]

We also experimented with further variables that may be expected to be related to the exceptionally poor performance of the Greek labour market. Controlling average educational qualifications, average workplace size, average tenure, and the share of private sector employees does not substantially affect the coefficient of our variable of interest. Also, these variables are only available in the latest waves of the EWCS, limiting our estimating sample. Thus, we can conclude, with a certain degree of confidence, that our puzzling result cannot adequately be explained by the usual factors that we can observe and account for. The only result that is certain is that part of the gap reflects the different macroeconomic conditions and, mainly, the different occupational and industrial structure of the Greek labour market.

In Columns 8–12, we estimate the same regression models for each job quality dimension separately. It can be seen that three of the five gaps, namely autonomy, the physical environment, and working time quality, are robust to the inclusion of our control variables, driving in this sense the robustness of the overall job quality gap. On the other hand, skill use and development and work intensity are similar in Greece and the average EU-28 country when all the previously mentioned controls are accounted for in the model.[9] Without further investigation, it is not possible to offer a strong explanation for these differential findings with regard to the different job quality dimensions.

To complement this analysis, a discussion of factors that may explain our findings but are not directly observable seems appropriate here. On the one hand, one could argue that the low quality of jobs in Greece, mainly with respect to the aspects related to skill use and development and job autonomy, reflect a particularly paternalistic and authoritarian managerial style, a significantly more Tayloristic organisation of work, and a limited use of high-involvement management in the country's workplaces (Ollo-López et al. 2011). However, this explanation does not convincingly solve the puzzle we have identified. The job quality gap between Greece and other European countries is also persistent when one compares Greece to significantly poorer European countries, where high-involvement management practices are limited too. This is documented again, and in a multiple regression setting, in Columns 13 and 14 of Table 5.2, where our standard model is estimated on the sample of the EWCS countries poorer than Greece (Column 13 excludes the union density variable that is not available for all countries and years). The coefficient of the Greece dummy is still large, negative, and statistically significant, confirming our concerns related to the validity of the proposed explanation.

On the other hand, one could put forward the argument that employees in Greece are particularly gloomy and pessimistic when they report their working conditions in a survey setting and that this may be the reason behind the persistent poor quality of performance observed in our data. There is some indication that this might be the case if we take into account survey evidence provided by other sources, such as the Eurobarometer surveys. In fact, in the Spring 2015 standard Eurobarometer survey (wave 83), Greece appears in the bottom of the EU's ranking regarding how well or badly the citizens perceive their personal job situation.[10] This, however, provides only circumstantial evidence, as it would require further exploration examining whether this particular pessimistic attitude is a result of the unprecedented crisis or a more permanent characteristic of pessimism, also apparent in the previous decades of relative affluence. In other words, one should be wary of *ad hoc* factors, which are reminiscent of some of the cultural explanations for the differences in HRM practices across countries (Vaiman and Brewster 2015). If there is any pessimism as a diachronic feature of workers' attitudes in Greece, then this is also an incomplete explanation. There is no *a priori* reason to assume that the way employees in Greece report their jobs in a survey setting should be any different from that of employees in the rest of the EU-28 or the EU candidate countries. Therefore, this seems to beg the question: what explains the higher level of pessimism around jobs in Greece compared to other countries? In short, without further exploration and a more detailed analysis, any argument based on cultural or attitudinal characteristics will likely appear as an easy and unconvincing way out of the relevant puzzle and debate.

This discussion implies a fascinating future research agenda that could address the various questions left unanswered here. More research is needed in addressing the puzzle revealed concerning the job quality performance of Greece relative to the rest of Europe. Research on the specific attitudes and practices of managers in Greek workplaces can certainly offer insights on the organisation of work, the design of jobs, and the management of human resources that takes place in Greece and may be the factor behind the results presented earlier. Also, the role of institutions in explaining the cross-country patterns in job quality can be a promising future research direction, following the lines of inquiry presented in Dobbin and Boychuk (1999), Gallie (2003, 2007), Ollo-López et al. (2011), and Esser and Olsen (2012), but with a focus on countries that are not easily categorised into specific "production" or "employment" regimes (such as Greece) and an extended array of job quality dimensions. Concerning institutions, in this chapter, we have only been able to account for relative union strength (captured by union density) in our effort to try and explain the puzzling result concerning the Greek labour market. However, as noted earlier, of equal importance are the structure, strategies, and overall attitudes of unions, something that cannot be easily addressed in a quantitative approach, such as the one presented in this chapter. A union concern about job quality is a broader issue (see Gallie 2003) that is only partially related to union strength or the access and presence of unions in a country's workplaces. Finally, a reconsideration of labour market policies is warranted. Apart from their impact and implications on the quantity side of the labour market, more research needs to focus on their relevance to the quality side, the everyday working experience of people employed, and how the latter reflects the relative power of the two actors in the employment relationship.

5 Conclusions

The aim of this chapter was to document and describe the comparative standing of the jobs of the Greek labour market in the job quality distribution of the EU jobs. In the process, we uncovered a relatively interesting puzzle. In nearly all of the relevant quality aspects (with the exception of the social environment of work), Greece is the only country among the EU-28 member states that is consistently placed at the bottom of the ranking for about the last 20 years. The present crisis made this picture even worse and led to a substantial widening of the "twin gap" (in both quantity and, to a lesser extent, quality) *vis-à-vis* the rest of the EU. The puzzle of why Greece appears as an *outlier* in job quality is further strengthened if one takes into account its relative level of economic development. Greece fares worse than several other countries, whether they are old member states, new member states, or EU candidate countries.

Our findings have theoretical, empirical, and policy implications. Theoretically, much remains unexplained regarding what drives the patterns of cross-country variation in job quality. As we saw earlier, we could not fully account for the relative position of Greece among the EU countries.[11] However, it appears that some relevant observable characteristics, particularly the industrial and occupational structure of the Greek labour market, may potentially offer an answer to our findings to some extent. This implies that much more theorising is required for the drivers of job quality and how the different actors and institutions of the labour market affect the quality content of a country's jobs (Gallie 2003, 2007). Empirically, we showed that recession does not necessarily mean that the worst jobs in an economy are destroyed, leaving only the best jobs available among the still employed population (Gallie et al. 2014). By contrast, rising unemployment, employers' cost-cutting strategies, and the changing balance of power between employers and employees in favour of the former can mean that the quality of jobs remaining in a crisis-stricken labour market declines. This decline may happen abruptly and swiftly, as what we observed to be the case in Greece between 2010 and 2015.

This latter point also reveals the problematic approach to labour market policy by the Troika and the successive Greek governments since the onset of the sovereign debt crisis and the implementation of the policies imposed by the loan agreements. Instead of boosting competitiveness and offering at least a partial answer to the problem apparent on the quantity side of the labour market, the implemented measures associated with labour market deregulation seem to have had negative implications for both the quantity and quality of jobs. Unemployment reached unprecedented levels while, as we documented in this chapter, the quality of existing jobs declined, in some respects quite dramatically. Hence, the policy agenda followed in the country not only led to reduction in the overall well-being of the population that lost their jobs and market incomes, but it also resulted in a less fulfilling and harsher reality for those still employed.

Notes

1 It should be noted that the findings that we report below concerning the relative standing of Greece in terms of its job quality do not depend on the specific choice of countries and it holds irrespective of the rest of the EU countries used for the comparison. We comment on the overall standing of Greece in the whole EU-28 throughout this section.
2 Earnings data is available in the EWCS in the 2010 and 2015 waves only. Apart from our research objective of focussing on non-wage aspects in this chapter, this is another reason why wages have not been investigated in more detail in this work.
3 All models are estimated by OLS. Standard errors robust to clustering at the level of the country are used throughout. Results are robust to the use of different modelling approaches, e.g. the use of fractional probit to take account of the 0–1 range of the dependent variable.
4 The results presented below do not change if we also include the non-EU countries available in the EWCS in various years in the estimations. We will only use these countries in parts of the analysis that follows.
5 The source of all macro-level variables is the World Development Indicators of the World Bank. See http://databank.worldbank.org/data/reports.aspx?source=world-development-indicators#.
6 Actually, the unemployment rate is a statistically insignificant determinant of the overall job quality. In contrast, there is a positive and significant relationship between GDP per capita and job quality.
7 Union density data is sourced from the online OECD database (see http://stats.oecd.org/). Missing data in this source is filled in by the estimates reported in Visser (2015). Note that union strength, however, is not a good proxy for union strategy concerning job quality. We return to this issue below.
8 The OECD's EPL index is only available for a subsample of the EU-28 countries and years. For this reason, there is a substantial reduction in the estimating sample (see Column 7 in Table 5.2).
9 The raw gaps (without controls) are negative and statistically significant in all cases.
10 See http://ec.europa.eu/commfrontoffice/publicopinion/archives/eb/eb83/eb83_publ_en.pdf (accessed: 23/06/2018).
11 A similar concern might be apparent for the ranking of Cyprus in the overall job quality distribution. See Figure 5.10.

References

Brown, A., Charlwood, A., and Spencer, D. A. (2012). 'Not All that It Might Seem: Why Job Satisfaction Is Worth Studying despite It Being a Poor Summary Measure of Job Quality'. *Work, Employment and Society*, 26(6): 1007–1018.

Burchell, B., Sehnbruch, K., Piasna, A., and Agloni, N. (2014). 'The Quality of Employment and Decent Work: Definitions, Methodologies, and Ongoing Debates'. *Cambridge Journal of Economics*, 38(2): 459–477.

Cazes, S., Hijzen, A., and Saint-Martin, A. (2015). 'Measuring and Assessing Job Quality: The OECD Job Quality Framework'. *OECD Social, Employment and Migration Working Papers*, No. 174. Paris: OECD.

Christopoulou, R. and Monastiriotis, V. (2014). 'The Greek Public Sector Wage Premium before the Crisis: Size, Selection and Relative Valuation of Characteristics'. *British Journal of Industrial Relations*, 52(3): 579–602.

Clark, A. (1997). 'Job Satisfaction and Gender: Why Are Women so Happy at Work?'. *Labour Economics*, 4(4): 341–372.

Clark, A. (2005). 'Your Money or Your Life: Changing Job Quality in OECD Countries'. *British Journal of Industrial Relations*, 43(3): 377–400.

Daouli, J., Demoussis, M., Giannakopoulos, N., and Laliotis, I. (2016). 'The 2011 Industrial Relations Reform and Nominal Wage Adjustments in Greece'. *Journal of Labor Research*, 37(4): 460–483.

Dedoussopoulos, A., Aranitou, V., Koutentakis, F., and Maropoulou, M. (2013). *Assessing the Impact of the Memoranda on Greek Labour Market and Labour Relations*. Working Paper 53. International Labour Office.

Dobbin, F. and Boychuk, T. (1999). 'National Employment Systems and Job Autonomy: Why Job Autonomy Is High in the Nordic Countries and Low in the United States, Canada, and Australia'. *Organization Studies*, 20(2): 257–291.

Esser, I. and Olsen, K. M. (2012). 'Perceived Job Quality: Autonomy and Job Security within a Multi-Level Framework'. *European Sociological Review*, 28(4): 443–454.

Eurofound. (2012). *Trends in Job Quality in Europe*. Luxembourg: Publications Office of the European Union.

Eurofound. (2017). *Sixth European Working Conditions Survey – Overview Report (2017 Update)*. Luxembourg: Publications Office of the European Union.

Felstead, A., Gallie, D., and Green, F. (eds.). (2015). *Unequal Britain at Work*. Oxford: Oxford University Press.

Forth, J., Bryson, A., and George, A. (2017). 'Explaining Cross-National Variation in Workplace Employee Representation'. *European Journal of Industrial Relations*, 23 (4): 415–433.

Gallie, D. (2003). 'The Quality of Working Life: Is Scandinavia Different?'. *European Sociological Review*, 19(1): 61–79.

Gallie, D. (2007). 'Production Regimes and the Quality of Employment in Europe'. *Annual Review of Sociology*, 33: 85–104.

Gallie, D., Felstead, A., Green, F., and Inanc, H. (2014). 'The Quality of Work in Britain over the Economic Crisis'. *International Review of Sociology*, 24(2): 207–224.

Green, F. (2004). 'Work Intensification, Discretion, and the Decline in Well-Being at Work'. *Eastern Economic Journal*, 30(4): 615–625.

Green, F. (2006). *Demanding Work*. Princeton, NJ: Princeton University Press.

Green, F., Mostafa, T., Parent-Thirion, A., Vermeylen, G., Van Houten, G., Biletta, I., and Lyly-Yrjanainen, M. (2013). 'Is Job Quality Becoming More Unequal?' *Industrial and Labor Relations Review*, 66(4): 753–784.

Holman, D. (2013). 'Job Types and Job Quality in Europe'. *Human Relations*, 66(4): 475–502.

ILO. (2013). *Decent Work Indicators: Guidelines for Producers and Users of Statistical and Legal Framework Indicators*. ILO manual: second version. Geneva: ILO.

ILO. (2014). *Greece: Productive Jobs for Greece*. Geneva: ILO.

Kornelakis, A. and Veliziotis, M. (2018). 'Job Quality in Europe: Regulation, Workplace Innovation and Human Resource Practices'. In: G. Suder, M. Riviere and J. Lindeque (eds.). *The Routledge Companion to European Business*. Series: Routledge Companions in Business, Management and Accounting. London: Routledge, pp. 173–189.

Kornelakis, A., Voskeritsian, H., Veliziotis, M., Kapotas, P., and Georgaki, K. (2017). *Prospects for a New Employment Relations and Labour Market Model in Greece*. Final Report for the London School of Economics, Hellenic Observatory, National Bank of Greece Small Grants Scheme. London: London School of Economics/ Hellenic Observatory.

Molina, O. (2014). 'Self-Regulation and the State in Industrial Relations in Southern Europe: Back to the Future?' *European Journal of Industrial Relations*, 20(1): 21–36.

Muñoz de Bustillo Llorente, R., and Fernández Macías, E. (2005). 'Job Satisfaction as an Indicator of the Quality of Work'. *The Journal of Socio-Economics*, 34: 656–673.

Ollo-López, A., Bayo-Moriones, A., and Larraza-Kintana, M. (2011). 'The Impact of Country-Level Factors on the Use of New Work Practices'. *Journal of World Business*, 46(3): 394–403.

Rosenthal, N. (1989). 'More than Wages at Issue in Job Quality Debate'. *Monthly Labor Review*, 112: 4–8.

Spencer, D. A. (2015). 'Developing an Understanding of Meaningful Work in Economics: The Case for a Heterodox Economics of Work'. *Cambridge Journal of Economics*, 39(3): 675–688.

Theodoropoulou, S. (2016). 'Severe Pain, Very Little Gain: Internal Devaluation and Rising Unemployment in Greece'. In: M. Myant, S. Theodoropoulou and A. Piasna (eds.). *Unemployment, Internal Devaluation and Labour Market Deregulation in Europe*. Brussels: ETUI, pp. 25–57.

Vaiman, V. and Brewster, C. (2015). 'How Far Do Cultural Differences Explain the Differences between Nations? Implications for HRM'. *The International Journal of Human Resource Management*, 26(2): 151–164.

Visser, J. (2015). *ICTWSS Data Base*. Version 5.0. Amsterdam: Amsterdam Institute for Advanced Labour Studies AIAS.

6 The rise of involuntary non-standard employment in Greece during the great economic depression[1]

Ilias Livanos and Konstantinos Pouliakas

1 Introduction

Over the past ten years, the Greek labour market has undergone dramatic changes. The impact of the economic crisis as well as the implementation of drastic product and labour market reforms linked to three economic "Memorandum" programs has created a climate of uncertainty not only for those in search of employment, but also for those already employed. In addition to the marked increase in unemployment rates experienced during the prolonged economic recession, another notable trend in the Greek labour market has been an accelerated move away from traditional (i.e. "standard") open-ended full-time contracts towards more flexible, non-standard employment contracts. On the one hand, such a trend in the Greek job market has been, to an exceptional extent, a necessary reaction to the need for cost-cutting on behalf of enterprises at the brink of closure and facing severe financial constraints. On the other hand, the striking and continued proliferation of non-standard employment in Greece is raising concerns about the country's ability to fully exploit its human resource potential and restore long-term growth.

In such times of economic crisis, the focus of labour market analysts and commentators has primarily been on unemployment and, of course, this has been with good reason. In particular, while unemployment had become a less urgent problem in Greece as it remained at levels below 10% before signing the first bailout agreement, it picked up dramatically thereafter, reaching record levels among all European Union countries. There were 440 thousand unemployed people in 2006 (an unemployment rate of about 9%), rising to a high of almost one million three hundred people in search of employment in 2013 (27.3% unemployment rate), falling slightly to 24.5% in 2015. In other words, the number of unemployed people in 2015 was 2.7 times higher than the respective number of 2006.[2]

On top of such high levels of unemployment, there have also been estimates that between 350–427 thousand Greeks have emigrated for purposes of finding work (Lambrianidis 2014; Lazaretou 2016). At the same time, contrary to past trends, it is the highly educated that have sought to leave the country for purposes of work, while the vast majority are young people (aged 18–25). Based on recent evidence, during the crisis years, 75% of the emigrants held a university degree, while 25% were people with post graduate degrees, many of which were doctors or graduates of polytechnic schools (Labrianidis and Pratsinakis 2016). This "brain drain" has contributed to the shrinkage of the total workforce. Given the aforementioned labour supply trends and the generalised lack of effective labour demand during the period of austerity, the total number of people in employment declined by approximately 20%.[3]

These numbers paint only a partial picture of the dire straits of the Greek labour market. Official unemployment statistics fail to take into account "discouraged" individuals, namely those who may have been actively searching for work for some time but eventually gave up trying, even though they wish to have a job, as they could not find any or suitable employment. But the weak job market also manifests in other forms of skill underutilisation, which extend beyond those linked to high levels of unemployed/inactive labour and affect the employed population. This is because some individuals, who at times of a stronger labour market would actively be seeking work (in other words, are counted as unemployed) but not compromise their reservation wage, are likely to accept jobs with pay levels, hours, and/or working conditions they would otherwise reject in periods of buoyant economic activity. This arises due to the need to sustain (minimum or target) living standards in the face of widespread wage cuts and low bargaining power associated with depressed job availability, high unemployment/vacancy ratios, and prolonged unemployment duration. Therefore, in addition to high levels of unemployed or discouraged inactive workers, concerns have been expressed about an increasing trend of other forms of "hidden" or "masked" unemployment in Greece, such as employed workers who are hours-constrained (i.e. would wish to work more hours than at present) or are over-qualified for their jobs (McGuinness and Pouliakas 2017; Pouliakas 2014). More importantly, there has been a striking increase in the share of workers accepting "involuntary non-standard employment contracts," namely individuals who are involuntarily employed in either part-time or temporary contract jobs.

Apart from serving as a potential pool of "reserve unemployed labour," the fact that there is a growing prevalence of involuntarily employed individuals is a cause of concern for the Greek economy. Evidence that preceded the economic crisis had already highlighted that such flexible forms of work had contributed to the creation of an underprivileged working class in Greece, fostering a segmented labour market (Pouliakas and Theodossiou 2005). High levels of involuntary forms of employment also tend to have a positive association with job insecurity, poor career development prospects and, in some cases, poor working conditions and lack of social security. Pouliakas and Theodossiou (2009) have also highlighted that the "utility" costs associated with non-standard forms of employment (and, in particular, the transition to such forms of atypical work) are often high and can be underestimated due to habituation and cognitive dissonance taking effect. Towards this end, some of the recent reforms implemented as part of the economic rescue programs (e.g. regulations concerning working hours and lowering of barriers to the use of part time and temporary contacts) are likely to have further facilitated labour market segmentation in Greece. The restructuring of the Greek economy that has taken place as a result of the economic crisis – in particular, the reduction of the public sector and the increasing share of sectors traditionally reliant on the use of such flexible contracts (e.g. retail sales, hospitality, catering and food services) – is also expected to have contributed to a rising incidence of non-standard employment.

The present chapter aims to shed some light on this relatively under-researched aspect of the Greek labour market by focusing on the extent, trend, and determinants of involuntary non-standard employment during the years of the "Great economic depression" (2009–2015).To do that, the paper builds on the work of Green and Livanos (2015), who employed a new typology of Involuntary Non-standard Employment (INE henceforth), adopting an "individual constrained choice approach". In other words, the focus of the work is on individuals who explicitly state that they have adopted non-standard forms of work (part-time or/and temporary), albeit on an involuntary basis (individuals state that they accepted such contracts because they could not find full-time or/and permanent work). Such an analysis aims to investigate aspects of the labour market that the official definitions and statistics often neglect, thus not capturing the full extent of the challenges the workforce is facing.

Using data from the Greek Labour Force Survey (LFS), covering the period 2006–2015, and adopting multivariate econometric techniques, the present work provides a measure of INE as a share of total employment across different groups of workers as well as regions of Greece. This chapter seeks to provide insights, using descriptive and econometric analyses, into the similarities and differences in the incidence and nature of INE across different population subgroups of Greece, taking into account individuals' socio-demographic and human capital characteristics, past labour market status, job conditions, and selected macro-indicators capturing key features of the economy at the regional and national level. In doing so, the article adds to knowledge about INE in Greece, providing in-depth analysis of the EU Member State most hardly hit by the 2008 global financial crisis. The findings of this study not only contribute to the literature, but they can also be used to learn about the design of suitable employment policies in Greece that would tackle the proliferation of so-called "precarious" employment at its root.

2 Literature review

2.1 Measurement and determinants of non-standard "precarious" employment

The academic interest in non-standard forms of employment has grown in recent years, mainly because of concern about the negative impact they may have on employee well-being. The growth in non-standard or atypical forms of employment, namely modes of work that deviate from what used to be conventional work (permanent/full-time job), can be attributed to various reasons. On the one hand, the intensification of atypical forms of work has been spurred by the need to increase flexibility in work organisations for both employers and employees (Kalleberg 2000). This enables agents to respond faster in the case of adverse economic contingencies as well as adapt to changing social preferences (e.g. mobility; teleworking; etc.). On the other hand, when taking a sociological or industrial relations standpoint, it can be argued that the prolonged economic crisis has challenged the bargaining position of workers (Glassner and Keune 2010). This empowers employers to offer temporary or part-time contracts even if they could in fact offer more jobs under standard contractual terms, exploiting any economic rents that can be made (e.g. recent evidence would point to some Greek employers employing workers on part-time jobs yet still requesting that they engage in eight-hour working days [ILO 2016; Kornelakis et al. 2016]). In light of the excess supply of labour in the Greek economy and the increased duration of a typical spell of unemployment due to constrained job availability, many workers are also likely to accept positions they would otherwise reject. Moreover, the growth in non-standard employment could be linked to changing structural characteristics of economies, such as variations in the industrial composition of employment, and to institutional factors (e.g. lack of access to or provision of affordable child care, employment protection legislation, working hour regulations or activation policies, etc.).

Interest in non-standard forms of employment is usually spurred by the fact that they tend to involve "precarious work". The latter is a rather controversial term, as it comprises a combination of elements that can be found in almost every job and work environment. Nevertheless, some jobs are considered more precarious than others, while some social and age groups are more likely to end up in such a status (Kretsos 2010). Precarious jobs capture elements related to, among others, working hours (e.g. involuntary part-time jobs, nightshifts/weekend work, short-time jobs, underemployment), type of contracts (e.g. involuntary temporary, temporary agency or informal contracts), skills underutilisation, as well as, more broadly, jobs involving low pay, job insecurity, and poor working conditions. Thus, given the complexity and multi-dimensionality of the notion of precarious employment (or, conversely, of "good jobs"), an all-inclusive measurement capturing all such aspects is difficult to achieve.

There is extensive literature focused on the measurement and trends of job quality, which has paid particular emphasis to operationalising the concept of precarious or "low-quality" work. This is typically done either using subjective job satisfaction measures (Pouliakas and Theodossiou 2010) or multi-dimensional indices (which take into account a wide array of measures, such as job insecurity, poor access to training and career prospects, low pay, lack of social protection, etc.) (Green 2006). At the policy level, indicators of job quality (such as the 2001 Laeken indicators of the European Commission) have also been an integral part of the European Employment Strategy, while the ILO's Decent Work Agenda has monitored such indicators closely (Davoine et al. 2008; EMCO 2010).

Given that precarious employment can extend to a wide array of potential indicators, the focus of the present study is on one narrow aspect of precariousness, which relates to the involuntary nature of non-standard employment. The reason for focusing on such involuntary non-standard employment (INE) is because firstly, it accepts that not all non-standard forms of work can be classified as "precarious". For instance, temporary work may be voluntary when it facilitates flexibility for certain workers (e.g. students) or when it serves a as "stepping stone" to more stable future employment (e.g. internship, working abroad to gain experience, etc.) (Nunez and Livanos 2015). Secondly, it also seeks to isolate (albeit in a subjective manner) the part of non-standard contracts that is linked to a "constrained individual choice" element from what is otherwise a very heterogeneous employment relation. Our investigation considers how such a narrower measurement is linked to other aspects of precariousness, such as poor job conditions, low pay, and access to social rights.

Alternative approaches in past literature have predetermined the precarious element of work by simply assuming that any form of atypical work is precarious instead (Da Silva and Turrini 2015). Furthermore, despite its merits, the "quality of work" approach raises questions about the validity of inclusion of some equilibrium outcomes (e.g. low wages or training provision) as proxies of job precariousness. In our study, we acknowledge that different approaches have both strengths and limitations, while also acknowledging as a starting point that a universally accepted definition, which can also be supported by available data at European level, is difficult to obtain.

Despite the fact that many studies investigating forms of non-standard employment do not distinguish between the voluntary/involuntary dimension, often due to data limitations, the academic interest has grown in recent years due to the ongoing economic crisis. Among the relevant studies that make such a distinction, Kauhanen and Nätti (2015) examine job quality and worker well-being for Finland. The authors find that workers in involuntary part-time and temporary work have weaker job quality indicators compared to those who are voluntarily in non-standard employment. With regard to involuntary part-time employment, most initial studies had focused on the relationship between involuntary part-time employment and unemployment at the macro level, finding a strong positive correlation between the two measures (Leppel and Clain 1988). Bednarzik (1975) found that in the US, younger people, the less educated, and females are more likely to be in involuntary part-time employment than average.

Some recent studies have focused on differences between voluntary and involuntary temporary workers using microeconomic data. Amuedo-Dorantes

(2000) studied the Spanish labour market and found that workers in temporary employment, many of whom involuntarily, have limited chances of career advancement. Skedinger (2011) investigated the impact of employment protection in 20 EU countries and concluded that greater stringency of employment regulations for "regular" work is associated with higher involuntary temporary employment. Using data from the 2010 UK Labour Force Survey, Cam (2012) found that involuntary part-time status is more frequently observed among males and single women. Nunez and Livanos (2015) investigated the causes of different types of temporary employment in Europe and found that rather than being "temps by choice", women, younger and single individuals, and non-nationals were more likely to be in temporary employment because they could not find a permanent contract.

Horemanas et al. (2016) focused their research on involuntary part-time work across EU member states, assessing its implications on poverty risk. A recent study by the European Parliament (2016) also assessed different types of employment and how they are connected to work precariousness. The study concluded that involuntary part-time is linked to relatively high levels of precarious employment (captured by a wide variety of indicators, notably in-work poverty, low pay, etc.). Finally, in a relevant study, Veliziotis et al. (2015) compared the incidence of involuntary part-time employment in Greece and the UK. The authors concluded that rising levels of the phenomenon observed in the post-crisis years can be attributed mostly to an economic trend effect. Nevertheless, important socio-demographic and job composition effects are also evident in their analysis. As the authors focused on the immediate time period (2008–2013) in which the Greek economy was exposed to the economic downfall, they observed that the determinants of involuntary part-time employment in the country were subject to greater "noise" than in the UK.

Our research follows these studies that have tried to capture different elements of precarious work. In particular, it builds on the work of Green and Livanos (2015), who grouped involuntary part-time and temporary contacts into a unique measure of involuntary non-standard employment (INE). The study subsequently investigated the impact of the economic crisis on INE across regions in the UK. The same research methodology has been extended to six European countries with distinctive labour market characteristics (Green and Livanos 2015). Kretsos and Livanos (2016) have also adopted this measurement at the EU-15 level by introducing job insecurity into the measurement of precarious work.

This approach measures INE by capturing only those who explicitly stated in the survey that they accepted non-standard work because they could not find alternative conventional employment (full-time, permanent). It considers non-standard work as voluntary when it occurs for reasons such as workers being in education or training, in a foreseen probationary period, illness or disability, family responsibilities, or other personal reasons.

2.2 *Non-standard employment in Greece*

Non-standard employment, captured mostly by temporary and part-time work, has traditionally remained at low levels in Greece relative to other European countries. This can be mainly attributed to the historical socio-economic structure of the Greek economy. In particular, the private sector has traditionally been organised around small family businesses, either agricultural units or small establishments, where helping hands could be drawn from within the circles of the extended family network without the need to sign a formal contract. At the same time, this production structure sustained relatively high levels of undeclared work. As for the public sector, a strong industrial movement has ensured that most public sector workers have remained covered by regular contracts, and it resisted the widespread proliferation of flexible forms of work. Moreover, female participation in the labour market has been considerably low, and up to recent years, the existence of a flexible contract was rarely seen as an opportunity for securing employment.

Nevertheless, this picture has changed over the last two decades, and both employers and employees have come to acknowledge some of the benefits of flexible contracts. At the same time, it has repeatedly been highlighted that the Greek labour market has suffered from low levels of flexibility that, in turn, keep employment at low levels (OECD 2007). Consequently, new flexible forms of work were slowly introduced in both the private and the public sector even before the onset of the crisis, while the legislative framework was changed to facilitate such contracts and ease the ability of employers to "hire and fire". This process has been further enabled by various laws introduced by the consecutive memorandum agreements signed in recent years between the Greek government and the Troika of institutions (ECB, European Commission, IMF). For instance, recent laws facilitate the further proliferation of part-time employment and extend the period of trial temporary employment without the obligation of the employer to offer compensation rights for contracts up to 12 months.

As a result of these regulations, but mainly due to the violent economic adjustment that took place in Greece since the economic collapse of 2009, both temporary and part-time forms of employment have seen their share in total employment increase. The national rate of part-time employment increased by almost 3% points between the onset of the economic crisis in 2009 (6%) and 2015 (9%) with some regional variations prevailing. Attica, Epirus, Western Greece, and Crete experienced the highest percentage point increases (6%, 5%, 4% and 3%, respectively). The patterns of temporary employment were less uniform during the same period across the regions, as the increase in the use of temporary work was sharper in the islands rather than the mainland. While the national rate of temporary employment has remained subdued at the national level, the rate increased from 19% to 27% in Crete, from 17.5% to 23% in the Ionian Islands, from 11.5% to 16% in the Northern Aegean, and from 24% to 31% in the Southern Aegean.[4]

3 Data and descriptive statistics

The analysis of the paper is based on microdata from the Greek Labour Force Survey (LFS), a household-level survey designed to gather information on the labour market conditions of the residents of the country. As with any survey, the LFS is subject to sampling errors, possible miscoding of answers, etc. In our analysis, we use data from the second quarter of each year over the period 2006–2015, as this quarter is considered to be more indicative about the labour market situation of an individual, while it is also the one used for estimating the annual rates of various statistics (e.g. the unemployment rate).

Given the focus on INE in the paper, our attention centres on individuals whom the LFS classifies as being employed under an employer's administrative control, i.e. individuals who

> during the reference week performed work, even for just one hour a week, for pay, profit, or family gain or were not at work but had a job or business from which they were temporarily absent because of, for example, illness, holidays, industrial dispute, and education and training.

There is no specific question of INE being in the LFS. Therefore, there is a need to combine information from a number of questions to create a variable indicating the INE status. The full-time/part-time distinction refers to the main job and is based on a spontaneous response by participants. The type of contract, temporary or permanent, is also self-assessed from the sample of employees only. According to the Eurostat definition, employees with limited contract duration are those whose main job will terminate either after a predetermined fixed period, or after a period not known in advance, but nevertheless defined by objective criteria such as the completion of an assignment.

LFS respondents are also subsequently required to declare the reasons for which they work under a part-time or temporary contract. For instance, they are asked whether they work part-time as a result of being unable to find full-time work and whether they work under limited duration contracts due to the inability to find a permanent job. Those answering that the "Person could not find a full-time job" and/or the "Person could not find a permanent job" are classified as being involuntary part-time and involuntary temporary workers, respectively. In our analysis, we have used this information in order to form two separate binary variables, taking the value 1 if someone is in involuntary part-time (temporary) work and 0 otherwise (such as when individuals have taken up non-standard employment due to any other "voluntary" reasons or are employed under a standard full-time/permanent contract[5]).

The two measures are hence combined to create a unique INE binary variable that follows the same dichotomous logic (1 if in INE and 0 otherwise). Even though temporary and part-time employment may differ substantially, in the sense that they attract a heterogeneous type of workforce faced with different preferences and constraints, a common denominator of such groups is the involuntary nature of their non-standard contract. Therefore, our analysis seeks to focus on the difficulty these individuals face in finding jobs in alignment with their preferences and prior endowments/constraints. This rationalises the choice of grouping together the two groups for statistical analysis.

For the econometric investigation undertaken in the next section, LFS data for the time period 2006 to 2015 is used, capturing different pre- and post-crisis periods of the economic cycle in which significant institutional changes and labour market reforms have been implemented. The sample of individuals used for the analysis concentrates on those aged 25–64. The choice to leave the group aged 15–24 out of the analysis is intentional, since more than half of all individuals aged less than 25 do not participate in the labour market or may be keener to work voluntarily in non-standard work. Keeping this segment of the active workforce in the analysis would thus distort the incidence and underlying determinants of INE experienced by the adult workforce in Greece. Moreover, it is important to note that due to the survey design, information about the incidence of INE is only available for employees in the sample. This can raise concerns about selectivity biases, as discussed further in the next section.

In principle, more flexible working patterns should have a positive impact on overall levels of employment and could be a preferable working arrangement for some individuals who wish to find gainful employment. However, looking more closely at the data, one can observe that in 2015, about two-thirds of those holding a temporary or part-time contract have been doing so involuntarily, namely they have accepted such a contract only because they could not find permanent or full-time work. At the level of the national economy, about 14% of all available workers are involved in involuntary non-standard employment. Such a high share of workers, which increased from 9.8% in 2009, can be conceived as a measure of underemployment or "hidden unemployment," which is there to top up the already dramatic rates of unemployment. Regional variations are evident, with the more decentralised areas (e.g. the Islands, Western Greece, and Macedonia) being more prone to INE. Moreover, as can be seen from the last columns of Table 6.1, most temporary and part-time workers in 2015 were in such contracts involuntarily (66% and 80%, respectively).

In addition to observing regional differences in INE across the 13 NUTS2 regions of Greece, different groups of workers also appear to have been affected. Table 6.2 presents the composition of workers across the samples of all individuals in employment as well as those in INE, involuntary temporary employment, and involuntary part-time employment. Some groups of workers are more likely to be found in involuntary forms of employment as opposed to regular employment. Younger workers (aged 25–34), singles, females, non-nationals, low-educated individuals, and service and elementary workers are characterised by a higher incidence of INE. Past labour market experience also

Table 6.1 Involuntary employment by region before and during the crisis

	INE TOTAL			Involuntary Part-Time Employment			Involuntary Temporary Employment		
	2009	2015	% point change	2009	2015	% point change	2009	2015	% point change
Northern Greece	11.2	16.1	4.9	68.7	77.4	8.7	73.5	78.8	5.2
Eastern Macedonia	9.0	13.5	4.5	78.2	79.5	1.3	68.3	76.4	8.1
Central Macedonia	10.6	14.6	4.0	68.4	81.1	12.7	71.9	76.1	4.2
Western Macedonia	13.9	20.6	6.7	56.1	62.1	6.1	74.4	86.0	11.6
Epirus	11.3	15.7	4.4	72.2	86.9	14.7	79.5	76.5	-3.0
Central Greece	**11.6**	**14.5**	**3.0**	**74.6**	**70.7**	**-3.9**	**72.7**	**78.4**	**5.7**
Thessaly	11.0	12.0	1.0	82.1	93.0	10.9	66.6	81.3	14.7
Ionian Islands	16.2	16.6	0.4	78.5	33.8	-44.7	81.6	76.7	-4.9
Western Greece	10.6	18.3	7.7	76.1	62.1	-14.0	75.9	77.8	1.9
Continental Greece	9.4	9.9	0.5	56.9	81.1	24.2	69.2	73.7	4.5
Peloponnese	10.6	15.8	5.2	79.3	83.4	4.1	70.2	82.3	12.1
Aegean and Crete	**14.4**	**17.1**	**2.7**	**53.8**	**81.6**	**27.8**	**73.1**	**57.8**	**-15.4**
Northern Aegean	8.1	15.1	7.0	32.7	72.9	40.2	70.3	75.8	5.5
Southern Aegean	20.6	14.1	-6.5	61.3	87.1	25.7	77.7	41.0	-36.7
Crete	14.6	22.1	7.5	67.4	84.9	17.6	71.4	56.5	-14.9
Attica	**7.8**	**11.4**	**3.6**	**67.3**	**79.6**	**12.4**	**71.8**	**59.3**	**-12.5**
Greece Total	**9.8**	**13.7**	**3.9**	**68.74**	**80.8**	**12.1**	**72.7**	**66.4**	**-6.3**

Source: Authors' estimations based on LFS data for individuals aged 25-64; sample of employees

seems to make a difference, as those previously in unemployment have a much stronger presence in involuntary forms of work compared to those in continuous employment. A stronger share of workers employed in medium-sized firms is in INE.

The descriptive statistics also indicate that the jobs of those in INE are subject to several elements of precariousness. For instance, a high share of

Table 6.2 Sample description

	All sample	INE	INE Temporary	INE Part-Time
Age group				
25–34	25.3	35.1	35.6	34.7
35–44	29.2	29.0	28.9	29.0
45–54	24.4	19.4	18.1	20.9
55–64	9.2	6.7	6.2	7.6
Marital status				
Single	27.7	34.7	35.9	33.4
Married	66.3	57.7	56.9	57.9
Female	43.2	55.7	51.4	66.1
Greek nationals	89.7	79.2	79.4	78.3
Level of education				
High	33.8	22.4	23.2	23.9
Medium	39.3	36.6	35.0	38.1
Low	26.9	41.0	41.9	38.0
Northern Greece	**7.2**	**7.4**	**7.3**	**8.1**
Eastern Macedonia	5.5	4.6	4.4	5.4
Central Macedonia	15.6	15.8	15.2	17.1
Western Macedonia	2.8	3.7	4.1	2.9
Epirus	5.1	5.7	5.5	7.0
Central Greece	**4.9**	**5.1**	**5.1**	**5.2**
Thessaly	6.2	6.2	6.4	5.6
Ionian Islands	1.9	2.9	3.6	1.7
Western Greece	5.3	5.0	5.0	5.4
Continental Greece	5.8	5.2	4.7	6.1
Peloponnese	5.4	6.2	6.1	7.3
Aegean and Crete	**4.2**	**6.5**	**7.7**	**3.6**
Northern Aegean	2.1	1.9	2.3	1.0
Southern Aegean	2.6	4.9	6.0	1.6
Crete	7.9	12.8	14.8	8.1
Attica	**25.0**	**25.0**	**21.9**	**30.8**
Occupation				
Legislators	1.8	0.3	0.4	0.2
Professionals	18.8	12.6	12.8	15.9
Associate professionals	10.5	5.2	5.3	5.0
Clerks	15.4	10.6	11.3	8.7
Service workers	17.5	22.5	20.4	23.6
Skilled agriculture	0.9	1.9	2.3	1.5
Craft	13.0	12.8	13.3	10.6
Plant operators	8.7	4.8	5.6	2.6
Elementary	11.2	29.1	28.5	31.8

(*Continued*)

Table 6.2 (Cont.)

	All sample	INE	INE Temporary	INE Part-Time
Status a year ago				
Employed	96.0	84.82	83.07	86.02
Unemployed	3.2	13.0	14.6	11.5
Student	0.3	0.6	0.6	0.6
Inactive	0.5	1.6	1.7	1.8
Shift work patterns				
Shift	21.8	19.2	19.2	16.5
Evening	45.7	51.2	49.9	53.8
Night	16.7	12.5	13.6	9.5
Saturday	45.9	56.2	57.2	51.1
Sunday	22.9	27.3	30.4	18.2
Company size				
<10	42.0	59.9	57.6	67.7
11 to 19	15.6	12.7	13.2	11.7
20 to 49	11.9	8.5	8.5	7.3
More than 50	17.2	9.4	10.8	5.3
Work-related				
Has more than one job	2.1	3.7	3.7	4.6
Wishes to work more	7.9	41.4	25.7	88.8
Tenure (in years)	11.0	3.7	2.8	5.1
Hours of work	39.2	32.9	37.0	20.2
Homework	4.0	2.9	2.9	3.5
Work uninsured	3.6	13.8	12.8	19.5
Supervisory role	11.3	2.8	3.1	1.6

Note: Authors' estimations based on LFS data for individuals aged 25-64; sample of employees, 2006–2015

such employees engage in evening or weekend work or, as expected, indicate that they are constrained in terms of their hours of work, inducing them to accept an extra/second job. A much smaller share of such employees holds a supervisory post in their organisation relative to the average worker.

4 Econometric methodology

The estimation of how different factors (e.g. demographic, socio-economic, work-related etc.) can explain the incidence of INE is complicated by the need to account for the potential selectivity bias that may arise due to the fact that the sample of individuals in INE is truncated. In particular, the dependent variable is only observed for a selected sample of labour market participants, in particular employees, among the original random sample of all individuals of working age. Typically, this complication is more prominent in a sample of females, as there is a greater share of economically inactive women in the population. The estimation of the determinants of INE using standard least squares estimators is therefore likely to suffer from sample selection bias, as factors influencing an individual's self-selection into the sample of employees may simultaneously affect the outcome variable equation (INE).

In particular, the econometric methodology used is one whereby the probability of observing that an individual i is in INE ($y_2 = 1$) is determined if an unobserved latent variable $y_2^* > 0$:

$$y_{i2}^* = \mathbf{x}_i \boldsymbol{\beta} + \phi T + u_{i2} \tag{1}$$

Here, $\mathbf{x}$ is a vector of relevant explanatory variables that influence the likelihood of INE; $\boldsymbol{\beta}$ is a set of regression parameters to be estimated; T are time dummy variables, one for each year of the sample period (2006–2015); and u_2 is an unobserved random error term $u_2 \sim N(0, \sigma_2^2)$. Sample selection bias occurs when the outcome variable is observed only for certain values of a selection variable y_1 ($y_1 = 1$), such as when the latter refers to an individual's participation in the labour market as an employee and is determined by equation (2) below:

$$y_{i1} = \mathbf{z}\gamma + \delta I_i + \lambda T + u_{i1} \tag{2}$$

Here, $\mathbf{z}$ is a vector of factors that affect the probability of selection into the workforce, γ is a vector of estimable regression coefficients, I is an extra identifying variable (one that determines selection but is uncorrelated with the outcome variable), T are time dummy variables, and $u_1 \sim N(0, \sigma_1^2)$, the random error term, may be correlated with unobserved factors in the main outcome equation $corr(u_1, u_2) \neq 0$.

Given the possibility of sample selection bias, a two-step Heckman procedure (Heckman 1979) should be used, which allows one to sequentially model the selection equation and the INE equation. As y_1 is a discrete choice variable, estimation of the likelihood of participation in the employee pool requires a Heckman-Probit estimator.[6] Subsequently, the coefficients of this first-step regression are used to estimate the conditional probability of being in INE. To ensure efficiency in estimation, the system of two equations is preferably estimated jointly via maximum likelihood.

A number of key demographic, socioeconomic, and regional variables are used in the estimation of equations (1) and (2), in accordance with previous literature. The need to use only those factors that can be observed for all individuals of working age as well as the overall data unavailability prevent us from deploying a list of desirable variables in the selection equation (2). For example, recent studies note that female participation can be influenced by the legal framework surrounding divorces (Bargain et al. 2010) and by housing prices (Johnson 2014). Nevertheless, our choice of variables covers most of those discussed in the literature (Humphries and Sarasua 2012). Furthermore, the selection of explanatory variables has been made so that analysis of their relationship with the incidence of INE should enable policymakers to draw evidence-based inferences, focused on how to improve the design of State policies to be more effectively targeted at different socioeconomic groups and to implement appropriate regional employment policies.

In particular, participation in the labour market as an employee is modelled by using a number of variables typically encountered in previous studies, such as gender, age, marital status, native status, number of young children in the household, highest level of educational attainment, prior labour market status (e.g. employed, unemployed, inactive, student, other), a set of regional dummies (at NUTS2 level), and whether the individual has recently participated in any lifelong learning activities.

Data constraints have prevented the use of theoretically compelling identifying variables in the selection equation. After confirming that the partial correlation between regional unemployment rates and the probability of INE is not statistically significant,[7] we have used regional unemployment rates as an additional, identifying variable in equation (2). This extra variable does indeed have a statistically significant negative influence on the chances of an individual being a paid employee.

The estimation of the main equation (1) includes, in addition to those used in the estimation of the selection equation, a list of job-related characteristics. These work-related variables include the social insurance status of the employee, type of sector (public or private), firm size, number of years of tenure with the current employer, number of hours of usual work, whether the jobholder has supervisory responsibilities, types of atypical work (shift work, evening work, nightshifts, Sunday shift, Saturday shift, working at home),[8] whether the worker has a second job or wishes to work more hours in his/her current job. A list of occupational dummies (ISCO 1 digit) and sectoral dummies (NACE 1 digit) are also taken into account. In total, three different models are estimated based on this specification, one for each type of INE (INE part-time, INE temporary, and total INE).

Similar concerns regarding the presence of selectivity bias are also present in relation to the examination of a second issue of concern in the paper, namely the impact of INE on individual-level wages (w_i). Specifically, the following wage equation has been estimated in order to investigate whether individuals who are in involuntary non-standard contracts experience any significant differences in pay relative to those in alternative contractual states (i.e. voluntary non-standard or core employment):

$$w_i = \theta\,INE_i + \mathbf{x_{iw}}\boldsymbol{\rho} + \vartheta T + u_{iw} \tag{3}$$

Here, $\mathbf{x_{iw}}$ is a vector containing a list of variables influencing individual earnings (e.g. gender, age, years of employer tenure, various job characteristics, industry, occupation, and region dummies), and ρ is the associated vector of the regression coefficients to be estimated. Given that earnings are only observed for the sample of employees, a standard two-step Heckman methodology has been employed, whereby a selection equation that is similar to (2) has been estimated at a first stage.

Identification of the selection equation is achieved in this case via the use of an extra variable that captures whether an individual is registered with a public employment office and receives unemployment benefits (relative to the omitted case whereby individuals do not receive unemployment benefits or are not registered at all). A priori, it is expected that individuals who receive unemployment insurance will be less likely to participate in the labour market as an employee, other things equal, relative to their counterparts who do not receive any such support. The reason is that the cost of job search is likely to be lower for the former group, whereas the latter will be faced with greater financial constraints, expediting their quicker return to the labour market. Moreover, it has also been confirmed that there is a statistically insignificant partial correlation between this identifying variable and wages.

5 Empirical results

5.1 The trend of involuntary non-standard employment

Table 6.3 outlines the regression coefficients and associated robust standard errors following the estimation of the main INE equation as well as the individual components of INE (INE part-time, INE temporary). As described in the previous section, a Heckman probit estimator was initially deployed to estimate the determinants of INE in the Greek sample. Nevertheless, weak evidence of joint significance between the outcome and selection equations was detected (the null hypothesis of independence between them cannot be rejected at the 5% level of significance, i.e., $\chi^2(1) = 3.33^*$). Taking this into account, Table 6.3 presents the results of estimation of the main INE equation (1) as well as its sub-components based on the use of a standard probit estimator.[9]

Prior to considering the impact of various determinants of INE, it is worth focusing on the estimated signs of the time dummies, which capture the impact of various unobserved time-varying factors on the incidence of INE, which are independent of the evolution of changing socio-demographic and job characteristics. When the probability of INE is regressed solely on the time dummies (not shown in Table 6.3), without controlling any of the observed characteristics of the employed population, it is clear that there has been a statistically significant upward trend in the incidence of INE in Greece since 2009, the year in which the debt crisis first unfolded. Nevertheless, the empirical estimation shown in Table 6.3 reveals that since 2012, the rise in the mean incidence of total INE can be partially attributed

Table 6.3 Economic results

	INE	INE 2006-2009	INE 2010-2015	INE Part-Time	INE Temporary
Personal characteristics					
Female	0.18***	0.19***	0.16***	0.24***	0.12***
	(0.014)	(0.021)	(0.019)	(0.032)	(0.014)
Single	0.12***	0.11***	0.13***	0.09***	0.11***
	(0.017)	(0.023)	(0.026)	(0.038)	(0.017)
Non-national	-0.04*	-0.14***	0.05*	-0.12***	-0.03
	(0.020)	(0.030)	(0.027)	(0.045)	(0.020)
Age group					
30–34	-0.05***	-0.04	-0.06**	-0.04	-0.04**
	(0.019)	(0.028)	(0.027)	(0.043)	(0.019)
35–39	0.01	0.01	0.01	-0.05	0.03
	(0.021)	(0.030)	(0.029)	(0.048)	(0.021)
40–44	0.04*	0.07**	0.02	-0.02	0.04*
	(0.022)	(0.033)	(0.030)	(0.050)	(0.023)
45–49	0.14***	0.16***	0.13***	0.04	0.12***
	(0.025)	(0.036)	(0.034)	(0.055)	(0.025)
50–54	0.18***	0.14***	0.21***	0.07	0.14***
	(0.028)	(0.043)	(0.038)	(0.060)	(0.029)
55–59	0.23***	0.19***	0.26***	0.15**	0.16***
	(0.033)	(0.051)	(0.044)	(0.070)	(0.035)
60–64	0.18***	0.21***	0.16**	-0.12	0.16***
	(0.051)	(0.078)	(0.068)	(0.105)	(0.053)
Status a year ago					
Unemployed	0.45***	0.44***	0.48***	0.09*	0.43***
	(0.025)	(0.040)	(0.033)	(0.053)	(0.024)
Student	0.07	0.02	0.15	0.27	0.06
	(0.093)	(0.130)	(0.134)	(0.174)	(0.092)
Inactive	0.14**	0.14*	0.12	-0.17	0.19***
	(0.068)	(0.082)	(0.116)	(0.141)	(0.060)
Level of education					
Medium	-0.13***	-0.17***	-0.10***	-0.05	-0.13***
	(0.016)	(0.023)	(0.021)	(0.035)	(0.016)
High	-0.24***	-0.22***	-0.25***	-0.15***	-0.23***
	(0.022)	(0.033)	(0.030)	(0.052)	(0.023)
Training (last 4 weeks)	-0.11**	-0.02	-0.18***	-0.20**	-0.03
	(0.049)	(0.069)	(0.070)	(0.100)	(0.047)
Working patterns					
Shift	-0.03*	-0.03	-0.04	-0.02	-0.02
	(0.019)	(0.030)	(0.025)	(0.043)	(0.020)

(Continued)

Table 6.3 (Cont.)

	INE	INE 2006-2009	INE 2010-2015	INE Part-Time	INE Temporary
Evening	-0.00	0.00	-0.00	-0.04	-0.01
	(0.016)	(0.023)	(0.022)	(0.033)	(0.016)
Night	-0.020***	-0.021***	-0.19***	-0.06	-0.19***
	(0.023)	(0.034)	(0.031)	(0.058)	(0.023)
Saturdays	0.18***	0.12***	0.22***	0.22***	0.08***
	(0.018)	(0.027)	(0.024)	(0.037)	(0.018)
Sundays	0.15***	0.18***	0.11***	-0.10*	0.14***
	(0.021)	(0.031)	(0.028)	(0.050)	(0.021)
Homework	-0.07*	-0.21***	0.06	-0.15**	-0.07**
	(0.036)	(0.053)	(0.049)	(0.073)	(0.035)
Company size					
Size of firm: <10	0.00	0.00	0.00	0.00	0.00
	0.00	0.00	0.00	0.00	0.00
Size if firm: 11-19	-0.04**	-0.01	-0.07***	-0.04	-0.03
	(0.018)	(0.026)	(0.026)	(0.039)	(0.019)
Size of firm: 20-49	-0.05**	-0.07**	-0.04	-0.12**	-0.06***
	(0.021)	(0.031)	(0.028)	(0.046)	(0.022)
Size of firm: >50	-0.05***	-0.08***	-0.02	-0.16***	-0.02
	(0.020)	(0.030)	(0.027)	(0.050)	(0.020)
Size of firm: unknown	-0.01	-0.04	0.01	-0.09*	-0.01
	(0.020)	(0.030)	(0.027)	(0.046)	(0.021)
Work-related characteristics					
Works uninsured	0.26***	0.036***	0.17***	0.13***	0.23***
	(0.027)	(0.039)	(0.037)	(0.049)	(0.026)
Public sector employee	0.11***	0.19***	0.04	-0.21***	0.25***
	(0.020)	(0.028)	(0.030)	(0.043)	(0.020)
Tenure (in years)	-0.09***	-0.09***	-0.08***	-0.03***	-0.10***
	(0.002)	(0.003)	(0.002)	(0.002)	(0.002)
Hours of work	-0.04***	-0.03***	-0.04***	-0.11***	-0.01***
	(0.001)	(0.001)	(0.001)	0.002	(0.001)
Supervisory role	-0.14***	-0.14***	-0.14***	-0.26***	-0.16***
	(0.029)	(0.043)	(0.041)	(0.083)	(0.030)
Has more than one job	0.26***	0.17***	1.02***	1.67***	0.48***
	0.019)	(0.035)	(0.024)	(0.030)	(0.021)
Wishes to work more	1.11***	1.25***	1.02***	1.67***	0.48***
	(0.019)	(0.035)	(0.024)	(0.030)	(0.021)
Region of residence					
Central Macedonia	0.23***	0.24***	0.023***	0.030***	0.021
	(0.031)	(0.045)	(0.043)	(0.059)	(0.039)

(Continued)

Table 6.3 (Cont.)

	INE	INE 2006-2009	INE 2010-2015	INE Part-Time	INE Temporary
Western Macedonia	0.38***	0.44***	0.31***	-0.07	0.42***
	(0.042)	(0.062)	(0.059)	(0.091)	(0.42)
Thessaly	0.24***	0.33***	0.15***	-0.07	0.42***
	(0.036)	(0.052)	(0.050)	(0.076)	(0.037)
Epirus	0.18***	0.27***	0.11**	0.27***	0.18***
	(0.037)	(0.054)	(0.051)	(0.068)	(0.039)
lonian Islands	0.30***	0.29***	0.29***	-0.02	0.036***
	(0.045)	(0.070)	(0.061)	(0.121)	(0.045)
Western Greece	0.09***	0.05	0.11**	0.25***	0.06
	(0.037)	(0.055)	(0.051)	(0.076)	(0.039)
Continental Greece	0.01	0.13**	-0.11**	0.19**	-0.05
	(0.037)	(0.054)	(0.051)	(0.073)	(0.039)
Attica	0.02	0.05	-0.01	0.19***	-0.05
	(0.029)	(0.043)	(0.041)	(0.056)	(0.030)
Peloponnese	0.21***	0.19***	0.22***	0.33***	0.21***
	(0.037)	(0.055)	(0.050)	(0.070)	(0.038)
Northern Aegean	0.45***	0.45***	0.44***	0.07	0.45***
	(0.050)	(0.081)	(0.066)	(0.145)	(0.051)
Southern Aegean	0.59***	0.53***	0.62***	0.07	0.57***
	(0.039)	(0.057)	(0.054)	(0.111)	(0.039)
Crete	0.40***	0.45***	0.35***	0.01	0.42***
	(0.032)	(0.047)	(0.045)	(0.068)	(0.033)
Sector dummies (NACE 1 digit	YES				
Occupations dummies (ISCO 1 digit)	YES				
Time dummies	YES				
Constant	0.24**	0.08	0.39**	0.36	-0.67***
	(0.105)	(0.149)	(0.152)	(0.130)	(0.103)
Observations	134,769	64,031	70,738	131,940	134,769

Note: Authors' estimations based on LFS data for individuals aged 25-64; sample of employees, 2006–2015; Reference categories : males, nationals, aged 25-29, low education, Eastern Macedonia

to the changing composition of jobs in the economy.[10] In particular, the estimates suggest that the statistically significant upward time trend of INE in the raw statistics reflects changes in various job characteristics (e.g. training, firm size, public sector, years of tenure, work hours, etc.) that took place in the post-crisis years in the Greek job market. Looking more closely at the individual components of INE (i.e. part-time INE, temporary INE), it becomes clear that although there is no evidence of a statistically significant increase in the share of persons holding involuntary temporary contracts, other things equal, since 2013, the probability of being involuntarily employed in a part-time job has become significantly greater.

5.2 The determinants of INE

In addition to the movement of INE over the business cycle, Table 6.3 further highlights a number of interesting associations of INE with various individual and job characteristics, as estimated on the basis of the whole sample (2006–2015). A key insight from the regressions is that the marginal impact of several explanatory variables varies markedly between the individual components of INE, namely whether non-standard employment is linked to the involuntary take-up of a part-time or temporary job. This is reasonable given that the individual decision-making processes underpinning the choice of either type of atypical form of employment, part-time or temporary work, are likely to be different among job-seekers.

Holding various other correlated factors constant, the empirical estimation highlights that female workers have a higher statistically significant probability of being involuntarily employed in their jobs. This is driven mostly by the higher readiness of female workers to accept involuntary part-time work. Relative to younger workers, who are more likely to accept non-standard employment contracts for voluntary reasons (e.g. to finance their education and training or to accumulate years of work experience), the empirical findings indicate that older-aged employees, especially older females, are more likely to take up non-standard, especially temporary, jobs involuntarily. This also holds true for non-married workers (especially males[11]), who are not faced with additional household constraints and can more readily accept the offer of non-standard contract jobs. While a markedly higher share of non-Greek nationals is concentrated in INE, the partial coefficient shown in Table 6.3 indicates that this positive raw relationship can be attributed entirely to the type of occupations/industries in which non-nationals are typically employed in the Greek job market. Indeed, once the influence of the type of occupation/industry on the probability of INE is stripped out, it is observed that Greek nationals, in particular females, have higher chances of ending up in INE. In particular, Greek nationals are more likely to accept involuntary part-time jobs.

The human capital characteristics of workers are also significantly related to their likelihood of being precariously employed. In particular, low-educated individuals are characterised by higher chances of being involuntarily employed in non-standard employment, both in the form of involuntary part-time and temporary work. Hence, it is clear that the accumulation of a higher skill level has acted as a shield against the need to accept a non-standard employment contract in Greece despite the severity of the economic downturn. This finding is in agreement with the recent analysis of Christopoulou and Monastiriotis (2016), who have highlighted that the market valuation of the productive characteristics of Greek workers, namely the wage returns to educational credentials, has risen in the years following the economic crisis. Furthermore, continuous adult training, taking place within the formal educational system, is found to be negatively related to INE, affecting female employees in particular. This may reflect that lifelong learning opportunities are less abundant in involuntary part-time jobs or that individuals in INE have lower incentives and face greater barriers to participating in continuing training.

Table 6.3 highlights further that a previous spell of unemployment (or inactivity) exerts a relatively large positive effect on the probability of INE. However, this positive impact is driven largely by the association with the involuntary take-up of a temporary contract, highlighting that a temporary contract is seen as a stepping stone into the formal job market (even if their preference would be to find a permanent job) for some job seekers.

A number of job characteristics also exhibit a statistically significant relationship with the probability of being in INE status. Specifically, involuntary contract jobs are found to be a particularly bad outcome for individuals (especially males) given that not only are they associated with less job security, but they also tend to entail limited or no social insurance. All other things equal, a worker who is in an involuntary, non-standard, job also has higher chances of not having either health or social insurance provided to him as part of his/her job. Public sector employees are also more likely to state that they are employed within voluntary temporary contracts but are less prone to involuntary part-time jobs as opposed to individuals in the private sector. The relationship of INE with the size of the local unit in which the individual is employed is also interesting, given that the propensity of being in INE (especially of males) is greater in micro-sized firms (i.e., those with fewer than 10 employees).

A negative association is observed between the number of years of employer tenure and the odds of being in involuntary employment, as is also the case with jobs characterised by more weekly usual hours of work. However, the fact that involuntary jobs are significantly and positively related to weekend work, or they are less likely to entail supervisory duties (in particular, among male employees), is testament to the fact that such jobs are inherently of lower quality.[12] Furthermore, in accordance with the theory of multiple jobholding (Pouliakas 2017), individuals who are constrained in terms of the hours of work in their primary job or those who wish to hedge against the risk of primary job insecurity, as is typically the case with people in INE, are more induced to take up a second job.

The empirical estimation further reveals a number of interesting associations in relation to the relationship of INE with the industrial/occupational composition of employment in Greece as well as observed regional differences in the incidence of INE. In particular, it is observed that individuals who are employed in the sectors of accommodation and catering, agriculture, construction, and transport and storage exhibit a higher propensity of being in INE relative to those in the wholesale and retail sector. Similarly, individuals in elementary occupations, skilled agricultural posts, crafts, or market services and sales also have a higher aptitude of being involuntary employed with atypical contracts in comparison to professionals. Finally, in relation to individuals working in the area of Attica, those employed in the Aegean and Ionian Islands and Crete as well as workers in Western Macedonia have higher chances of being in INE.

5.3 Changes in the determinants of INE across time

The prolonged economic crisis in Greece has not only had a remarkable impact on levels of economic activity, but it has also resulted in a significant change in the composition of the Greek labour force. As discussed in Christopoulou and Monastiriotis (2016) and confirmed in our sample, since the outbreak of the recession in 2009, the Greek workforce has become older (due to the rise of youth unemployment and the premium placed by employers on work experience) and more qualified (reflecting a premium placed on higher qualifications). It is less male-dominated and a smaller number of employees are employed in micro-sized firms post-crisis (due to widespread business closures of small enterprises). Moreover, a significantly lower share of employees is now employed in the manufacturing and construction sector, while more people have found jobs in the accommodation and catering and wholesale and retail sectors. Overall, the occupational distribution of employment has exhibited a move towards high-skilled professional services and market services and sales.

In light of such marked structural changes, it is reasonable to expect that some of the determinants of INE in the post-crisis era may be different relative to the reality that prevailed before 2009. Table 6.3 examines this hypothesis by comparing the estimated marginal impact of the determinants of INE between the pre-crisis (2006–2009) and post-crisis years (2010–2015).[13] It is clear from the table that the probability of selecting INE has decreased among females between the two periods. This is presumably due to the fact that as the females share in the total workforce has increased, more males have been forced to accept involuntary contracts among the shrinking pool of available jobs. Similarly, the chances of being in INE have risen for older employees aged 50–60. The likelihood of involuntarily accepting a job has become greater for non-married workers in recent years, while non-nationals have greater chances of being in INE in the post-crisis era.

As a testament to the value of higher education in the Greek job market, the marginal effects shown in Table 6.3 demonstrate that tertiary graduates enjoyed even fewer chances of being employed in INE since the crisis. By contrast, since medium-qualified graduates have been partly crowded-out by those with higher skills (Pouliakas 2014), the probability that they will end up in INE has risen over time.

Other interesting changes related to the quality of involuntary non-standard contracts include the fact that employees in INE have a higher propensity to work on Saturdays and engage in multiple jobholding in the post-crisis period. However, a smaller share of employees is also observed to lack any form of social insurance coverage in INE jobs during the 2010–2015 period. Finally, whereas INE tended to be heavily concentrated in the public sector in the years before the onset of the recession, since 2010, no statistical differences exist in the incidence of INE between public and private sector employees.

5.4 Impact of INE on wages

As mentioned in Section 4, many individuals may self-select non-standard forms of employment due to their own preferences or attitudes towards risk. The choice of employment in a part-time job may, for some, reflect their own optimal labour-leisure choice, taking into account the relative weight of the pay received per hour worked in relation to other budget and personal (e.g. family responsibilities; lack of child care) constraints. Similarly, in equilibrium, some may be willing to trade off the extra job insecurity associated with temporary contracts for additional compensating pay (Pouliakas and Theodossiou 2009) or may select a temporary job (e.g. an apprenticeship contract) as a stepping stone to regular employment.

Although such occurrences among adult employees are expected to result, other things equal, in the receipt of lower mean wages relative to comparable workers employed in "core" (permanent/full-time) employment, individuals who are in involuntary non-standard employment should not, a priori, experience any extra wage penalty in comparison with other workers also employed under non-regular contracts. By contrast, if one can observe from the data that those employed in INE receive lower mean wages relative to individuals with similar demographic and socio-economic characteristics who have voluntarily accepted atypical contracts, then this constitutes evidence that the jobs of the former group are genuinely of "lower quality," reflecting an added layer of labour market segmentation.

Putting this hypothesis to the test, Table 6.4 outlines the results of the econometric estimation of earnings regressions for the Greek labour market over the time period 2006–2015. The estimations examine the *ceteris paribus* relationship between the net monthly earnings of Greek employees and INE status.[14] In addition to regressing real net monthly earnings on INE status, Table 6.4 further explores the extent of the wage differential that exists between involuntary and voluntary forms of non-standard employment relative to core (full-time/permanent) employees.[15]

What is clear from the data is that the real monthly earnings of Greek workers who are employed involuntary under non-standard contracts are,

Table 6.4 Heckman wage regression

Dependent var: log real net monthly earnings		Section eq: prob employee	
INE	-019***		
	(0.003)	Receipt of unemployment benefits	-1.45***
VNE	-0.13***		(0.030)
	(0.005)	Female	-0.32***
Female	-0.06***		(0.005)
	(0.004)	30–34	-0.01
Age group: 30–34	0.03***		(0.010)
	(0.004)	35–39	-0.07***
40–44	0.07***		(0.010)
	(0.004)	45–49	-0.17***
45–49	0.08***		(0.010)
	(0.004)	50–54	-0.36***
50–54	0.10***		(0.011)
	(0.006)	55–59	-0.68***
55–59	0.11***		(0.011)
	(0.009)	60–64	-1.34***
60–64	0.16***		(0.013)
	(0.016)	Single	0.06***
Single	-0.04***		(0.007)
	(0.003)	Non-national	0.59***
Non-national	-0.12***		(0.009)
	(0.007)	Edu: Medium	0.31***
Edu: Medium	0.01		(0.006)
	(0.004)	Edu: High	0.70***
Edu: High	0.04***		(0.006)
	(0.008)	Unemployed a year ago	-0.89***
Tenure	0.01***		(0.010)
	(0.000)	Training	0.35***
Tenuresq	-0.00***		(0.022)
	(0.000)	Uninsured	-0.47***
Unemployed a year ago	0.03***		(0.011)
	(0.011)	Regional dummies	YES
Training	0.00	Times dummies	YES
	(0.007)	Lambda	-0.10***
Uninsured	-0.07***		(0.015)
	(0.007)	Constant	-0.25***
Public	0.08***		(0.015)

(*Continued*)

Table 6.4 (Cont.)

Dependent var: log real net monthly earnings	Section eq: prob employee	
	(0.003)	
Size : 11–19	0.02***	
	(0.003)	
20–49	0.04***	
	(0.003)	
>50	0.09***	
	(0.003)	
Unknown	0.07***	
	(0.003)	
Supervisor	0.08***	
	(0.003)	
Hours	0.01***	
	(0.000)	
Sector dummies (NACE 1 digit)	YES	
Occupation dummies (ISCO 1 digit)	YES	
Region dummies	YES	
Time dummies	YES	
Constant	6.47***	
	(0.020)	
Observations	361,606	
Standard errors in parentheses ***p<0.01, **p<0.05, *p<0.1		

Note: Authors' estimations are based on LFS data for individuals aged 25-64; 2006-2015; INE = Involuntary non-standard contract; VNE = Voluntary non-standard contract; Reference categories: regular (full-time/permanent) contract, males, married, nationals, aged 25-29, low education, size <10 employees

on average, about 19% lower in relation to comparable employees in other forms of contracts. In general, workers who have regular contracts receive higher net monthly earnings in the Greek job market for the offer of the same number of work hours, relative to those in non-standard employment. However, it is also evident that individuals who are involuntarily employed with a non-standard contract experience a larger wage penalty (in the order of about 21%) in comparison to core employees, whereas the wages of voluntary non-standard workers are about 14% lesser than this common reference group.[16] Assuming the absence of any significant difference in unobserved characteristics between voluntary and involuntary non-standard contract workers, which would introduce endogeneity bias in the estimated wage returns, the significantly lower wages received by individuals in INE status would constitute evidence that this group of employees is susceptible to labour market segmentation. In other words, such employees are not only in non-standard jobs involuntarily, but they are also penalised by receiving a lower wage relative to comparable employees in similar jobs and with the same contract type.

6 Conclusions

The pronounced economic crisis in Greece, along with the rapid deregulation (e.g. cuts in minimum wages, institution of firm-level collective bargaining, ease of firing, etc.) that was carried out in the country as part of the implementation of the bailout programs, has accentuated and amplified a number of rigidities and failures in the Greek economy and labour market. Perhaps the most pronounced effect that the Great Recession has had is the marked and sustained increase in the national (especially youth) unemployment rate. Yet, another side-effect of the slack labour market, which often receives less attention, is the stark rise in underemployment, such as non-standard forms of employment occurring involuntarily. During the prolonged economic downturn, the Greek labour market has witnessed marked increases in the share of individuals who are involuntarily employed with part-time or temporary contracts or in informal work. Similar increases have also been evident in the incidence of workers wishing to work more hours in their current jobs or as larger over-qualification rates among higher-educated graduates. All of these indicators paint a bleak picture of severe skill underutilisation and eroded job security/quality linked to ineffective aggregate demand in Greece.

In this paper, we have examined the determinants and evolution of one such form of precarious employment, namely involuntary non-standard employment. In particular, this study has looked into flexible work arrangements, such as temporary and part-time contracts, isolating the involuntary element. These two forms of work are examined individually as well as in combination. Even though they consist two heterogeneous forms of employment, when they occur involuntarily, they share common grounds: the lack of choice or an element of precarity. For the purposes of our research, data from the Greek labour force survey has been used, with suitable econometric techniques applied. The focus of the analysis has been on examining the evolution of INE throughout the economic crisis and how it has been distributed across regions and particular groups of workers.

It has been shown that the share of Greek adult workers who are involuntarily employed under non-standard contracts – in particular, involuntary part-time contracts – has risen significantly during the last 7–8 years. Much of this increase can be attributed to the changing composition and characteristics of available jobs in the labour market, which have shifted towards greater insecurity, rather than to an altering mix in the supply of skills. On average, individuals in INE, apart from having to accept non-standard contracts involuntarily, are found to receive lower mean wages (compared to those in non-standard jobs voluntarily) while having higher chances of not being covered by any type of social/health insurance. At the same time, workers in INE are often involved in occupations/sectors (typically lower skilled) that enjoy lower job quality. Thus, our findings strengthen the argumentation that workers in INE are susceptible to attributes of precarious employment and signal that labour market segmentation has become ingrained in the Greek labour market during the Great Economic Crisis.

As a consequence of this, while Greece is facing unprecedented levels of unemployment and full attention has been paid to tackling joblessness, an important segment of the labour force is also accepting low quality jobs or is seeing its employment conditions deteriorate significantly. This phenomenon calls for policy intervention as the fear of skill obsolescence, further brain-drain, and an increasingly discouraged workforce has marked implications for productivity and may constitute a further barrier to Greece's recovery from the economic crisis.

Notes

1 Contact information, CEDEFOP, Europe 123, Thessaloniki (Pylaia), 55 102; Tel: +030 490 292; email: ilias.livanos@cedefop.europa.eu; konstantinos.pouliakas@cedefop.europa.eu. The views expressed in the paper are solely the authors' and do not necessarily represent those of the European Centre for the Development of Vocational Training (Cedefop). The usual disclaimer applies. The authors would like to thank Dr. Giovanni Russo, participants at a 2015 meeting of the Greek Labour Market Research Network (GLMRN) held at the London School of Economics, and two anonymous referees for their useful comments and insights.
2 Authors' estimations based on Greek LFS microdata.
3 Authors' estimation based on Greek LFS microdata.
4 Authors' estimations based on Greek LFS microdata.
5 Even though we refer to some forms of non-standard contracts as "voluntary", on the basis that the underlying motives for accepting such contractual forms of work are not related to the unavailability of full-time or permanent employment, we acknowledge that some of the residual reasons for picking atypical work (e.g. care for children or other dependents, illness or disability, other personal or family reasons) may also reflect a "constrained" set of choices. Nevertheless, as our concern is primarily focused on the inability of effective demand to be in alignment with individual preferences for contract choices, we follow the conventional wisdom in literature here.
6 In particular, the two equations are estimated jointly using the command "heckprob" in STATA.
7 This has been confirmed by running a separate probit regression of equation (1), in which the regional unemployment rate has been added as an explanatory variable together with all other possible determinants of INE (e.g. age, gender, education, industry, occupation, etc.).

8　The inclusion of variables capturing various types of atypical work (e.g. shift work, evenings or weekend work, working from home) has been made on the grounds that they are typically used in literature as proxies of the "quality of work" and may constitute additional (complementary) measures of functional flexibility used by employers in addition to reliance on non-standard contracts.

9　Due to space constraints, the results of the Heckman probit estimation are available from the authors upon request. It has been confirmed that there are no significant differences in the sign and test statistics of the regression coefficients obtained when using the two-step methodology that corrects for sample selection bias and those reported in Table 6.3. All empirical coefficients in the selection equation are in accordance with prior expectations. For instance, a positive yet non-linear association is found between the number of children and the probability of being an employee. Younger individuals, non-nationals, higher-educated individuals, and those in continuous employment are more likely to be in the workforce.

10　This can be deduced by the fact that when the estimation of INE on the time dummies takes place and various demographic (e.g. sex, age, migrant status) or other individual characteristics of the workforce (e.g. past labour market status) are taken into account, the estimated coefficients of the time dummies remain positive and statistically significant. By contrast, when various job characteristics (e.g. training, firm size, public sector, years of tenure, work hours, occupation, industry etc.) are included in the specification, the time dummies for the years 2012–2015 become statistically insignificant.

11　Although the breakdown of the empirical estimations by gender is not shown here due to space constraints, it is available from the authors upon request.

12　An interesting finding is that in the whole sample, there is a negative, albeit weak, association between home working and the chances of INE. This association appears to be largely driven by the substitutability between the ability to work from home and the need to involuntarily accept a part-time job, although the effect has largely vanished during the post-crisis years. No significant gender effects are found.

13　The comparison between the two time periods has been done for clarity of exposition and due to space constraints in the paper. The regression coefficients when performing a multivariate regression analysis of the determinants of INE for each year in the sample are also available from the authors upon request.

14　In the Greek LFS, respondents are requested to provide information about their total net monthly pay within a limited number of wage bands. Following Livanos and Pouliakas (2010), a continuous variable has been derived for the purposes of the regression analysis by assigning the mid-point of the respective band to each employee. When interested in the hourly rate of pay, we transform monthly earnings by dividing the figure by 4.3 times the usual weekly hours. The values have been subsequently deflated in 2015 prices using the harmonised index of consumer prices (HICP).

15　The analysis has also looked into the differences in earnings between individuals who are employed under all possible contractual states of non-standard and standard employment, in particular, full-time/permanent employment, full-time/involuntary temporary, full-time/voluntary temporary, voluntary part-time/permanent, involuntary part-time/permanent, involuntary part-time/involuntary temporary, involuntary part-time/voluntary temporary, voluntary part-time/involuntary temporary, voluntary part-time/voluntary temporary. The results have confirmed that any form of contract (either part-time or temporary) that contains an involuntary element is associated with a larger wage penalty relative to the same type of contract combination that is voluntarily accepted. Results are available from the authors upon request.

16 It has been confirmed that the higher wages received by voluntary non-standard contract workers relative to those in INE are statistically significant at the 1% level of significance.

References

Amuedo-Dorantes, C. (2000). 'Work Transitions into and Out of Involuntary Temporary Employment in a Segmented Market: Evidence from Spain'. *Industrial & Labor Relations Review*, 53(2): 309–325.

Bargain, O., Gonzalez, L., Keane, C. and Ozcan, B. (2010). Female Labor Supply and Divorce: New Evidence from Ireland. IZA Discussion Paper no. 4959.

Bednarzik, R. W. (1975). 'Involuntary Part-Time Work – Cyclical Analysis. *Monthly Labor Review*, 98(9): 12–18.

Cam, S. (2012). 'Involuntary Part-Time Workers in Britain: Evidence from the Labour Force Survey'. *Industrial Relations Journal*, 43(3): 242–259.

Christopoulou, R. and Monastiriotis, V. (2016). 'Public-Private Wage Duality during the Greek Crisis'. *Oxford Economic Papers*, 68(1): 174–196.

Da Silva, D. and Turrini, A. (2015). 'Precarious and Less Well-Paid? Wage Differences between Permanent and Fixed-Term Contracts across the EU Countries'. *European Economy, Economic Papers 544*, European Union.

Davoine, L., Erhel, C., and Guergoat-Lariviere, M. (2008). 'Monitoring Quality in Work: European Employment Strategy Indicators and Beyond'. *International Labour Review*, 147: 2–3.

EMCO. (2010). Quality in Work: Thematic Review 2010 Brussells.

Glassner, V. and Keune, M. (2010). Negotiating the Crisis? Collective Bargaining in Europe during the Economicdownturn. *DIALOGUE working paper*. Geneva, ILO. 10.

Green, A. and Livanos, I. (2015). 'Involuntary Non-Standard Employment Employment and the Economic Crisis: Regional Insights from the UK'. *Regional Studies*, 36(1): 44–66.

Green, F. (2006). *Demanding Work: The Paradox of Job Quality in the Affluent Economy*. Princeton, NJ: Princeton University Press.

Heckman, J. (1979). 'Sample Selection Bias as a Specification Error'. *Econometrica*, 47(1): 153–161.

Horemanas, J., Marx, I., and Nolan, B. (2016). 'Hanging In, but Only Just: Part-Time Employment and In-Work Poverty Throughout the Crisis'. *IZA Journal of European Labor Studies*, 5(5) https://doi.org/10.1186/s40174-016-0053-6.

Humphries, J. and Sarasua, C. (2012). 'Off the Record: Reconstructing Women's Labor Force Participation in the European Past'. *Feminist Economics*, 18(4): 39–64.

ILO. (2016). *Diagnostic Report on Undeclared Work in Greece*. Geneva: ILO.

Johnson, W. (2014). 'House Prices and Female Labor Force Participation'. *Journal of Urban Economics*, 82(c): 1–11.

Kalleberg, A. L. (2000). 'Nonstandard Employment Relations: Part-Time, Temporary and Contract Work'. *Annual Review of Sociology*, 26: 341–365.

Kauhanen, M. and Nätti, J. (2015). 'Involuntary Temporary and Part-Time Work, Job Quality and Well-Being at Work'. *Social Indicators Research*, 120(3): 783–799.

Kornelakis, A., Veliziotis, M., Voskeritsian, H. and Kapotas, P. (2016). *Prospects for New Employment Relations and Labour Market Model in Greece*. London: Hellenic Observatory, LSE.

Kretsos, L. (2010). 'The Persistent Pandemic of Precariousness: Young People at Work'. In: J. Tremmel. *A Young Generation Under Pressure?* New York: Springer, pp. 3–22.

Kretsos, L. and Livanos, I. (2016). 'The Extent and Determinants of Precarious Employment in Europe'. *International Journal of Manpower*, 31(1): 25–43.

Labrianidis, L. and Pratsinakis, M. (2016). *Outward Migration from Greece during the Crisis*. London: Hellenic Observatory, LSE.

Lambrianidis, L. (2014). 'Investing in Leaving: The Greek Case of International Migration of Professionals'. *Mobilities*, 9(2): 314–335.

Lazaretou, S. (2016). 'Brain Drain: The Modern Trend of Migration of Greeks during the Years of Crisis'. *Bank of Greece Economic Bulletin*, 43: 33–58.

Leppel, K. and Clain, S. H. (1988). 'The Growth in Involuntary Part-Time Employment of Men and Women'. *Applied Economics*, 20(9): 1155–1166.

Livanos, I. and Pouliakas, K. (2010). 'Wage Returns to University Disciplines in Greece: Are Greek Higher Education Degrees Trojan Horses?'. *Education Economics*, 19(4): 411–445.

McGuinness, S. and Pouliakas, K. (2017). 'Deconstructing Theories of Overeducation in Europe: A Wage Decomposition Approach'. *Research in Labor Economics*, 45: 81-127.

Nunez, I. and Livanos, I. (2015). 'Temps "By Choice"? an Investigation of the Reasons behind Temporary Employment among Young Workers in Europe'. *Journal of Labor Research*, 36(1): 44–66.

OECD. (2007). *Economic Surveys: Greece*. Paris: OECD.

Parliament, E. (2016). *Precarious Employment in Europe: Patterns, Trends and Policy Strategies*. Brussels: Directorate General For Internal Policies.

Pouliakas, K. (2014). A Balancing Act at Times of Austerity: Matching the Supply and Demand for Skills in the Greek Labour Market. *Discussion papers 7915*. Bonn, Institute for the Study of Labor: IZA.

Pouliakas, K. (2017). 'Multiple-Job Holding: Career Pathway or Dire Straits?' *IZA World of Labour*, 356: https://wol.iza.org/articles/multiple-job-holding-career-pathway-or-dire-straits/long.

Pouliakas, K. and Theodossiou, I. (2005). 'Socio-Economic Differences in the Job Satisfaction of High-Paid and Low-Paid Employees in Greece'. *Bank of Greece Economic Bulletin*, 24: 91–132.

Pouliakas, K. and Theodossiou, I. (2009). 'Measuring the Utility Cost of Temporary Employment Contracts before Adaptation: A Conjoint Analysis Approach'. *Economica*, 77(308): 688–709.

Pouliakas, K. and Theodossiou, I. (2010). 'Socio-Economic Differences in Job Satisfaction of High-Paid and Low-Paid Workers in Europe'. *International Labour Review*, 1: 1–35.

Skedinger, P. (2011). *Employment Consequences of Employment Protection Legislation IFN Working Paper 865*. Stockholm: Research Institute of Industrial Economics.

Veliziotis, M., Matsaganis, M., and Karakitsios, A. (2015). Involuntary Part-Time Employment: Perspectives from Two European Labour Markets. *ImPRovE Working Papes*. 15.

7 Unemployment experiences and coping strategies of the unemployed in crisis-ridden Greece

Christina Karakioulafis

1 Introduction

The Greek debt crisis combined with austerity measures have led to rising – and unprecedented for the Greek labour market – unemployment levels and a labour market landscape marked by increasing employment precariousness and deregulation of labour relations. This situation, in addition to wage cuts, increased taxes, and a shrinking welfare state, exacerbated the overall socio-economic insecurity of Greek households.

However, in Greece, the scientific analysis of unemployment and precariousness is mainly of a statistical, economic, and journalistic nature. Thus, unemployment statistics dominate, while experiences of unemployment become the "dark" and "silent" face of statistics (Araujo 2013). Nevertheless, although statistical analysis allows us to register and measure households or individuals affected by situations such as unemployment, they do not allow us to see the ways in which these households and unemployed persons manage to handle the economic consequences of the crisis (Paugam 2016).

This chapter explores how men and women experience and cope with unemployment and loss of work as well as the way they perceive their present and future general working (or non-working) situation. The aim is to highlight both subjective experiences and significations of unemployment and loss of work as well as the coping strategies of the unemployed.

Deriving from "qualitative studies," the emphasis is on how individuals "narrate" their experiences and perceptions of their situation. Even though one could be tempted to reduce the respondents' discourse to mere personal testimonies, the experiences of the unemployed are comprehended as part of processes that surpass them largely. According to Araujo-Guimarães et al. (2010: 17):

> references must not be reduced to subjective experiences or, on the other hand, to the cultural models that frame those individual experiences. They must be considered the joint product of both institutional structures and subjective experiences, of the strategies of individual actors and collective regulations, of subjective worlds and normative constraints.

In this sense, individual unemployment experiences reflect and are considered in the light of broader socio-economic factors, affecting the way individuals perceive, deal, and cope with their condition (Yvon and Clot 2001).

More particularly, this chapter addresses three main issues: how do the economic crisis and the rising unemployment rates in Greece influence unemployment experiences; what are the main "sentimental" and "material" coping strategies of the unemployed; what is the role of "traditional" support networks (such as the family) during the economic crisis? To address these questions, face-to-face in-depth interviews were carried out with unemployed men and women during 2012–2014 and in 2016.

The chapter is structured as follows. The next section provides a brief literature review of the main theoretical frameworks related to this study. Subsequently, after explaining the research context and the methodology followed, an analysis of the findings regarding unemployment experiences and the coping strategies of the unemployed takes place. Finally, the results of the research are discussed.

2 Unemployment experiences and coping strategies of the unemployed: a literature review

Unemployment experiences have occupied a considerable number of theoretical and empirical studies already since the 1930s. As Gallie and Paugam (2000) pointed out, unemployment is an issue that draws the interest of researchers much more in periods of economic recession than in periods of prosperity. Thus, the increasing unemployment rates due to the Great Depression boosted the interest of social scientists regarding the social consequences of unemployment.

Despite differences, various studies showed that unemployment is generally a detrimental experience profoundly affecting not only the well-being of the individual concerned, but also their immediate environment. For Jahoda (1982) and the Marienthal study researchers (Lazarsfeld et al. 1933[1975]), unemployment signified "a state of deficit in relation to a set of 'enduring human needs' that are provided by paid work" (Cole 2007: 1134). Unemployment "causes psychological distress because it deprives people of the latent functions that employment provides ...," such as a shared experience; a structured experience of time; collective purpose, status, and identity; and required regular activity (Waters and Moore 2002: 15). The question of time is central in unemployment research. In their study of the unemployed in Marienthal, researchers pointed out the disruptive consequences of unemployment in the daily time structure. Relevant studies demonstrate the sentiment of boredom and idleness, the loss of a sense of time, as well as the paradox of having a lot of time and little to do with it (or of doing nothing because there is so much time) (Lazarsfeld et al. 1933[1975]; Engbersen et al. 2006). The Marienthal study is of particular interest as it refers to the psychosocial consequences of unemployment in the context of extreme economic recession.

Furthermore, the Marienthal study demonstrated the inability to perceive the unemployed as a homogenous group and talk about a common experience of unemployment. In their study, the authors have identified four different attitudes and behaviours of the unemployed families: the "resigned," who had lost their future orientation and no longer made plans; those "in despair," who had given up on finding work and displayed much more emotional despair, depression, and hopelessness compared to the first group of families; the "apathetic," who reacted to unemployment with apathy, showed carelessness towards themselves and their children and had no future plans; and finally the "unbroken," who were more active, maintained hope, and continued to have future plans (Lazarsfeld et al. 1933[1975]).

Thus, unemployment experiences differ according to a variety of factors, such as age, gender, marital and family status, educational level of the unemployed, the duration of unemployment, or the economic situation of the household. Moreover, the existent policies and institutions regarding unemployment and the type of unemployment benefits may also contribute to diversified experiences. In other words, unemployment does not affect all the unemployed in the same way.

As Demazière (2006) points out, the experience of unemployment depends on the complex combination of heterogeneous factors: the position of the unemployed in the life cycle, one's social status or position in a social path, the subjective predictions of the unemployed regarding the future and the available social networks, as well as the objectively possible social positions. According to Pahl (1992), unemployment experiences depend on several factors, such as the duration of employment time, the stage of the life course when the period of unemployment began, the alternative identities available for the unemployed, the previous occupational identity, the culture of the unemployed, and the system of social protection.

Regarding the issue of gender, status, and identity, initially, it was assumed that men suffer more from unemployment because it hurts their "masculinity" and is opposed to the "male breadwinner model". During the 1930s and early 1940s, some studies were published focusing on the consequences of unemployment for unemployed men – with reference to the dominant "male-breadwinner model" – such as the study of Bakke in the communities of Greenwich (1934) and New Haven (1940) or the study of Mirra Komarowsky (1940) in an industrial city outside New York. On the other hand, women were supposed to be better able to cope with unemployment because they would find substitute activities easier (such as domestic work and taking care of the children). However, relevant research has shown that in the case of unemployed women, domestic work and taking care of the children does not appear as a voluntary substitute activity but more as a forced one, while the return to the "housewife" status is not experienced well and involves social isolation (Schnapper, 1994 [1981]).

In what follows, we will focus on studies dealing with the heterogeneity in unemployment experiences to comprehend how the unemployed perceive and narrate their conditions. We will also focus on literature that examines the coping strategies of the unemployed as well as the role of social support networks.

Regarding the first issue, a body of the relevant literature examines dominant unemployment experiences creating "ideal types" or a "cartographies" following the "Marienthal study" tradition in a direct or indirect way. For example, in France, Schnapper (1994 [1981]), a "path-defining study" (Monticelli et al. 2016: 139) that marked a new phase in unemployment studies (Gallie and Paugam 2000) distinguished three types of "unemployment experience": "absolute unemployment," which implies the loss of previous social status, isolation, a rupture of social bonds, as well as feelings of humiliation, emptiness, and failure; "inverted unemployment," where paid work is in second order compared to other activities offered for individual fulfilment; and "differentiated unemployment," concerning unemployed executives. "Absolute unemployment" ("chômage total") corresponds to the typical image of an unemployed person and seems to be predominant among working-class people, whose social status and identity is derived mainly from work, whereas people belonging to middle and upper social classes found it easier to develop a social replacement status by mobilising their educational and/or social capital.

In their research, Demazière et al. (2013) (see also Araujo-Guimarães et al. 2010; Demazière, 2013a, 2013b) examine the variety of unemployment experiences in different national contexts. The study is based on a comparative investigation in three metropolitan areas (Paris, Tokyo, Sao Paolo). Considering the cultural and institutional differences between national contexts as well as social dissimilarities among the unemployed, the authors tried to show the ways in which the unemployed "narrate" the experience of unemployment and the meanings they attribute to this experience. They created a sort of a "map of significations" that aims to emphasise the changes, the heterogeneity, and the ambivalence of the ways the unemployed use to interpret their situation. Despite differences, three major significations seem to prevail: "discouragement" (*découragement*), "competition" (*compétition*), and "inventiveness" (*débrouillardise*).

Discouragement corresponds to the experience of "absolute" unemployment. In that case, the unemployment experience is dominated by a certain fatalism and a feeling of incapacity to change the current situation, find a job, and plan a future. "As the vain attempts to escape unemployment pile up, job deprivation is experienced as being more and more unbearable and insurmountable". The unemployed "feel trapped in a dead end" and "crushed by a ubiquitous unemployment against which it has become impossible to fight". In the case of inventiveness, individuals "invest in" or "invent" "survival" strategies and activities in an effort to resist the negative consequences of labour deprivation. Here, a certain form of withdrawal from employment is observed, while at the same time, the person concerned valorises activities that offer a sense of social utility to "erase unemployment, lastingly if not permanently, by eclipsing the job search and filling all their spare time". Besides that, individuals tend to reconvert to professional activities, which differ from those they occupied before. Finally, with regard to competition, individuals – being generally optimistic – focus on a strategic job search and reintegration into the labour market:

> the job search is related as being the person's main activity, giving meaning to their real-life situation, occupying all their waking hours, and leads to their vision of their future employment. It is a discourse that dilutes unemployment in the activity of searching for work and in the competition to succeed.
>
> (Araujo-Guimarães et al. 2010: 12, 13, 14 & 17)

These three major significations help us better understand unemployment experiences in the actual Greek context.

Besides dominant unemployment experiences and significations, the preceding issues are also relevant to the ways in which the unemployed cope sentimentally and materially with their condition. In other words, unemployment experiences are strongly related to coping practices, sometimes making it difficult to distinguish one from another.

Coping has become a crucial point of unemployment analysis as researchers try to better understand the efforts of disadvantaged individuals in coping with hardships. Most particularly, in the case of the unemployed, scholars tried to comprehend the way they learn to live with their condition; recompense the absence of job, income, and recognition (originating from work); and try to preserve a decent life status. Social support is one of the main protective elements and coping resources examined (Lahusen and Giugni 2016).

In addition to individual factors, sentimental coping depends, among others, on existing support networks, social values regarding unemployment, or even the general – economic – context. As for material coping, it seems to depend on official welfare benefits, help from informal support networks, and available alternative solutions outside the official "wage labour" system.

Sentimental coping is strongly related to the following question: who is to be blamed? This is a question that shapes the opinion of the unemployed about their condition, the society's perception of unemployment, and the potential stigmatisation of the unemployed. According to Furnham (1988) and Furnham and Rawles (1996) (in Bendassolli et al. 2015), there are three main types of reasons given for unemployment by the unemployed: individualistic, societal, and fatalistic (inevitable) reasons. Whether people blame themselves or the system is often connected to contextual or institutional factors (Sharone 2013).

The question of "blame" is also relevant to the stigmatisation of the unemployed. It appears that the extent to which the unemployed feel stigmatised depends on the social context. As Pahl (1992: 219) points out, the unemployment experience "is a socially constructed identity. Family, friends and neighbours can determine, to a very large extent how stigmatised the individual may feel". Usually, unemployment is related to a stigmatised social status (Price et al. 1998). Additionally, the unemployment problem, related to a wider "responsibilising ethos" "has been primarily discursively configured as the 'problem of the unemployed,' residing to the individual himself rather than to contextual factors (such as social, economic, or political conditions)" (Laliberte-Rudman and Aldrich 2016: 2).

In times such as the Great Depression, where unemployment rates were higher, being unemployed seems to be less stigmatising than in periods of prosperity. Thus, the social context shapes and guides the opinions of individuals about unemployment and is decisive in understanding how people react to and experience unemployment (Price, et al., 1998). As Lorenzini and Guigni (2016: 84) point out, even if a negative representation of the unemployed exists in the society, it is diminished if unemployment rates increase and "everyone knows someone who is unemployed". As the authors show, referring to the Swiss context, low unemployment rates underline negative stereotypes regarding the unemployed even among family members ("the idea that they are not making enough efforts to find a job; if they really want to find a job, they can; or they are taking advantage of the system").

As for material coping, the question concerns the available forms of relief for the unemployed. Gallie and Paugam (2000) pointed out the fact that in order to understand unemployment experiences, one should take into account the particular economic, social, and political context, which can differ from one country to another. Taking into account three dimensions – welfare regime, family, and market – the authors distinguish between various welfare regimes and forms of intervention of the welfare state (sub-protective, liberal-minimal, employment-centred, universalistic) depending on coverage, levels of compensation, and the extent of activation policies; models of family residence (dependence model, model of relative autonomy between generation, model of advanced inter-generational autonomy); and variations concerning the general economic development and/or sectoral development.

With regard to welfare regimes, Greece is considered a sub-protective welfare state offering the unemployed less than the minimum protection required for their subsistence. In this system, few of the unemployed receive unemployment benefits, while the amounts of these benefits are low (Gallie and Paugam 2000). Concerning the role of the family, Greece is marked by an extended inter-generational dependence model of family residence. Taking these two features into account, informal coping strategies and unemployment reliefs seem to play a key role.

In a recent comparative research in seven European countries, Paugam et al. (2014) (see also: Paugam 2016) focused on the coping strategies of the unemployed. According to the authors:

The experience of unemployment, especially when it lasts longer than the statutory period of benefit, threatens the organic participation tie with post-industrial society as the material and symbolic recognition of work and the social protection stemming from employment may to some extent be called into question. Unemployed people then face the risk of social disqualification.

(Paugam et al. 2014: 8)

But while the organic participation tie (or bond) is essential for the attachment of individuals to groups and society, it is not the only bond through which individuals integrate into society. So, to understand the unemployment experiences and coping strategies of the unemployed, one must also consider the so-called lineal bond ("between parents and children"), elective participation bond ("between peers or persons chosen because of their affinities"), and citizenship bond ("between individuals sharing the same basic rights and duties within a political community"). The question is whether unemployment implies not only a breakdown of the organic participation bond but also a breakdown of the other types of bond. In other words, the question is whether there is a "chain reaction" ("unemployment is a cumulative process of breakdown of the four types of tie") or a mechanism compensating for the breakdown of the organic participation bond, further compensated for by the persistence or even reinforcement of the other form of bonds (Paugam et al. 2014).

Thus, regarding "coping," social support is supposed to moderate the detrimental consequences of unemployment. The issue of social relations is also crucial in unemployment research. As pointed out by Lahusen and Giugni (2016: 4), "the relationship between unemployment and social support is a complex one …". On the one hand, social support is a factor that diminishes the detrimental effects of unemployment both in terms of sentimental and material relief. On the other hand, the risk of social isolation is strong among the unemployed and cannot be comprehended independently from voluntary or non-voluntary feelings of "self-blame," stigmatisation, and economic deprivation. Frequently, the unemployed have to cope with a rupture of their social ties and bonds (Gallie, et al. 2003; Lorenzini and Giugni 2016; Paugam 2008, 2016).

Nevertheless, it is generally considered that families and peers may provide social capital (Grimmer 2016) and can be considered a source of resources that permit the unemployed to live a decent life and offer a central "antidote" or "vaccine" against social isolation, psychological suffering, and a negative perspective of the future (Lahusen and Giugni 2016: 3). In that case, social capital mainly refers to material resources originating from social relations or networks. Thus, the intensity of social contacts influences the amount of social capital (Grimmer 2016).

Vis-à-vis the coping strategies of the unemployed in the southern European countries, Paugam et al. (2014: 89–90) point out the importance of undeclared work that is considered a sort of "resourcefulness". It has always been seen: "especially in working class circles, as a more or less normal way of topping up one's income". In southern European countries, such as in Greece, undeclared work among unemployed people seems to be "a part of daily life" and people had "no problem talking about it openly".

This contextual factor is pointed out in the works of Pardo (2004) and Pahl (1992). Pahl also points out the role of the regional context as well as the importance of the existence of possibilities for alternative forms of work outside (official) employment. It appears that:

> where employment has been traditionally seasonal and transitory then alternative survival strategies will have become well-established in the local culture. Again, by contrast, where there is no tradition of unemployment and likewise no alternative support system the consequences can be very serious.
>
> (Pahl 1992: 219)

As pointed out by Pahl (1992), in communities where unemployment and underemployment are high and of long duration, people develop survival strategies to help them cope with the instability and fluctuations of local employment opportunities. These strategies may include migration, seasonal employment, and periods free from wage labour.

3 Methodology

As mentioned earlier, findings emerged from face-to-face in-depth interviews carried out with unemployed men and women during 2012–2014 and in 2016. A part (20) of the interviews with unemployed men and women were carried out in the framework of a research program on unemployment and employment precariousness financed by the Labour Institute of the General Confederation of Greek Workers (GSEE) (Karakioulafi et al. 2015). Subsequently, 17 interviews were carried out by the author.

Respondents were mostly recruited through the "snowballing" method, and the sample includes men and women of different ages issued various professional environments. The only selection criterion was to have a minimum employment experience. Most of the interviewees were women, while in the case of men, it was difficult to conduct interviews with older unemployed men. This was not the result of a methodological choice but of a "practical" difficulty of finding older unemployed men who were available to participate. This "difficulty" seems consistent with the findings regarding the unemployment stigma in the case of unemployed men.

The face-to-face interview schedule covered a wide range of questions on issues related – more or less directly – to unemployment issues. Thus, the participants were asked not only about their unemployment condition in a strict sense, but also about the general socioeconomic situation in Greece over the last years as well as about their household condition. More broad questions regarding, for example, the general socioeconomic condition of the households where the unemployed lived, helped "put" narrations in a context. Questions related to the general socioeconomic situation in Greece facilitated the discussion and seemed to have made it easier for respondents to talk about their unemployment condition.

Further questions concerned their previous professional path and employment condition; the specific experience and instant of job loss, where we asked them to narrate the moment of job loss (in order to see who they blame and how they experienced this moment); the actual unemployment experience in order to examine issues such as the time use or the unemployment stigma; their job-seeking practices and/or strategies; their future professional and non-professional plans and their perceptions about the future; the ways they try to cope sentimentally and materially with unemployment; and, finally, the extent and role of family support.

The analysis of the interviews draws on sociological and socio-anthropological literature addressing unemployment experiences and coping strategies of the unemployed. The body of the literature examined concerns mostly other national contexts – since relevant research in Greece is limited and of a more statistical and economical character. The analysis follows the methodological tradition of Lazarsfeld et al. 1933[1975] in their renowned Marienthal study, using qualitative methods of empirical research and analysis.

4 Experiencing and narrating unemployment

4.1 Discouragement and pessimism: dominant sentiments among the unemployed

Most of the unemployed interviewed declared to be pessimistic not only about finding a job but also regarding the type of job they will be able to find. Amid crisis, "discouragement" prevails over other significations of unemployment, and the experience of "absolute unemployment" is much more pronounced.

> At first, I didn't want to believe that I won't find a job again; now I begin to be convinced: it is out of question that I'll be able to find a job again; it's finished. [...] A few days ago, I thought that something will happen, that I will find something, but now I am disappointed.
>
> (D., male, 38 years old, married, one child)

> Unfortunately, I'm not positive at all. I don't like saying that, but that's it. Everything is finished. Jobs in the private sector, in the public sector, in the construction industry, everything is finished.
>
> (N., male, 25 years old, unmarried, no children)

It seems that although there is a great desire to work, to do any kind of work, jobs are rare, temporary, and precarious (Balourdos and Spyropoulos 2012).

> Every time I find a job I try to put a little money aside. But in the end, this does not happen, or it happens just for a moment. Those are precarious jobs. Without professional horizon, without stability.
>
> (G., male, 28 years old, unmarried, no children)

Among the unemployed people interviewed, there is a widespread conviction that even if they find a job, it will be of poorer quality both in terms of wages and working conditions.

T., a 25-year-old unemployed man (unmarried, no children), describes his experience during his job search:

> I'm trying to find a job for a long time, both in the sector I worked before, as seller, as well as in other sectors. [...] But I still can't find anything. And some jobs that I found were in companies that didn't pay well. Less money per month than the unemployment benefit.

His testimony is consistent with that of the following respondent:

> (The employer) told me "at present the company doesn't pay wages. Come to work, I will hire you and you will eventually get paid". [...] I would leave my house, to work for 12 hours, plus 2 hours the time to go to work. I would be absent for 14 hours from home without earning any money.
>
> (D., male, 38 years old, married, one child)

At the same time, they are certain they have to make many concessions and accept jobs they would have previously refused.

> I'm to find a job. It's impossible! Today it is difficult to find a job. I would accept any job.
>
> (C., female, 37 years old, married, two children)

> There is nothing [...] All my friends who are looking for a job, like me, find jobs where the wages are low, below the unemployment benefit [...] Yes of course (I would have done concessions), regarding wages and working hours. (I would) work part time in the afternoon. Before, I would never have accepted such a thing.
>
> (A., female, 40 years old, married, two children)

> You are just trying to find a job. The situation we knew in the past, where you had the possibility to choose, is gone. Now, you bow down, you say yes to everything, regardless if you like it or not. What can you do? [...] We don't have the choice.
>
> (P., male, 45 years old, married, one child)

Feelings of discouragement, disappointment, and vanity of their efforts strengthen as time passes. The number of CVs sent without positive response seems to intensify these feelings.

> Since mid-August I have sent 70–80 CVs [The interview was carried out in early October]. [...] I was invited in five job interviews.
> (V., female, 26 years old, unmarried, no children)

> I also send CVs. I counted them before coming (to the interview) [...] 212 CVs, and during these years I was called for four interviews.
> (Th., female, 35 years old, married, two children)

> I spoke to a friend who is a head hunter and who has a huge database with contact details of companies [...] (He told me) "Give me your CV. I'll put it in the database so that it circulates everywhere". [...] I received five responses among 1,500 companies.
> (T., female, 43 years old, unmarried, no children)

The no-response from employers, as we can see from the previous citations, as well from the one that follows, is equal to a negative response:

> The bad thing about CVs is that you don't get a response. You can send them up to five CVs a day in different kind of jobs, and you get no answer. I have been searching for work during the whole summer, only one (employer) called to tell me that the job was taken. But at least he called!
> (E., female, 26 years old, unmarried, no children)

4.2 Age as a major obstacle in finding a job

The insecurity and pessimism about the fact of finding work intensifies in the case of unemployed men and women of a certain age. As evidenced by the following quotations, respondents consider their age as a disadvantage because in their view, a potential employer would consider them as being more "expensive" and "less productive" than younger employees.

> Then you tell yourself "I'm 40 years old. Who will hire me?" If you see the job ads for sellers, they ask for people up to 25 years.
> (G., female, 40 years old, divorced, one child)

> I am 43 years old. The reactions regarding my age were so intense that I had to remove my age from my CV. Because I was told that when employers see the CV of a person of my age, they don't even look at it. They rumple it and throw it in trash. [...] My age is "forbidden".
> (T., female, 43 years old, unmarried, no children)

I have searched for another job, but as I have told you they didn't hire me because of my age [...] The first thing they asked me is how old I was. And when they heard my age, it was as if I had told them that I'm 60 or 70 years old. And I couldn't lie. I can't hide to you, that this disappointed me a lot.

> (M., female, 54 years old, lives with her partner, unemployed,
> works only during summers in a hotel)

All job ads mention that they are searching for young women. Ok, I feel young but I'm not young. So, when I call them and I tell them that I'm calling for the job ad, the first thing they ask me is: "how old are you?". And when I tell them that I'm 50 they are answering "But we are looking for a young woman". [...] My age is a hindering factor.

> (N., female, 50 years old, divorced, two children)

However, this causes feelings of insecurity among younger unemployed as well:

In many companies where I had a job interview, they told me that they prefer employees younger than 25 years old because their wages are lower.

> (M., female, 26 years old, unmarried, no children)

In other cases, especially in the case of the unemployed close to retirement, we find a version of the experience of "discouragement" (Demazière et al. 2013; Demazière 2013a, 2013b). Here, the discouragement leads to a gradual "withdrawal" or "exit" from the labour market:

Now I prepare my papers for the retirement. I tried desperately to find a job.

> (X., female, 55 years old, married, one child)

Generally, I try (to work), but ... [...] And I don't know to do anything else. And besides, as I am getting older, I do not have the flexibility to work elsewhere or to undergo training to do something else.

> (Z., female, 52 years old, married, no children)

4.3 Imputing blame on the employer

Regarding the question "who is to be blamed?", most of the respondents tend to blame and impute responsibility on their ex-employers and on the generalised economic crisis.

Almost all respondents think that their ex-employer could have avoided the layoffs. Those laid off under the pretext of the crisis believe that even if the crisis exacerbated the problems, (financial) problems pre-existed. From their point of view, the "bad" economic performance of enterprises and lay-offs are the result of failed investments made by their former employers. There is a common feeling that the employer could manage the company's problems differently and thus avoid layoffs.

> There is always a more proper way (for one) to announce your dismissal. He can tell you: "Look, I can't cope with the problems. Tell me what can be done?" [...] The other imputes the responsibility on you. It's your fault and it is for you to find the solution.
>
> (X., female, 55 years old, married, one child)

> All these years we worked there, and the company was making money, we were close to each other, we had contacts even outside of work. [...] And when work came to a bitter end, there have been changes in their behaviour. [...] Then we became the bad guys who had no compassion for the company.
>
> (A., female, 37 years old, married, two children)

4.4 The retreat of the unemployment "stigma"

On the other hand, there is a generally accepted idea: anyone regardless of their qualifications and skills may be unemployed. Thus, the crisis "protects" from a certain stigma that traditionally accompanied the unemployed and discharges them of humiliation or of feelings of personal responsibility regarding their situation.

> I think that the economic crisis has become a shelter for people who are facing work problems [...] In 2006–2007 an unemployed was marginalised. Now you are not marginalised. Many people now talk openly: "I have no job, I have no money. I won't go this year on vacations, because I have no money". In previous years, this was a taboo in Greek society. It was not said. It was unmentionable.
>
> (D., male, 38 years old, married, one child)

In his eyes, the image of an increasing number of people picking up their children from school during periods that are normally working hours is evidence of the extent of the problem.

> Of course, I talk to the parents of my son's classmates [...] (Among them] there are many whose both parents are unemployed. And I see many men. [...] I see many men who are unemployed. Seventy percent of the parents who pick up their children from school are men. And I can understand it [the fact that they are unemployed] from their outfit. The fact that they pick up their child from school dressed in sweatpants and unshaved. In other words, you see that the other doesn't work.

And we discuss. The one is unemployed, the other one works in the construction industry. One day he works, another he doesn't. Everyone is in the same situation.

(D., male, 38 years old, married, one child)

Look, at first, I was a little annoyed that they didn't hire me, because I felt that it was a question of pride in a sense that "Okay, guys, I'm not that useless, I've done so many things". Then, you realise what is happening. I can see that now. In the past, if you said that you were unemployed, it was a little embarrassing because the others were thinking "Okay, you're in Athens, there are so many jobs, so what are you looking for?". Now that you see so many people (being unemployed) you say to yourself, "Okay, something is wrong there is no healthy company, there is no one to hire you".

(Th., female, 35 years old, married, two children)

In general, we can talk about a shift from an individual to a more collective interpretation, where the "blame" for unemployment is imputed on the crisis that leaves no one unaffected. Thus, although unemployment is generally considered a condition that is experienced in a solitary way, its massiveness seems to create a kind of bonding among those who are between unemployment or at least share a common experience.

Most of us are in the same situation. Either we are unemployed, or we experience pay cuts and working hours cuts.

(A., female, 40 years old, married, two children)

4.5 Dismissal and the "chronicle of a death foretold"

Concerning the way in which the unemployed perceive their condition, a factor that appears to influence their perception is that in most cases, there were signs of what would happen as the "chronicle of a death foretold":

The big problems began in 2008. [...] those losing their job could not find another. Doors opened just to dismiss people and never to hire someone

(T., female, 43 years old, unmarried, no children)

In some cases, pay cuts had taken place earlier or there had been significant delays regarding the payment of wages. Elsewhere, work had diminished, or the company had lost customers. In some cases, there was a reduction in personnel or a change in the employment contract. Hence, almost all respondents experienced a precarisation of their employment condition before being dismissed.

It all started with a delay in the payment of wages. [...] Meanwhile the employer had closed half of its stores and had dismissed people. But you know, everyone had a hope that they will get off.

(A., female, 40 years old, married, two children)

Once there was a question of reducing our wages [...] And our question was, "Well, we will accept the reduction, but will we be paid on time?" [...] At that moment, we saw a refusal on his part. [...] Then, he began to threaten us that he will make us work on a rotational basis, etc.

(C., female, 37 years old, married, two children)

We all understood that things were not going well. You could see this. But no one told us anything. They were telling us all the time that everything goes well. But we worked there, we could see [what will happen].

(P., male, 42 years old, married, one child)

Even if they felt or understood that the company was facing problems, it didn't mean that they were prepared for their dismissal. In other words, even if there were signs of what would happen, the respondents experienced the dismissal as a shock. Despite the signs – and although much of the responsibility for their situation is imputed on their employer – all this does not moderate the "trauma" of dismissal. Some were furious, while others felt that someone "has pulled the rug under their feet" or didn't realise immediately what has happened. Nevertheless, in all cases, whatever the reaction and although this was not explicitly stated, there was a widespread feeling that dismissals had been selective (Trotzier 2006) and the predominant question was: "Why me and not someone else?"

[The first feeling] was the shock. For someone who has learned to work from the age of 19 and was in a job where everything was going well [..] it's a shock. It is also the fear. Suddenly you find yourself in an unknown situation.

(A., female, 37 years old, married, two children)

I felt that I was literally rebuffed. After six years. [...] I think I was rebuffed, that I don't matter as a person or as a character.

(F., female, 38 years old, married, one child)

It was suffocating. I felt lost. I didn't know how to handle it. The fact that you have been working for 17 years and that they are firing you.

(G., male, 42 years old, married, two children)

The day they announced my dismissal it was my day-off. They announced my dismissal over the phone. When I picked up the phone, they just coldly told me that I was fired because the company wasn't doing well. I didn't expect them to treat me like this. [...] I felt very bad. Psychologically I was a wreck. I didn't expect them to fire me, since I had a good evaluation [...] I didn't expect them to treat me like this, since I was very good at my job.

(K., male, unmarried, 26 years old)

4.6 *The uncertain future and the cancellation of life plans*

The deprivation of a stable and continuous income for unemployed people as well as their inability to provide for basic needs are factors affecting the way they perceive their future situation.

Faced with a general feeling of cancellation or change of life plans, the respondents demonstrate a certain anxiety (and in some cases, pessimism) regarding their future financial and social situation.

Currently we pay our rent with the unemployment benefit that will end in a few months. From the moment I will stop receiving the unemployment benefit and don't find a job, I can no longer stay in Athens. [...] I am starting to become anxious about what I'll do if I cannot find a job.

(Th., female, 35 years old, married, two children)

The survival issue stresses me. I am not alone. I have a family to support, I have a small child asking for something every day. I want to be able to offer him things. [...] We adults, we can deprive ourselves from cigarettes and coffee, [...]. But a small child is a small child! He needs things, and that is what makes me anxious.

(D., male, 45 years old, married, one child)

I am optimistic, but I also feel insecure. The one does not exclude the other. I feel insecure because I want to be OK towards my child and my wife.

(D., male, 38 years old, married, one child)

In the case of the young unemployed, we can discern a feeling of frustration and lack of prospects in relation to their professional future. More generally, as also demonstrated by Paugam et al. (2014), young people believe that the crisis hinders their plans and aspirations.

I cannot make plans. [...] I am quite disappointed regarding the question of work. I searched a lot, I did not find anything, I don't know what to do.

(T., male, 25 years old, unmarried, no children)

We aren't searching for a job that will satisfy us. We are just searching for a job. So, our expectations are limited. But most of us don't even achieve this objective. Therefore, I can't be optimistic.

(V., female, 26 years old, unmarried, no children)

S. (female, 27 years old, unmarried, no children) refers to that situation of extreme impermanence and temporariness marking the professional and general life biography of young adults.

> [Regarding my professional future] that's disappointing. [...] In fact you enter a temporary situation. I'll be here or there temporarily. I'll do this temporarily. [...] You don't have this security [...] And all this instability has a permanent character. And I think people of my age begin to take a path of instability, to create their world and to organise their daily lives based on this instability. Insecurity becomes an experience, you internalise it. Thus, automatically you enter a process where you learn not to have a lot off expectations. You restrain, in fact, your expectations.
>
> Now, my life isn't based on anything. The only standard I have is that every six months I change jobs. This doesn't give you the possibility to put your life into a path, to stabilise. Having a stable job, gives you the possibility ... to do things for yourself.

(A., male, 28 years old, unmarried, no children)

Although some knew that it would be difficult to find a job, they hoped things would get better:

> In fact, when I finished my studies I knew that we didn't have the same available opportunities I had in mind when I started my studies. I was aware of that because we were already in a crisis period. [...] From the beginning I had no expectations. However, I thought that with effort and intensive research [...] things would improve. Things did not improve and in fact the whole procedure (of trying to find a job) makes me tired.

(S., female, 27 years old, unmarried, no children)

> The first 2–3 months (of unemployment) I was theoretically OK until I realised that I was once again (a) dependent (family member). I couldn't choose anymore how I was going to spend my time and I had to make savings on everything. I had a mini depression [...] I began to see a psychologist because I thought it was my fault. As if it was me who had not done enough (to find a job) [...] I know it's silly to think in such a way especially during this period.

(V., female, 26 years old, unmarried, no children)

In some cases, the disappointment resulting from the inability to find a job makes them think of a change of plans in relation to their future career or even a retraining. Both can be understood as strategies of "inventiveness".

> Now I feel less guilty, in the sense that even though I do not have a career or even a job in my field of expertise, at least I can see and do something else.
>
> (S., female, 27 years old, unmarried, no children)

> I also thought to cease practicing law. I gave myself a certain time margin. Another year. If in the meantime I don't find (a job) that will allow me to have a certain standard of living, I'll stop. […] I cannot think that all this will be permanent. […]. I will put an end to all that […] I want to move forward. Now I feel I'm in a stagnant situation.
>
> (V., female, 26 years old, unmarried, no children)

At times, as in the case with the following respondent, the plans become more concrete:

> I give private lessons to children. I thought, at least I will be occupied with something that I really like […] even if I earn less money. At least, I'm doing something that I like […].
>
> (C., female, 32 years old, married)

However, sometimes "inventiveness" gives way to "discouragement":

> The more you sit, the more you step back […] [There is an] Inactivity. […] And that irritates me. […] I started English courses, I continued for half a year and I stopped. I wasn't in the mood […] It makes you step back.
>
> (A., woman, 33 years old, married, one child)

Respondents talk of returning to their hometowns or seeking work abroad. These two options are perceived as possible solutions, even if it doesn't mean that they undertake concrete initiatives in one direction or the other.

> [I think of] going back to L. [hometown] […] Because there, I have a house. I think that there I could do something. For example, my father is a priest, he's got land, we will have something to eat. At least I will not be hungry.
>
> (C., female, 33 years old, married, two children)

> An alternative is to go to L. [hometown of her husband]. The idea is to return there for a certain time, if we cannot pay the rent anymore. We

are thinking of doing this, but not in a very intense way [...] We also think of going abroad.

> (Th., female, 35 years old, married, two children)

For the younger unemployed, the search of work abroad seems like the only alternative if they are not able to find employment in Greece in the next one to two years.

> With my friends, we discuss a lot (the issue of unemployment). In fact, it is the main subject of our discussions. Most of us think of going abroad.
> (S., male, 27 years old, unmarried, no children)

> I'm thinking of going abroad but this is not so easy.
> (V., female, 26 years old, unmarried, no children)

4.7 Undeclared work as a coping strategy

In some cases, unemployment and undeclared work coexist, securing a little extra income for the unemployed. This extra income becomes essential when they are no longer entitled to unemployment benefit or have never been entitled to it (for example, professionals or self-employed workers, or those who worked for a long time in "undeclared" jobs). Thus, "undeclared work" emerges as a "survival" or "coping" strategy and corresponds to an effort to be in occupied activities that intend to reduce the negative effects of unemployment.

> I would accept any job [...]. For example, now I will work for a few days as a cleaning lady in a neighbour's house.
> (Z., female, 52 years old, unmarried, no children)

> This morning I was paid for the [therapeutic] massages I do. Something that I do occasionally. [...] Undeclared! It was a great feeling to have money. And I thought it would be nice to have a steady income [...] that would give me security.
> (G., male, 28 years old, unmarried, no children)

> Particularly, when you send CVs and you get no response, you feel very useless and you turn towards undeclared work to cope.
> (G., male, 25 years old, unmarried, no children)

> I receive the unemployment benefit for the last 8 months. The last 3 months I also did undeclared work because I couldn't cope financially, since the unemployment benefit was around 280 euros per month.
> (G., male, 24 years old, unmarried, no children)

Z. (female, 28 years old, married, two children) explains that even though she has been working for a long time in a hair salon, she is not entitled to unemployment benefits:

> No [I'm not entitled to the unemployment benefit], because in Greece undeclared work prevails and it is difficult for someone to gather the necessary social insurance contributions to be entitled to unemployment benefits.

However, income from undeclared work is uncertain because in most cases, it concerns low-paying jobs that do not provide secure and sufficient compensation.

> I found a job in a medical practice three times a week as a secretary. I must work unofficially because otherwise I would have to pay more [the respondent refers to contributions for social security] [...] From this work I earn about 250 euros per month.
>
> (T., female, unmarried, 43 years old)

> In reality, I am not unemployed, but I don't have a stable job the last two years. I work three times a week to earn some money. On weekends, I clean a house, I cook and take care of their child and every Wednesday I clean two medical practices. [...] I earn 60 euros the weekend, another 40 from the medical practices. 100 euro a week.
>
> (E., female, 47 years old, married, two children)

Th. (female, 35 years old, married, two children) gives private lessons to children. This is something she already did before losing her job to supplement the family income but that at present is a critical – but also uncertain – source of income:

> I have always done this [giving lessons] as a kind of additional work. Now it has become my principal work, but it is a rather uncertain work.

4.8 Family support more needed than ever ... but also under extreme pressure

The role of informal social networks, particularly that of families in Greek societies, has been mentioned by numerous studies before the crisis. As discussed earlier, Greece is considered a "sub-protective" welfare regime marked by an extended inter-generational dependence (Gallie and Paugam 2000). In recent years, family networks continued to support their members in various ways, such as direct financial assistance, indirect support, or housing. Therefore, it seems that in times of crisis and with a social state whose support decreases, family networks bear the burden of the economic and social problems (Balourdos and Spyropoulos 2012) and the "informal social state" absorbs most of the social effects of the crisis (Lyberaki and Tinios, 2012).

> My mother started immediately to help me to live decently [...] She is helping me all these years, she brings me food.
>
> > (T., female, 43 years old, unmarried, no children)

> Luckily, we have our sponsors, the retired grandparents.
>
> > (A., female, 40 years old, married, two children)

> Without the help of grandparents, we wouldn't be able to cope. My mother buys us a few things from the supermarket. And when we needed a little money, it was my parents-in-law who gave us that money.
>
> > (Th., female, 35 years old, married, two children)

Regarding the younger unemployed, the return to the parental home or the delayed departure from it becomes almost inevitable.

> Having a family support gives me the opportunity to have some expectations from the kind of work I seek. [...] I have a little shelter. It bothers me, but I feel gratitude for having it.
>
> > (V., female, 26 years old, unmarried, no children)

According to Paugam et al. (2014: 59), in southern European countries, the "normative obligation of extended cohabitation concerns both parents and children". In fact, children are not able to set up their own homes and/or to live with their partners till they are sure to have some kind of stable work. In these contexts, it is considered quite normal for adult children to live with their parents and participate in household life.

Nevertheless, they feel a deep frustration because their unemployment condition delays emancipation. Their inability to leave the parental home, the fact that they must return to it, or not having the necessary income to secure their own accommodation and to support themselves creates feelings of distress.

K. (male, 32 years old) describes his return to his parental home as follows:

> I returned to my parents' house. Without work and having to pay the rent and bills. It was out of the question. [...] And you return at home with your parents. And you have that nagging again [...] You don't have your space [...] It is like before, as if you were a small child, but at the time it didn't bother you.

The whole situation causes them additional embarrassment since they know that their parental family is also facing economic difficulties.

V. (female, 26 years old, unmarried, no children) describes her situation as follows:

> I live with my parents because I cannot do otherwise. They both work and, also, sustain me. [To have to depend on them] bothers me enormously.

This is also the case for the following respondents:

> I'm forced to live with my parents. [...] Well, I receive the unemployment benefit and I give them a part for the household's expenditures. But they also can't get by.
>
> (T., male, 25 years old, unmarried, no children)

> My parents are helping me, but for how long will they be able to help me? They have their everyday expenses and they are having difficulties to fulfil their obligations.
>
> (K., male, 26 years old, unmarried, no children)

> Yes [my parents] are helping me. But not a lot. Few things. They also have difficulties getting by. My father is retired. He receives the OGA pension.[1] He does some agricultural work with my mother to provide for themselves.
>
> (N., male, 25 years old, unmarried, no children)

Although the appeal to family solidarity is a quasi-normality in Greece, it becomes problematic during the crisis (Papadopoulos and Roumpakis 2013). What changed compared to the pre-crisis period is that more and more people rely on the help of family networks, while these latter often fail to fulfil this "traditional" role, since they also suffer the impact of the crisis and their possibilities of financial support are limited. In this context, the family support often provokes an embarrassment to the unemployed.

> My parents sent us meat and vegetables from the village and my husband's parents will give gifts to our children or lend us money. Obviously, they cannot afford this. They are retired.
>
> (A., female, 33 years old, married, one child)

> I miss having my own money. Not to depend on anyone. I want to buy cigarettes and I'm hesitating to ask, "Dad, give me 3 euros to buy cigarettes". It is humiliating! I'm 40 years old. I'm not 20 to ask my father for money.
>
> (G., female, 40 years old, divorced, one child)

> You feel differently when you see that the one who is helping you also has financial problems. You feel like a parasite, even though it's not your fault.
>
> (F., woman, unmarried, 33 years old)

5 Discussion and conclusions

Following the narrations of the interviewees, one can understand that the economic crisis plays a crucial role in shaping the way individuals experience and cope with job loss and their unemployment condition as well as how they perceive their present and future working (or no-working) situation. In other words, unemployment experiences cannot be examined irrespective of the general developments in the Greek labour market, society and economy during the crisis. In fact, one could speak of a "collective experience of crisis" (Raveyre 2005). This seems to affect unemployment experience in two ways.

On the one hand, it reduces expectations and aspirations either of finding work (at all) or "decent" work in terms of wages or general labour relations. Unemployed people demonstrate a certain pessimism with respect to their ability to escape their unemployment situation or to find a "good" job. There is a kind of fatalism and lack of confidence among the "victims" of the current crisis, such as that experienced by the victims of the crisis of 1929 in Marienthal (Lazarsfeld et al. 1933[1975]). Thus, unemployment is experienced and lived more negatively, and discouragement prevails upon other significations, while the interviewees' words demonstrate their pessimism and anxiety regarding their future.

On the other hand, the extended unemployment and the widespread deregulation of the Greek labour market appears to moderate feelings of humiliation or personal failure among the unemployed in the sense that nowadays, everyone can become unemployed. In general, the interviewees' narrations give us the image of a certain retreat of the unemployment stigma. One can observe a shift from individualist to more collective interpretations, where the "blame" for unemployment is imputed on "crisis," which leaves no one unaffected and feelings of "self-blame" retreat. Thus, although unemployment is generally considered a condition experienced in a solitary way, its extent seems to create a kind of tie among those who are unemployed, or at least a sense of a shared experience.

Concerning the interpretation of their unemployment situation, a factor that appears to influence how the unemployed perceive their status is that in most cases, there was evidence of what will happen. However, even when there were signs of what would happen, the respondents experienced the dismissal as a shock.

It is the context of the economic crisis that creates feelings of anxiety and a lack of optimism among the unemployed regarding their future. These feelings seem to be very intense among "older" unemployed, who see their possibilities finding a job diminish, but they are also intense among young unemployed, as they are in a phase of their biographical development "where they are not yet fully integrated into social life as independent citizens and autonomous individuals" and unemployment has a sort of "scarring effect" on them (Lahusen and Giugni 2016: 2).

Regarding the ways in which unemployed cope with their situation, informal coping strategies and unemployment reliefs are of particular interest in national and social contexts such as Greece, where formal institutions, such as state support for the unemployed and unemployment benefits, are less developed or play a marginal role (Gallie and Paugam 2000). In fact, informality seems to play a crucial role in contexts of "thin institutional apparatus for unemployment relief" (Leontidou, 1993: 93). Nevertheless, the role of informal practices and institutions seems to be problematic in the context of economic crisis.

First, the role of offering social assistance to face the crisis was delegated to the family (Lyberaki and Tinios 2012). Nevertheless, in this context, it is not only the providential role of the state that was weakened but also the providential role of society, something that should make us think about the consequences of the crisis on family solidarity and on the capacity of families to substitute the lack of a formal welfare state (Araujo 2013). As Lyberaki and Tinios (2012: 194, 199) point out, the Greek crisis "acts as a stress test of relations" between the formal and the informal system: "The formal part places more insistent demands while at the same time squeezing the liquidity of the informal system". So, the two authors question whether the informal support and protection can "become 'bankrupt'".

According to Paugam (2016), in order to benefit from family support, the family must be in a financial situation that allows the provision of such a support. In other words, even if the family is willing to help, family solidarity and intergenerational redistribution is challenged and subjected to strain. Thus, in a crisis context, those who were protected from poverty in the past and could help out their unemployed children might suddenly find themselves under severe economic pressure (Paugam 2016).

In view of this, while "families remain the last line of defence in times of hardship" (Chabanet, et al., 2016: 27), the unemployed experience this support negatively. In case of the younger unemployed, this support has a frustrating effect and "is not only experienced as a blessing but also as a problem of dependence, which can inhibit personal development" (Lahusen and Giugni 2016: 4), while in the case of "older" unemployed, this support has an embarrassing and humiliating effect.

Second, with regard to informal employment, it appears to be a strategy of a last resort to escape involuntary unemployment due to the absence of viable alternatives (Günther and Launov 2012; Leonard 2000) rather than the result of the voluntary choice of the workers. Informal work may be considered both as a survival strategy as well as a proactive strategy to cope with unemployment as a sphere of "opportunities and motivations for encouraging paid work within the hidden economy among unemployed people" (Sixsmith 1999: 259).

Nevertheless, one should not assume that the income from informal work is "plentiful and inexhaustible manna from heaven" (Paugam et al. 2014:90). More often, it concerns small and not very well-paid jobs, which are not enough for people to survive on, while within economic crisis, possible resources from informal work have also dried up (Paugam et al. 2014). However, the "poverty escape" type of undeclared work seems to prevail among the unemployed. In other words, undeclared work becomes the main source of income and a way to avoid extreme poverty (Pfau-Effinger 2009).

Note

1 *OGA* (Agricultural Insurance Organisation) grants *pensions* to all persons who hold a job in the agricultural sector. The OGA pensions are very low pensions.

References

Araujo, P. (2013). 'Destins tracés et contraction des horizons: être chômeuse au Portugal'. *Genre, sexualité et société*, Automne 2013 .Retrieved from: https://journals. openedition.org/gss/2992

Araujo-Guimarães, N., Demazière, D., Hirata, H., and Sugita, K. (2010). 'Unemployment, a Social Construction: Institutional Programs, Experiences and Meanings in a Comparative Perspective'. *Economic Sociology, The European Electronic Newsletter*, 11(3): 10–24.

Bakke-Wight, E. (1934). *The Unemployed Man: A Social Study*. New York: Dutton & Co., Inc.

Bakke-Wight, E. (1940). *The Unemployed Worker: A Study of the Task of Making A Living without A Job*. New Haven: Yale University Press.

Balourdos, D. and Spyropoulos, N. (2012). 'Portraits of Poverty in Greece during the Crisis'. In: A. Mouriki, D. Balourdos, O. Papaliou, N. Spyropoulos, and E. Fagadaki (eds.). *The Social Portrait of Greece 2012: Aspects of the Crisis*. Athens: EKKE, Institute of Social Policy,pp. 161-183.

Bendassolli, P., Gondim, S., Guedes, M., and Coelho-Lima, F. (2015). 'Attributions of Causes for Unemployment by Unemployed Workers'. *Análise Psicológica*, 33(2): 153–164.

Chabanet, D., Cinalli, M. and Richard, D. (2016). 'Youth Long-Term Unemployment in France: Challenging Common Trends'. In: C. Lahusen and M. Giugni (eds.). *Experiencing Long-Term Unemployment in Europe*. London: Palgrave Macmillan, pp. 17-38.

Cole, M. (2007). 'Re-Thinking Unemployment: A Challenge to the Legacy of Jahoda et al.'. *Sociology*, 41(6): 1133–1149.

Demazière, D. (2006). *Sociologie des chômeurs*. Paris: La Découverte.

Demazière, D., Guimarães, N. A., Hirata, H. et Sugita, K. (2013). *Etre chômeur à Paris*. São Paulo, Tokyo: Une méthode de comparaison internationale, Paris: Presses de Sciences Po.

Demazière, D. (2013a). 'Le chômage at-il encore un sens? Enseignements d'une comparaison dans trois métropoles'. *Sociologie du Travail*, 55(2): 191–213.

Demazière, D. (2013b). 'Typologie et description. À propos de l'intelligibilité des expériences vécues'. *Sociologie*, 4(3): 333–347.

Engbersen, G., Schuyt, C. J. M. and Timmer, J. (2006). *Cultures of Unemployment: A Comparative Look at Long-Term Unemployment and Urban Poverty*. Amsterdam: Amsterdam University Press.

Furnham, A. (1988). *Lay Theories: Everyday Understanding of Problems in the Social Sciences*. Oxford: Pergamon Press.

Furnham, A. and Rawles, R. (1996). 'Job Search Strategies, Attitudes to School and Attribution about Unemployment'. *Journal of Adolescence*, 19, 355-369.

Gallie, D., and Paugam, S. (eds.). (2000). *Welfare Regimes and the Experience of Unemployment in Europe*. Oxford: Oxford University Press.

Gallie, D., Paugam, S. and Jacobs, S. (2003). 'Unemployment, poverty and social isolation: Is there a vicious circle of social exclusion?'. *European Societies*, 5(1), 1-32.

Grimmer, B. (2016). 'Being Long-Term Unemployed in Germany: Social Contacts, Finances and Stigma'. In: C. Lahusen and M. Giugni (eds.). *Experiencing Long-Term Unemployment in Europe*. London: Palgrave Macmillan, pp. 39–72.

Günther, I. and Launov, A. (2012). 'Informal Employment in Developing Countries Opportunity or Last Resort?' *Journal of Development Economics*, 97(1): 88–98.

Jahoda, M. (1982). *Employment and Unemployment: A Social-Psychological Analysis*. Cambridge: Cambridge University Press.

Karakioulafi, C. Spyridakis, M., Karalis, D., Giannakopoulou, E. and Soros, G., (2015). *Unemployment and Job Insecurity. Dimensions and Implications in Times of Crisis*. Athens: INE-GSEE (in Greek).

Komarowsky, M. (1940). *The Unemployed Man and His Family*. New York: Dryden Press.

Lahusen, C. and Giugni, M. (2016). 'Experiencing Long-Term Unemployment in Europe: An Introduction'. In: C. Lahusen and M. Giugni (eds.). *Experiencing Long-Term Unemployment in Europe*. London: Palgrave Macmillan, pp. 17–38.

Leontidou, L. (1993). 'Informal strategies of unemployment relief in Greek cities: the relevance of family, locality and housing'. *European Planning Studies*, 1(1), 43-68.

Monticelli, L., Baglioni, S. and Bassoli, M. (2016). 'Youth long-term unemployment and Its social consequences in Italy:'In a world that does Not belong to Me''. In: C. Lahusen and M. Giugni (eds.). *Experiencing Long-Term Unemployment in Europe*. London: Palgrave Macmillan, pp. 139-169.

Laliberte-Rudman, D. and Aldrich, R. (2016). '"Activated, but Stuck": Applying a Critical Occupational Lens to Examine the Negotiation of Long-Term Unemployment in Contemporary Socio-Political Contexts'. *Societies*, 6(3): 1-17.

Lazarsfeld, P. F., Jahoda, M., and Zeisel, H. (1933[1975]). *Die Arbeitslosen von Marienthal – Ein soziographischer Versuch über die Wirkungen langandauernder Arbeitslosigkeit*. Frankfurt am Main: Suhrkamp.

Leonard, M. (2000). 'Coping Strategies in Developed and Developing Societies: The Workings of the Informal Economy'. *Journal of International Development*, 12(8): 1069–1085.

Lorenzini, J. and Guigni, M. (2016). 'Long-Term Unemployed Youth in Switzerland: Coping with Exclusion from the Labor Market in a Country with Low Unemployment'. In: C. Lahusen and M. Giugni (eds.). *Experiencing Long-Term Unemployment in Europe*. London: Palgrave Macmillan, pp. 74–106.

Lyberaki, A. and Tinios, P. (2012). 'The Informal Welfare State and the Family: Invisible Actors in the Greek Drama'. *Political Studies Review*, 12(2): 193–208.

Pahl, R. E. (1992). 'Does Jobless Mean Workless? A Comparative Approach to the Survival Strategies of Unemployed People'. In: C. H. A. Verhaar, L. G. Jansma, M. P. M. de Goede, J. A. C. van Ophem, and A. de Vries (eds.). *On the Mysteries of Unemployment. Studies in Operational Regional Science*. Dordrecht: Springer, pp. 209–224.

Papadopoulos, T. and Roumpakis, A. (2013). 'Familistic Welfare Capitalism in Crisis: Social Reproduction and Anti-Social Policy in Greece'. *Journal of International and Comparative Social Policy*, 29(3): 204–224.

Pardo, I. (2004). 'Unemployed and Hard Workers: Entrepreneurial Moralities between 'Shadow' and 'Sunlight' in Naples'. In: A. Procoli (ed.). *Workers and Narratives of Survival in Europe: The Management of Precariousness at the End of the Twentieth Century*. New York: State University of New York Press, pp. 121–146.

Paugam, S. (2008). *Le lien Social*. Paris: PUF.

Paugam, S., Giorgetti, C., Gloukoviezof, G., Guerra, I., Laparra, M., Papadopoulos, D., Tucci I., and Vlase, I. (2014). *The Crisis and Its Impact on Unemployed People in Europe – Qualitative Survey in Seven EU Member States*. Luxembourg: Publications Office of the European Union.

Paugam, S. (2016). 'Social Bonds and Coping Strategies of Unemployed People in Europe'. *Italian Sociological Review*, 6(1): 27–55.

Pfau-Effinger, B. (2009). 'Varieties of Undeclared Work in European Societies'. *British Journal of Industrial Relations*, 47(1): 79–99.

Price, R. H., Friedland, D. S. and Vinokur, A. D. (1998). 'Job loss: Hard times and eroded identity'. In: J.H. Harvey (ed.). *Perspectives on Loss: A Sourcebook*. Philadelphia: Taylor & Francis, pp. 303-316.

Raveyre, M. (coord.) (2005). 'Introduction: Restructurations. Nouveaux Enjeux'. *La revue de l'IRES*, 47: 7–17.

Schnapper, D. (1981 [1994]). *L'épreuve du chômage*. Paris: Gallimard.

Sharone, O. (2013). 'Why Do Unemployed Americans Blame Themselves while Israelis Blame the System?' *Social Forces*, 91(4): 1429–1450.

Sixsmith, J. (1999). 'Working in the Hidden Economy: The Experience of Unemployed Men in the UK'. *Community, Work & Family*, 2(3): 257–277.

Trotzier, C. (2006). 'Le choc du licenciement: femmes et hommes dans la tourmente'. *Travail, Genre et Sociétés*, 16: 19–37.

Waters, L. and Moore, K. A. (2002). 'Reducing Latent Deprivation during Unemployment: The Role of Meaningful Leisure Activity'. *Journal of Occupational and Organizational Psychology*, 75: 15–32.

Yvon, F. and Clot, Y. (2001). 'Le travail en moins. Une approche psychologique de l'activité'. *Cités*, 8: 63–73.

8 Too poor to leave the nest?

The Greek family as a safety net for young adults before and during the crisis

Rebekka Christopoulou and Maria Pantalidou

1 Introduction

The Greek "great recession" has been widely documented as the most severe and prolonged recession in the advanced world during peacetime. Over 2009–2015, the Greek economy lost all growth since its Eurozone entry, with GDP per capita contracting to levels not seen since 1999 and unemployment rates climaxing at 27%. Not surprisingly, youths were among those affected particularly hard. Youth unemployment peaked at shocking rates in 2013, exceeding 58% among 15–24-year-olds, 43% among 25–29 year-olds, and 30% among 30–34 year-olds (Eurostat LFS-series). This disproportionate deterioration in labour market outcomes and the consequent economic distress put youths at an increased risk of depression and suicide (Drydakis 2015; Economou et al. 2013, 2016), while, among those who kept their sanity, many fled the country to look for work elsewhere, with the trend including mostly the high-skilled (see, for example, Ifanti et al. 2014 for the brain drain of young Greek doctors). The majority did remain, however, and managed to pull through even though there were hardly any public safety nets on which they could rely (Matsaganis 2013, 2015). In this chapter, we study the only safety net that has been consistently available to struggling youths both before and during the recent crisis: the Greek family. Our main research question is whether Greek families have increased their support to their young members during the crisis and, if so, to what degree and in what form. In investigating this question, we also provide evidence on the demographic, economic, and cultural factors that instigate intergenerational dependency.

The transition to adulthood for young Greeks has traditionally been slow and supported by the family to a great extent. Researchers have shown that Greece fits well into the standard South-North divide of European families. Youths in Southern Europe, on the one hand, continue to co-reside with their parents well beyond their adulthood, even in periods of rather favourable economic and labour market conditions. Those in Northern Europe, on the other hand, leave their parental home much earlier (see Iacovou 2002 for evidence from the mid-1990s). While families in Southern Europe also give young adults cash transfers, the predominant form of support they provide is in terms of housing, in contrast to Northern Europe, where the data shows the opposite pattern (Albertini et al. 2007 study cross-country differences in 2004; Isengard et al. 2017 do the same for 2015). This latter characteristic, however, is relatively muted in the case of Greece. In comparison to Italy and Spain, for example, the difference in prevalence of co-residence and intergenerational transfers in Greece is small. Thus, the Greek family can be seen as a special case of the South-European paradigm, supporting vulnerable youths by providing cash or shelter or both.

Focusing on living arrangements, Giuliano (2007) argued for – and empirically substantiated – a cultural interpretation for the observed cross-country patterns, whereby familial co-residence depends on social norms about family structure. Strong and close-knit family ties in South European countries yield higher intergenerational co-residence rates, whereas the emphasis on individualism and independence in countries of Northern Europe yields lower co-residence rates. Although this interpretation is broadly convincing, economic factors are also at play. A large empirical literature has demonstrated that young adults decide whether or not to leave their parental home based on rental prices (Börsch-Supan 1986, Ermisch 1999, Ermisch and Salvo 1997, Haurin et al. 1993, Rogers and Winkler 2014), their own labour outcomes and incomes as well as those of their parents (Becker et al. 2010, Chiuri and Del Boca 2010, Dettling and Hsu 2014, Engelhardt et al. 2016, Manacorda and Moretti 2006, McElroy 1985), and general economic cycles or labour market conditions (Bilter and Hoynes 2015, Card and Lemieux 2000, Lee and Painter 2013, Matsudaira 2016, Wiemers 2017). Economic factors are also highly responsible for the determination of intra-family financial transfers. Young adults are more likely to receive cash from their parents when their parents' income is high, their own income is low, or when they face borrowing constraints (Altonji et al. 1997, Cox 1990, Cox and Jappelli 1990, McGarry 2016, McGarry and Schoeni 1995, Rosenzweig and Wolpin 1994, Schoeni 1997; Zilcha 2003). However, some findings suggest that, all else equal, parents may give more generous transfers when their children's incomes are higher in exchange for receiving reciprocal support from them in old age or when in need (Cox 1987, Cox and Rank 1992).

The present chapter adds to this large literature by examining the unique perspective of the Greek experience. Given that Greek families have a long tradition of supporting young adult members, the tremendous variations in economic conditions before and during the great recession allows us to reassess the influence of economic factors relative to that of culture on intergenerational dependency. Specifically, we draw data from the Labour Force Survey (LFS) to create a panel of the 13 Greek regions and 15 years (from 2002, when the country entered the Eurozone, until 2016). We use this panel to test (i) the long-run relationship of the youth unemployment rate with the share of youths who live with their parents (which measures familial interdependence); (ii) the long-run relationship of the youth unemployment rate with the share of youths who live with their parents and receive intra-household monetary transfers (which measures youth dependence on parents); and (iii) whether there is a structural break in these two relationships related to the crisis. This exercise serves as a close counterpart to a different study, where we focus on the co-residence-employment relationship and test for structural breaks at a more disaggregated level of analysis, i.e., by using pooled cross-sections of the individual-level LFS data (Christopoulou and Pantalidou 2017).

To our knowledge, this is the first study that comprehensively examines the role of the family as a fallback mechanism for young Greeks and its dynamic evolution. An earlier paper by Karagiannaki (2011) provides an informative outlook on the living arrangements of individuals aged 65 and older before Greece's entry into the Eurozone. In comparison to the present research, however, its focus is rather narrow as it analyses only co-residence outcomes and only for those youths who live with elderly parents. Among the cross-country studies that include Greece, none tests for the cyclicality of familial support by exploiting temporal variation (e.g. Albertini et al. 2007; Isengard et al. 2017 rely on cross-country variation at a certain point in time). Finally, among other country-specific studies that do test for cyclicality effects, none finds a statistically significant change of intergenerational dependency during a recession period. Our study is also distinct in this regard.

The analysis reveals that before the crisis, the Greek families had been characterised by a two-way intergenerational dependency whereby the generation that had the means supported the generation in need. This dependency, however, has been strengthened further during the crisis and has turned asymmetrical, with young people mostly becoming the recipients rather than the providers of support. Thus, although a strong family safety net existed before the crisis, when labour market conditions became critically adverse, families responded cyclically, taking extra action to shield their young members from the impact of the crisis. Notably, families responded by providing housing only (instead of both housing and monetary transfers), which was most likely by necessity and not by choice, as the generalised economic hardship also affected older adults. Another interesting result is that the crisis induced families to protect young men more than young women, a result that illustrates the role of cultural norms. Unlike men, stereotypical young women co-reside with their parents and receive their financial support irrespective of the crisis, i.e., even when there are employment opportunities in the labour market that would enable them to live independently.

The chapter is structured as follows: section 2 gives a description of the data, presents descriptive statistics, and discusses the method of estimation; section 3 presents our results; and section 4 provides concluding remarks.

2 Empirical strategy

2.1 Data

As already mentioned, our analysis derives data from the Greek Labour Force Survey (LFS). We focus on individuals aged 18–35 to capture the extended transition to adulthood in Greece, though our results are robust to limiting the sample to ages 18–25 as per the standard statistical definition of the population of young adults. Taking the second quarter of the LFS as representative for each year, we use the mother ID, father ID, and spouse ID variables to identify those youths who co-reside with their parents or parents-in-law. We also use self-reports of income sources to identify those youths who receive cash transfers from other household members.[1] With this data, we calculate the share of youths who co-reside, and the share of youths who co-reside and receive transfers[2] for each of the 13 Greek regions in each year over 2002–2016. Likewise, for each region and year, we calculate the youth unemployment rate using self-reports of employment status. To give a sense of the temporal evolution of these variables, we plot the country-level means in Figure 8.1.

Over 2002–2008, youth unemployment (dashed line) was more or less stable at 10% for men and 20% for women, but as soon as the crisis began, these rates started growing exponentially. Youth unemployment peaked in 2013, reaching 35% for men and 44% for women, and fell somewhat thereafter.[3] Notably, the shares of young adults who co-reside with parents (solid line) and the share of youths who co-reside with parents and receive

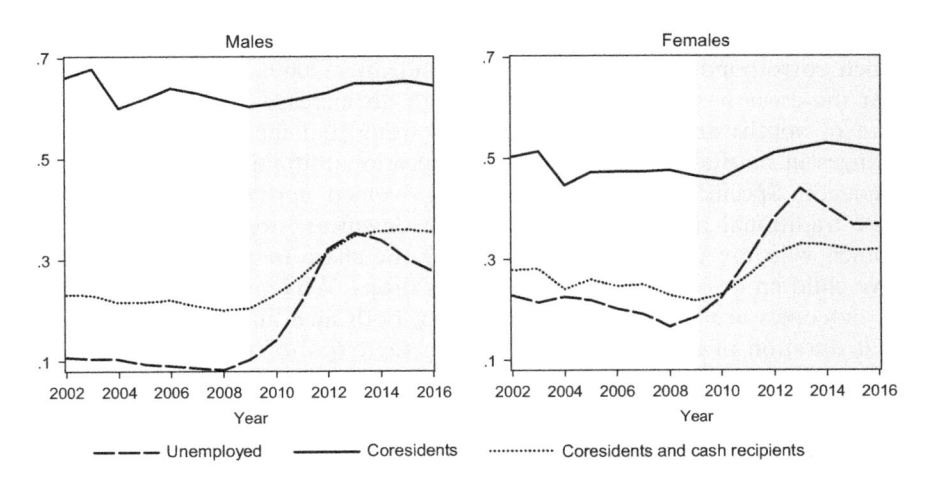

Figure 8.1 Youth unemployment rate and the share of youths who co-reside only or co-reside and receive intra-family transfers

intra-family transfers (dotted line) followed similar patterns, though temporal changes were less pronounced. Before the crisis, around 60% of young men and 47% of young women shared housing with parents, whereas during the crisis these shares showed a moderately upward trend followed by a faint downward trend. Likewise, before the crisis, around 21% of young men and 24% of young women lived with parents and received intrafamily cash transfers, but when the crisis hit, these shares jumped by 14 and 11 percentage points, respectively, and fell slightly thereafter. Over the entire period of study, the unemployment rate of young men (women) has a correlation of 0.306 (0.491) with the share of co-resident youths and 0.869 (0.755) with the share of financially dependent co-resident youths.

It is conceivable that this positive correlation can disappear once one controls for demographic factors, migration, housing prices, etc. To control for such factors in our regressions, we use the LFS data to create weighted averages for a range of characteristics of the youth population and of the population aged 40–60, which we treat as the parents' generation.[4] We complement this data with regional indicators from other sources, namely the growth rate of real GDP, net migration per capita, and two rental price indexes measuring the minimum and maximum rental cost in each region, i.e., the cost in the upmarket and down-market neighbourhoods, respectively. We draw data on GDP growth and net migration from the Eurostat, whereas the rental price indexes are our own calculations as there are no available indicators of housing or rental cost at the regional level for Greece. Several drawbacks of the regional indicators, including the fact that none is available for the entire period of interest, render them imperfect for the purpose of our study (for further details, see Christopoulou and Pantalidou 2017).

Table 8.1 presents summary statistics of the demographic trends for the young population in selected years. Specifically, we report statistics for 2009, the year that marked the beginning of the crisis, and for 2005 and 2013, which correspond to four years before and after 2009. The statistics show that the crisis has not only coincided with an increase in the interdependence of youths and parents regarding housing and income, but also with changes in marital outcomes, fertility, educational attainment, and place of residence. Specifically, after 2009, young women appear to abstain from their traditional role as homemakers: the downward trend in the share of women who are married accelerates, and the share of young women who have children or self-report as housewives drops. While no changes in marital outcomes are apparent for young men, both men and women increased their duration of studies and moved from the cities to rural areas after the crisis started.

2.2 Methods

The first step of our empirical analysis is to test whether the correlation of the youth unemployment rate and intergenerational dependency survives

Table 8.1 Weighted means and frequencies of selected variables

	Males			Females		
	2005	*2009*	*2013*	*2005*	*2009*	*2013*
Unemployed (rate)	0.09	0.10	0.35	0.22	0.19	0.44
Co-residents	0.62	0.60	0.65	0.47	0.47	0.52
Co-residents and cash recipients	0.22	0.21	0.35	0.26	0.22	0.33
Age	27.2	27.3	27.5	27.1	27.4	27.3
Married	0.25	0.21	0.18	0.43	0.40	0.35
Have child(ren)	0.16	0.14	0.13	0.33	0.33	0.28
Divorced/widowed	0.00	0.00	0.01	0.02	0.02	0.02
Housewives				0.16	0.15	0.10
Students	0.18	0.20	0.20	0.19	0.21	0.23
Completed education (years)	11.7	11.9	12.4	12.3	12.6	13.1
Residents in city	0.42	0.42	0.40	0.44	0.44	0.42
Residents in rural area	0.18	0.17	0.19	0.15	0.14	0.16
Income earners from assets	0.02	0.01	0.03	0.03	0.02	0.02
Income earners from benefits	0.01	0.01	0.02	0.02	0.03	0.03
Disabled	0.01	0.01	0.01	0.01	0.01	0.01

when we condition both on the observable control factors we mentioned earlier and on region-specific and year-specific unobservables. To do this, we estimate two-way fixed-effects panel-data models of the following form:

$$Y_{rt} = \beta_1 U_{rt} + \delta_1 X_{rt} + \varphi_r + \phi_t + \eta_{rt} \tag{1}$$

Here, Y_{rt} is a measure of intergenerational dependency (either the share of co-resident youths or the share of youths who co-reside and receive some income from other household members) in region r and year t; U is the youth unemployment rate; X is a vector that includes all other explanatory variables, i.e., the macro-level indicators and the characteristics and outcomes of youths and prime-age adults aged 40–60 (the population we treat as the parents' generation); φ_r represents the unobserved time-invariant region effect, ϕ_t is the region-specific year effect, and h_{rt} is the error term. In every case, we estimate (1) for men and women separately.

Our second step is to test whether the relationship between Y and U changes after the beginning of the crisis. To do this, we modify (1) in two equivalent ways:

$$Y_{rt} = \beta_2 U_{rt}{}^*(1 - Crisis) + \gamma_2 U_{rt}{}^* Crisis + \delta_2 X_{rt} + \varphi_r + \phi_t + \eta_{rt} \tag{2}$$

$$Y_{rt} = \beta_3 U_{rt} + \gamma_3 U_{rt}{}^* Crisis + \delta_3 X_{rt} + \varphi_r + \phi_t + \eta_{rt} \qquad (3)$$

Here, 1 is an all-ones vector and *Crisis* is a dummy variable that takes values zero in all years before 2009 and one in all other years (i.e., during the crisis). These two equations give the same information in slightly different forms. The coefficients β_2 and β_3 are equal and reflect the correlation of Y and U before the crisis; γ_2 gives the correlation of Y and U during the crisis; and γ_3 is the difference between β_2 and γ_2. All other coefficient estimates of the two equations are equal. Essentially, equation (2) tests the statistical significance of the correlation between Y and U separately in the pre-crisis and crisis periods, whereas equation (3) is an easy way to test the statistical significance of the difference in the correlation between Y and U between the two periods.

3 Results

3.1 Conditional correlations of intergenerational dependency and youth unemployment

We start with the estimation of equation (1) using the percentage of youths who share a home with their parents as the dependent variable. Table 8.2 reports the results from three alternative specifications estimated separately for men (columns 1–3) and women (columns 4–6). For each gender, the first specification includes only those control variables that we construct from the LFS data, and thus, the estimation sample covers the entire period of interest from 2002 to 2016. The second specification adds to the set of regressors the net migration per capita and the real GDP growth indicators, both of which are unavailable for 2016, and therefore, the sample size decreases from 195 to 182. Finally, the third specification includes the two rental cost indexes as additional control variables. These indexes are missing in all years before 2007, which causes the sample size to decrease further to 117 observations and to be dominated by the period of the crisis. Despite this loss of observations, the third specification is our preferred one because it is the most conservative and it maintains maximum precision.

Encouragingly, we find that the conditional correlation between youth co-residence and unemployment rate is robust irrespective of the specification we estimate. While the correlation is always positive and statistically significant for young men, for young women, it is statistically indistinguishable from zero, and gender differences are always significant. The estimated coefficient in the preferred specification for young men implies that for every increase in the youth unemployment rate by 1 percentage point, the share of co-resident youths increases by an average of 0.445 percentage points.

Table 8.2 Fixed effects regressions of the share of youths who live with parents

	Males			Females		
	(1)	*(2)*	*(3)*	*(4)*	*(5)*	*(6)*
Youth unempl. rate	0.303***	0.260***	0.455***	0.095	0.089	0.059
	(0.049)	(0.049)	(0.091)	(0.055)	(0.054)	(0.068)
Unempl. rate of parents generation	0.025	-0.073	-0.186	0.041	0.044	0.098
	(0.226)	(0.244)	(0.199)	(0.137)	(0.144)	(0.188)
Mean characteristics of youths						
Age	-0.004	-0.004	-0.028***	-0.014	-0.013	-0.020
	(0.006)	(0.007)	(0.007)	(0.012)	(0.014)	(0.014)
Study	-0.015	-0.058	-0.008	-0.615***	-0.535***	-0.699***
	(0.183)	(0.242)	(0.235)	(0.082)	(0.099)	(0.146)
Years of education	-0.009	-0.003	-0.009	-0.016**	-0.014**	-0.014
	(0.009)	(0.013)	(0.012)	(0.006)	(0.005)	(0.009)
Married/ Cohabitating	-0.749***	-0.714***	-0.573**	-0.764***	-0.697***	-0.811***
	(0.169)	(0.175)	(0.203)	(0.129)	(0.144)	(0.192)
Divorced/ Widowed	-0.568	-0.429	-0.716	-0.819**	-0.599*	-1.011*
	(0.473)	(0.527)	(0.596)	(0.296)	(0.327)	(0.494)
Have child(ren)	0.079	0.034	0.055	0.011	-0.079	0.107
	(0.252)	(0.227)	(0.257)	(0.103)	(0.116)	(0.105)
Metropolitan area	-0.128	-0.188	-0.249	-0.443*	-0.467	-0.542**
	(0.171)	(0.223)	(0.323)	(0.227)	(0.278)	(0.196)
Rural area	0.058	0.090	0.073	0.160***	0.212***	0.163*
	(0.045)	(0.054)	(0.099)	(0.031)	(0.018)	(0.088)
Income from assets	0.191	0.208	0.211	-0.311**	-0.422***	-0.382
	(0.221)	(0.240)	(0.462)	(0.121)	(0.094)	(0.285)
Income from benefits	0.018	-0.140	0.029	0.123	0.269**	0.378
	(0.234)	(0.320)	(0.339)	(0.111)	(0.106)	(0.226)
Housewives				-0.049	-0.025	0.015
				(0.055)	(0.052)	(0.092)
Disabled	0.793*	1.017**	1.039*	-0.333	-0.336	-1.170**
	(0.391)	(0.410)	(0.493)	(0.417)	(0.341)	(0.447)
Mean characteristics of parents generation						
Age	0.000	0.005	0.002	0.003	0.005	-0.026

(Continued)

Table 8.2 (Cont.)

	Males			Females		
	(1)	*(2)*	*(3)*	*(4)*	*(5)*	*(6)*
	(0.024)	(0.028)	(0.021)	(0.012)	(0.010)	(0.024)
Years of education	-0.026*	-0.022	-0.024*	-0.016*	-0.019	-0.019
	(0.013)	(0.016)	(0.011)	(0.009)	(0.011)	(0.014)
Married/ Cohabitating	0.246	0.236	0.163	0.052	0.163	0.379
	(0.326)	(0.386)	(0.329)	(0.118)	(0.122)	(0.232)
Divorced/ Widowed	-0.070	-0.101	-0.479	0.153	0.152	0.665
	(0.343)	(0.396)	(0.536)	(0.298)	(0.246)	(0.542)
Pensioner	-1.286***	-1.209***	-1.966***	-0.459*	-0.557**	-0.295
	(0.279)	(0.368)	(0.324)	(0.242)	(0.201)	(0.296)
Income from assets	-0.147	-0.185	-0.270	0.035	0.020	-0.050
	(0.158)	(0.165)	(0.246)	(0.075)	(0.067)	(0.115)
Income from benefits	-0.602	-0.410	-0.855	-0.071	-0.023	0.330
	(0.481)	(0.430)	(0.736)	(0.230)	(0.317)	(0.542)
Disabled	0.710	0.908*	1.234***	-0.252	-0.211	-0.351
	(0.497)	(0.474)	(0.364)	(0.371)	(0.346)	(0.412)
Net migration per capita		-1.439	-2.821		-2.673***	-1.454
		(2.107)	(3.221)		(0.661)	(2.668)
Growth rate of real GDP		-0.144*	-0.176		-0.013	-0.124
		(0.067)	(0.105)		(0.048)	(0.104)
Minimum rental cost index			0.735***			-0.030
			(0.231)			(0.194)
Maximum rental cost index			0.030			0.048**
			(0.026)			(0.021)
Constant	1.101	0.752	1.525	1.511**	1.259**	2.723**
	(1.051)	(1.381)	(1.256)	(0.610)	(0.473)	(0.913)
Observations	195	182	117	195	182	117
R-squared adjusted	0.623	0.611	0.705	0.792	0.807	0.830

Notes: Robust standard errors in parentheses. ***p<0.01, **p<0.05, *p<0.1. Controls: region & year dummies.

For all other explanatory variables, the results show slight differences across specifications, but virtually all statistically significant coefficients are plausible. Focusing on the preferred specification, we find that for men, co-residence decreases with the mean age of the youth population; the share of youths who are married; the share of pensioners; and the mean years of education in the parents' generation. In contrast, co-residence among young men increases with the share of the disabled both in the youth population and in the parent's generation, and with the rental cost in the downmarket neighbourhoods. For women, co-residence decreases with the share of youths who live in urban areas and the share of youths who are married, divorced, or enrolled in education and increases with the share of youths who live in rural areas and with the rental cost in the upmarket neighbourhoods. A somewhat puzzling result, which goes contrary to what we find for men, is that disability and co-residence rates for women are negatively associated; i.e. in years and regions where the share of disabled young women is higher, the share of young women who live with their parents is lower.

The differences in the results between men and women point to factors that may influence intergenerational co-residence, which we have not addressed effectively. To start with, co-residence may be unresponsive to youth unemployment because it is simply determined by cultural norms, which may well be gender-specific. The result of co-residence among young women being lower in years and in regions with more rural residents or less urban residents is consistent with this explanation. Rural societies are typically more traditional, and young women who live in such societies are under stricter parental supervision and may not be allowed to live independently.[5] Also consistent with this explanation is the result that co-residence among young males decreases with the rental cost in the downmarket neighbourhoods, whereas co-residence among young women decreases with the cost in the upscale neighbourhoods. Assuming that the cheaper neighbourhoods are relatively unsafe, young women who adhere to cultural gender stereotypes will arguably avoid living there.

Moreover, co-residence may be driven by the dependency of parents on their children rather than the reverse – a fact that could also be culture-related and gender-specific. In the regressions of Table 8.2, we have tried to address reverse causality by controlling for the unemployment rate of the parents' generation, which is statistically insignificant in all cases, and a range of other characteristics of that generation. It is reasonable, however, that the mismatch between the actual parents and the parents' generation imposed by the data limitations render these controls inadequate. Limiting the estimation sample to those young people who live with their parents and receive intra-family cash transfers is one way to circumvent this problem. These youths are plausibly the (net) beneficiaries rather than the (net) benefactors of the co-residence arrangement and, therefore, their population share can be treated as a measure of youth dependency on their parents as opposed to the share of co-resident youths, which captures both directions of intergenerational dependency.

We present the corresponding estimation results in Table 8.3. That is, we estimate equation (1) using the percentage of youths who share a home with their parents and receive intra-family transfers as the dependent variable and report the same specifications as in Table 8.2 and in the same order. Again, the conditional correlations of interest are robust across specifications, but this time, they are positive and statistically significant for both men and women, though magnitudes differ significantly between genders. The preferred specification suggests that for every increase in the unemployment rate of young men by 1 percentage point, the share of young men who depend on parents for both housing and income increases by an average of 0.509 percentage points, whereas the corresponding increase for young women is only 0.250 percentage points.

The results of Table 8.3 allow us to gain insight into the influence of both reverse causality and unobserved cultural factors on the relationship of interest. First, the fact that the estimated conditional correlations between youth dependency and unemployment for young men are of similar magnitude as those reported in Table 8.2 suggests that reverse causality is not an important issue. In contrast, for women, the correlation is statistically insignificant in Table 8.2 and significantly positive in Table 8.3, which suggests that reverse causality plays a role. Excluding young women who may co-reside with parents to provide, rather than receive, support from the estimation sample causes the conditional correlation to increase. It follows that for the excluded sample, the relationship between unemployment and co-residence is negative; i.e., young women are more likely to co-reside with dependent parents when youth labour market conditions are favourable and vice versa. This plausibly reflects that when labour market conditions are favourable, young women can find work and earn income with which they can support parents in need.

Second, our finding that reverse causality is relevant only in the case of women illuminates the role of culture in intergenerational dependency. It suggests that it is mostly women, not men, who act as carers for vulnerable parents – a gender-role that is consistent with the paradigm of South European familism, according to which "most of the caring needs of individuals – children, infirm older and disabled persons, but also healthy adult men – are defined as best served by the caring of wives, mothers, and/or daughters" (Saraceno 1994: 60), but it is also prevalent in countries outside Southern Europe (see, for example, Mellor 2001 for evidence from the US). Even after we address reverse causality, gender differences in the conditional correlations persist, suggesting that young women's dependency on parents is less responsive to labour market conditions than that of young men. Considering our lack of suitable controls for cultural norms, this result is also consistent with a cultural interpretation: young women

Table 8.3 Fixed effects regressions of the share of youths who co-reside and receive intra-family transfers

	Males			Females		
	(1)	*(2)*	*(3)*	*(4)*	*(5)*	*(6)*
Youth unempl. rate	0.534***	0.476***	0.509***	0.281***	0.257***	0.250**
	(0.092)	(0.076)	(0.074)	(0.079)	(0.066)	(0.086)
Unempl. rate of parents generation	-0.256	-0.374*	-0.357*	-0.111	-0.168	-0.121
	(0.153)	(0.186)	(0.174)	(0.150)	(0.123)	(0.175)
Mean characteristics of youths						
Age	-0.023**	-0.034***	-0.032**	-0.017	-0.020	-0.020
	(0.009)	(0.010)	(0.014)	(0.015)	(0.016)	(0.019)
Study	0.110	-0.013	-0.048	-0.230	-0.199	-0.208
	(0.159)	(0.197)	(0.232)	(0.164)	(0.179)	(0.175)
Years of education	0.013	0.017	0.023	-0.019**	-0.017*	-0.024**
	(0.009)	(0.011)	(0.017)	(0.008)	(0.009)	(0.008)
Married/ Cohabitating	-0.005	-0.001	0.181	-0.339***	-0.267**	-0.272
	(0.164)	(0.153)	(0.170)	(0.102)	(0.102)	(0.189)
Divorced/ Widowed	0.918**	0.968*	0.764	-0.408	-0.249	-0.368
	(0.400)	(0.496)	(0.463)	(0.231)	(0.273)	(0.437)
Have child(ren)	-0.002	0.033	-0.231	-0.026	-0.120	-0.108
	(0.148)	(0.120)	(0.147)	(0.127)	(0.109)	(0.126)
Metropolitan area	0.078	-0.236	-0.204	-0.168	-0.057	-0.095
	(0.127)	(0.144)	(0.210)	(0.105)	(0.067)	(0.191)
Rural area	0.028	0.005	-0.119	0.012	0.095*	0.062
	(0.069)	(0.071)	(0.111)	(0.049)	(0.044)	(0.064)
Income from assets	-0.271	-0.072	-0.076	-0.124	-0.276*	-0.168
	(0.178)	(0.137)	(0.298)	(0.162)	(0.142)	(0.300)
Income from benefits	0.155	0.104	-0.124	0.377**	0.543***	0.565***
	(0.199)	(0.278)	(0.384)	(0.140)	(0.145)	(0.170)
Housewife				0.074	0.109	0.171
				(0.076)	(0.074)	(0.120)
Disabled	0.978**	0.968**	1.209***	-1.361***	-1.598***	-2.608***
	(0.439)	(0.410)	(0.303)	(0.435)	(0.300)	(0.562)
Mean characteristics of parents generation						
Age	0.009	0.002	0.018	-0.020	-0.014	-0.021

(Continued)

Table 8.3 (Cont.)

	Males			Females		
	(1)	*(2)*	*(3)*	*(4)*	*(5)*	*(6)*
	(0.016)	(0.021)	(0.022)	(0.016)	(0.014)	(0.020)
Years of education	-0.009	-0.007	-0.024	0.001	-0.002	-0.006
	(0.011)	(0.014)	(0.018)	(0.012)	(0.011)	(0.011)
Married/ Cohabitating	0.184	0.111	-0.030	-0.050	0.082	0.233
	(0.281)	(0.322)	(0.351)	(0.209)	(0.213)	(0.342)
Divorced/ Widowed	0.198	0.334	-0.220	0.537	0.394	1.014*
	(0.437)	(0.461)	(0.543)	(0.475)	(0.459)	(0.536)
Pensioner	-0.905***	-0.577	-0.835	-0.711**	-0.984***	-1.088**
	(0.212)	(0.331)	(0.513)	(0.318)	(0.265)	(0.367)
Income from assets	0.419**	0.382**	0.420	0.139	0.146	0.180
	(0.157)	(0.160)	(0.243)	(0.132)	(0.116)	(0.160)
Income from benefits	-0.700	-0.879	-0.683	-1.364**	-1.118**	-0.474
	(0.552)	(0.525)	(0.846)	(0.454)	(0.477)	(0.645)
Disabled	0.083	0.042	-0.261	-0.240	-0.293	-0.776
	(0.304)	(0.299)	(0.477)	(0.386)	(0.369)	(0.588)
Net migration per capita		0.441	-0.138		-3.128***	-4.141**
		(1.421)	(2.368)		(0.977)	(1.500)
Growth rate of real GDP		-0.038	-0.132		-0.110	-0.267***
		(0.106)	(0.109)		(0.064)	(0.081)
Minimum rental cost index			0.474			0.004
			(0.322)			(0.272)
Maximum rental cost index			0.014			0.022
			(0.027)			(0.029)
Constant	0.057	0.776	0.060	2.127**	1.798*	2.075**
	(0.902)	(1.257)	(1.399)	(0.896)	(0.899)	(0.924)
Observations	195	182	117	195	182	117
R-squared adjusted	0.867	0.859	0.893	0.758	0.772	0.803

Notes: Robust standard errors in parentheses. ***p<0.01, **p<0.05, *p<0.1. Controls: region and year dummies.

may live with and off their parents irrespective of the available employment opportunities simply because they are culturally bound to do so (see also Christopoulou and Pantalidou 2017).

Only a few of the remaining explanatory variables in Table 8.3 are statistically significant, especially when one looks at the preferred specification. Interestingly, the share of young men who depend on parents for both housing and income has a significant association with the unemployment rate in the parents' generation and in the expected direction. The more adverse the labour market conditions for the parents' generation, the lower the share of dependent young men. Dependency of young men also decreases with the average age in the youth population and increases with the share of disabled youths. Contrary to men, whether young women rely on parents for housing and income is unrelated to the unemployment rate in the parents' generation. The share of dependent young women increases with the share of young women who receive income from benefits and with the share of divorced or widowed individuals in the parents' generation, and it decreases with youth educational attainment, the share of pensioners in the parent's generation, net migration per capita, and the growth rate of real GDP. The odd result that dependency among young women decreases as the share of disabled young women increases, which we observed in Table 8.2, is also present here. We are inclined to interpret this result as a spurious correlation caused by a confounding variable that is not immediately evident, searching for which is beyond the scope of this analysis.

3.2 Changes in the dependency-unemployment correlations related to the crisis

Next, we test whether and to what degree the conditional correlations between dependency and unemployment change after the beginning of the economic crisis. In Table 8.4, we report estimates of equations (2) and (3) using both the share of co-resident youths (panel A) and the share of financially dependent co-resident youths (panel B) as the dependent variable. These estimates result from specifications that control for all available characteristics of youths, all available characteristics of the parent's generation, net migration, and GDP growth (i.e., they correspond to the specifications reported in columns [2] and [5] in Tables 8.2 and 8.3). The reason we choose this specification is that it is the most conservative among those that leave a large enough sample to allow a viable test (this concerns the pre-crisis sample particularly). As previously, we estimate regressions for young men and women separately.

Our results reveal that the statistically significant co-residence-unemployment correlation that we found for men in Table 8.2 is driven by the period of the crisis, whereas the statistically insignificant correlation we found for women is driven by the period before the crisis. More precisely, before the

Table 8.4 Testing for a crisis effect

Fixed-effects regressions of % of co-residents and transfer recipients, aged 18–35, 2002–2015

		Males		*Females*	
		A. Share of youths who co-reside			
Youth unemployment rate					
	Pre-crisis	-0.109	-0.109	0.019	0.019
		(0.145)	(0.145)	(0.065)	(0.065)
	Crisis	0.402***		0.134**	
		(0.080)		(0.050)	
	Difference		0.511**		0.115**
			(0.199)		(0.040)
Observations		182	182	182	182
R-squared adjusted		0.643	0.643	0.811	0.811
		B. Share of youths who co-reside and receive intra-family transfers			
Youth unemployment rate					
	Pre-crisis	0.501***	0.501***	0.258***	0.258***
		(0.141)	(0.141)	(0.068)	(0.068)
	Crisis	0.466***		0.256***	
		(0.072)		(0.075)	
	Difference		-0.035		-0.001
			(0.135)		(0.058)
Observations		182	182	182	182
R-squared adjusted		0.859	0.859	0.771	0.771

Notes: Controls: as in columns (2) and (5) in Table (2) and (3). Robust standard errors in parentheses, ***p<0.01, **p<0.05, *p<0.1.

crisis, youth unemployment is statistically unrelated with the share of co-resident youths, and this holds for both men and women. During the crisis, the correlation becomes statistically significant for both genders – though, once again, it is much higher for men than for women, reminding us about the pertinence of culture and reverse causality. The difference in the correlations between periods is also statistically significant for both genders. The implication is that the crisis has caused the intergenerational dependency in the Greek families to strengthen; i.e., it has led to an increase in the share of youths who co-reside with their parents because they cannot afford to live independently. We note that it is possible that there is a small pre-crisis correlation between co-residence and unemployment that is not picked up by the data due to their aggregate nature and the short time-span of the sub-periods. Regardless, the main message remains: the beginning of the crisis coincides with a structural break that leaves more vulnerable young Greeks sharing housing with parents. This finding is unique in the empirical literature to our knowledge and stems from the severity of the Greek recession and the shortage of alternative safety nets for young Greeks. For example, Bilter and Hoynes (2015) carried out the same test for structural breaks using data from the United States over 1981–2014; i.e., their sample included both the recessions of the 1980s and the recent "great" recession, but none of their structural-break hypotheses were supported by their results.

Interestingly, our result does not survive when we limit the sample to those young co-residents who receive some income from other family members. The conditional correlations between youth unemployment and the share of youths who live with and off their parents are statistically significant both before and during the crisis and statistically equal when comparing the two periods. This result has two important implications. First, it implies that the exceptionally adverse labour market conditions for young adults brought about by the crisis caused more Greek families to provide housing for their young adult members, but it did not cause more Greek families to provide both housing and income. The economic hardship induced by the crisis, however, was so generalised that this does not come as a surprise. Adults of all ages saw significant cuts in their wages (Christopoulou and Monastiriotis 2014, 2016) and older individuals saw cuts in pensions and increases in the retirement age (Leventi and Matsaganis 2016). Therefore, financially supporting their young members was not an option for most Greek families.

The second implication is that reverse causality for young men, which could not be detected before breaking the sample into sub-periods, is evidently present before the crisis. Excluding those who do not receive cash transfers from the sample of co-resident youths (i.e., those who potentially co-reside in order to support vulnerable parents) causes the pre-crisis correlation to increase for both men and women, whereas during the crisis, this happens for women only. Thus, reverse causality is relevant for both genders before the crisis, but during the crisis, it disappears completely for men and weakens for women. To put it in simpler terms, the intergenerational dependency before the Greek crisis ran in both directions; i.e., better-off youths would support parents in need and better-off parents would support youths in need. However, after the crisis started, the intergenerational dependency for men became one-directional, with youths being on the receiving end of support, whereas for women, it remained two-directional but also skewed towards youths. This result is clearly symptomatic of the disproportionate economic distress imposed upon the younger relative to the older generations during the crisis.

4 Conclusion

Despite the extremely adverse conditions in the youth labour market during the Greek crisis, the youth population held out better than one would expect. In this chapter, we examined whether and to what degree this became possible due to intra-familial support, given that the Greek family has traditionally operated as the primary safety net available to vulnerable youths. To carry out our analysis, we estimated correlations of youth unemployment with two main variables: the share of young people who co-reside with their parents, as a proxy of two-way intergenerational dependence, and the share of young people who co-reside with their parents and receive intra-familial transfers, as a proxy of one-way dependence (of youths on their parents).

Our results showed that the influence of youth unemployment on co-residence is virtually non-existent before the crisis and positive and significant thereafter. In contrast, youth unemployment and the share of financially dependent co-resident youths have a positive and significant correlation throughout the period of study, and there is no change in this correlation after the beginning of the crisis. In both cases, the correlations are higher for men relative to women and are conditional on a range of characteristics of young people and their parents' generation and on several other regional indicators that capture developments outside the labour market.

These results have a number of important implications. They confirm that familial interdependence was the norm in Greece well before the crisis, but they also show that the crisis worked to reinforce this interdependence and altered its nature. Before the crisis, financially comfortable youths would support vulnerable parents, and financially comfortable parents would support vulnerable youths. During the crisis, youths became mostly beneficiaries and parents became mostly benefactors. In fact, to protect their adult children from the impact of the crisis, parents responded by providing housing and not by providing both housing and income, which is telling of their own financial difficulties. Interestingly, parents "rescued" more young men than women, but this was likely because young women were already safely protected in the parental nest, adhering to their traditional gender role.

Appendix

Table 8A.1 Region-specific fixed effects from the regressions presented in Table 8.2

	(1)	(2)	(3)	(4)	(5)	(6)
Central Macedonia	0.155	0.193	0.269*	0.352***	0.370***	0.345***
	(0.121)	(0.150)	(0.160)	(0.105)	(0.114)	(0.125)
Western Macedonia	0.058**	0.056*	0.156***	0.054***	0.038**	0.068**
	(0.027)	(0.029)	(0.051)	(0.017)	(0.018)	(0.030)
Epirus	0.061**	0.056*	0.186***	0.007	0.000	0.030
	(0.030)	(0.032)	(0.055)	(0.017)	(0.018)	(0.033)
Thessaly	0.099***	0.097***	0.117***	0.070***	0.072***	0.072***
	(0.028)	(0.031)	(0.030)	(0.014)	(0.016)	(0.023)
Ionian Islands	0.018	0.015	-0.265**	-0.040*	-0.052**	-0.020
	(0.040)	(0.042)	(0.103)	(0.023)	(0.024)	(0.085)
Western Greece	0.039	0.036	-0.232**	0.047***	0.036**	0.067
	(0.026)	(0.028)	(0.099)	(0.017)	(0.018)	(0.085)
Central Greece	0.064**	0.061*	0.130***	0.012	0.020	0.013
	(0.029)	(0.032)	(0.036)	(0.015)	(0.015)	(0.026)
Attica	0.243	0.287	0.366	0.534***	0.564***	0.448**
	(0.189)	(0.235)	(0.250)	(0.157)	(0.171)	(0.194)
Peloponnese	0.112***	0.109***	0.040	0.043***	0.049***	0.035
	(0.033)	(0.037)	(0.052)	(0.015)	(0.015)	(0.041)
North Aegean	0.031	0.018	-0.041	-0.022	-0.024	-0.010
	(0.030)	(0.034)	(0.048)	(0.016)	(0.018)	(0.046)
South Aegean	0.051**	0.050*	0.155***	-0.009	-0.011	-0.088**
	(0.024)	(0.028)	(0.043)	(0.015)	(0.016)	(0.040)
Crete	0.041*	0.043	0.128***	-0.005	0.001	-0.010
	(0.024)	(0.026)	(0.040)	(0.014)	(0.013)	(0.029)

Note: reference category is Eastern Macedonia and Thrace.

Table 8A.2 Region-specific fixed effects from the regressions presented in Table 8.3

	(1)	(2)	(3)	(4)	(5)	(6)
Central Macedonia	0.023	0.197*	0.204	0.137	0.082	0.068
	(0.103)	(0.108)	(0.141)	(0.098)	(0.100)	(0.140)
Western Macedonia	0.043**	0.049**	0.107**	0.062***	0.043**	0.061*
	(0.021)	(0.023)	(0.045)	(0.017)	(0.020)	(0.035)

(Continued)

Table 8A.2 (Cont.)

	(1)	(2)	(3)	(4)	(5)	(6)
Epirus	0.060***	0.060**	0.125**	0.029*	0.015	0.029
	(0.021)	(0.024)	(0.048)	(0.016)	(0.021)	(0.043)
Thessaly	0.039**	0.031	0.035	0.039***	0.037**	0.040
	(0.018)	(0.023)	(0.029)	(0.014)	(0.015)	(0.027)
Ionian Islands	0.016	0.018	-0.141	-0.043	-0.070**	-0.059
	(0.031)	(0.032)	(0.125)	(0.029)	(0.028)	(0.108)
Western Greece	0.024	0.029	-0.152	0.029	0.016	0.015
	(0.020)	(0.024)	(0.119)	(0.019)	(0.020)	(0.109)
Central Greece	0.053**	0.043*	0.065*	0.015	0.016	0.029
	(0.023)	(0.025)	(0.033)	(0.015)	(0.015)	(0.028)
Attica	0.019	0.276	0.265	0.178	0.101	0.047
	(0.160)	(0.170)	(0.239)	(0.149)	(0.152)	(0.218)
Peloponnese	0.053**	0.045	-0.000	0.017	0.011	0.017
	(0.026)	(0.029)	(0.060)	(0.019)	(0.018)	(0.050)
North Aegean	0.012	0.010	-0.062	0.003	-0.013	-0.005
	(0.020)	(0.026)	(0.060)	(0.021)	(0.023)	(0.056)
South Aegean	0.018	0.015	0.058	-0.016	-0.024	-0.053
	(0.019)	(0.022)	(0.043)	(0.019)	(0.019)	(0.045)
Crete	0.006	-0.004	0.049	-0.016	-0.016	-0.029
	(0.018)	(0.020)	(0.037)	(0.016)	(0.016)	(0.036)

Note: reference category is Anatoliki Makedonia and Thraki.

Notes

1 This variable refers to income from other household members and not specifically from parents because the LFS data does not allow us to identify who exactly is the donor of the cash transfer. This is somewhat problematic for our analysis, as we cannot tell apart married youths who live with their parents but share financial resources with their spouses from married youths who rely on their parents for both cash and shelter.

2 The LFS data does not allow us to identify youths who receive cash transfers from their parents when they live independently.

3 This "super-cyclicality" of youth unemployment is consistent with a general consensus in the literature that labouor demand for young workers is more responsive to macroeconomic developments compared to labor demand for prime-age adults (e.g. Blanchflower and Freeman 2000; Choudhry et al. 2012; Christopoulou 2008, 2013; Christopoulou and Ryan 2008).

4 We cannot control for mean characteristics of the actual parents because in the LFS data, we observe only those parents who co-reside with their children and not those whose children have left the household. Unavoidably, when controlling forregional means of characteristics of the parents' generation, we assume that youths and parents live in the same region. For those youths who, at the time of survey, lived in a region different from their parents, we incorrectly control forthe

characteristics of the generation of parents who live in that same region. This weakens the explanatory power of these controls.

5 It is also common to interpret the region-specific fixed-effects as reflecting cultural differences because culture is presumed to change slowly over time. However, in our results, this reasoning proves too simplistic. In Tables 8A.1 and 8A.2 in the Appendix, we report estimates of the region-specific effects that correspond to the regressions of Tables 8.2 and 8.3, respectively. The results are mixed for both men and women, and it is not straightforward to link either the regional differences for each gender or the resulting gender differences within each region to corresponding differences in cultural norms (e.g. there is no clear divide in the results between touristic and non-touristic regions or between regions with large cities, such as Athens and Thessaloniki, and regions with smaller towns).

References

Albertini, M., Kohli, M., and Vogel, C. (2007). 'Intergenerational Transfers of Time and Money in European Families: Common Patterns – Different Regimes?' *Journal of European Social Policy*, 17(4): 319–334.

Altonji, J. G., Hayashi, F., and Kotlikoff, L. (1997). 'Parental Altruism and Inter Vivos Transfers: Theory and Evidence'. *Journal of Political Economy*, 105(6): 1121–1166.

Becker, S. O., Bentolila, S., Fernandes, A., and Ichino, A. (2010). 'Youth Emancipation and Perceived Job Insecurity of Parents and Children'. *Journal of Population Economics*, 23(3): 1047–1071.

Bilter, M. and Hoynes, H. (2015). 'Living Arrangements, Doubling Up, and the Great Recession: Was this Time Different?' *American Economic Review: Papers & Proceedings*, 105(5): 166–170.

Blanchflower, D. G. and Freeman, R. B. (2000). 'The Declining Economic Status of Young Workers in OECD Countries'. In: D. Blanchflower and R. Freeman (eds.). *Youth Employment and Joblessness in Advanced Countries.* Chicago, IL: University of Chicago Press, 19–59.

Börsch-Supan, A. (1986). 'Household Formation, Housing Prices, and Public Policy Impacts'. *Journal of Public Economics*, 30: 145–164.

Card, D. and Lemieux, T. (2000). 'Adapting to Circumstances: The Evolution of Work, School, and Living Arrangements among North American Youth'. In: D. Blanchflower and R. Freeman (eds.). *Youth Employment and Joblessness in Advanced Countries.* Chicago, IL: University of Chicago Press, 171–214.

Chiuri, M. and Del Boca, D. (2010). 'Home-Leaving Decisions of Daughters and Sons'. *Review of Economics of the Household*, 8(3): 393–408.

Choudhry, M. T., Marelli, E., and Signorelli, M. (2012). 'Youth Unemployment Rate and Impact of Financial Crises'. *International Journal of Manpower*, 33(1): 76–95.

Christopoulou, R. (2008). 'The Youth Labor Market Problem in Cross-Country Perspective'. In: G. DeFreitas (ed.). *Young Workers in the Global Economy: Job Challenges in North America, Europe and Japan.* Cheltenham, UK: Edward Elgar, 21–58.

Christopoulou, R. (2013). 'Why Have Labor Market Outcomes of Youth in Advanced Economies Deteriorated?' *The B.E. Journal of Economic Analysis & Policy, De Gruyter*, 13(1): 203–238.

Christopoulou, R. and Monastiriotis, V. (2014). 'The Greek Public Sector Wage Premium before the Crisis: Size, Selection and Relative Valuation of Characteristics'. *British Journal of Industrial Relations*, 52(3): 579–602.

Christopoulou, R. and Monastiriotis, V. (2016). 'Public-Private Wage Duality during the Greek Crisis'. *Oxford Economic Papers*, 68(1): 174–196.

Christopoulou, R. and Pantalidou, M. (2017) 'The Parental Home as Labor Market Insurance for Young Greeks during the Crisis'. *GLO Discussion Paper Series* 158. Global Labor Organization (GLO).

Christopoulou, R. and Ryan, P. (2008). 'Youth Outcomes in the Labor Markets of Advanced Economies Decline, Deterioration, and Causes'. In: I. Schoon and R. K. Silbereisen (eds.). *Transitions from School to Work*. London: Cambridge University Press, 67–94.

Cox, D. (1987). 'Motives for Private Income Transfers'. *Journal of Political Economy*, 95(3): 508–546.

Cox, D. (1990). 'Intergenerational Transfers and Liquidity Constraints'. *The Quarterly Journal of Economics*, 105(1): 187–217.

Cox, D. and Jappelli, T. (1990). 'Credit Rationing and Private Transfers: Evidence from Survey Data'. *The Review of Economics and Statistics*, 72(3): 445–454.

Cox, D. and Rank, M. R. (1992). 'Inter-Vivos Transfers and Intergenerational Exchange'. *The Review of Economics and Statistics*, 74(2): 305–314.

Dettling, L. and Hsu, J. (2014). 'Returning to the Nest: Debt and Parental Co-Residence among Young Adults'. Federal Reserve Board. Working paper 80.

Drydakis, N. (2015). 'The Effect of Unemployment on Self-Reported Health and Mental Health in Greece from 2008 to 2013: A Longitudinal Study before and during the Financial Crisis'. *Social Science & Medicine*, 128: 43–51.

Economou, M., Angelopoulos, E., Peppou, L. E., Souliotis, K., and Stefanis, C. (2016). 'Suicidal Ideation and Suicide Attempts in Greece during the Economic Crisis: An Update'. *World Psychiatry*, 15(1): 83–84.

Economou, M., Madianos, M., Peppou, L. E., Patelakis, A., and Stefanis, C. N. (2013). 'Major Depression in the Era of Economic Crisis: A Replication of A Cross-Sectional Study across Greece'. *Journal of Affective Disorders*, 145(3): 308–314.

Engelhardt, G. V., Eriksen, M. D., and Greenhalgh-Stanley, N. (2016). 'The Impact of Employment on Parental Co-residence'. *Real Estate Economics*. doi:10.1111/1540-6229.12152.

Ermisch, J. and Salvo, P. D. (1997). 'The Economic Determinants of Young People's Household Formation'. *Economica*, 64(256): 627–644.

Ermisch, J. F. (1999). 'Prices, Parents, and Young People's Household Formation'. *Journal of Urban Economics*, 45(1): 47–71.

Giuliano, P. (2007). 'Living Arrangements in Western Europe: Does Cultural Origin Matter?' *Journal of the European Economic Association*, 5(5): 927–952.

Haurin, D., Hendershott, P., and Kim, D. (1993). 'The Impact of Real Rents and Wages on Household Formation'. *Review of Economics and Statistics*, 75: 284–293.

Iacovou, M. (2002). 'Regional Differences in the Transition to Adulthood'. *Annals of the American Academy of Political and Social Science*, 580: 40–69.

Ifanti, A. A., Argyriou, A. A., Kalofonou, F. H., and Kalofonos, H. P. (2014). 'Physicians' Brain-Drain in Greece: A Perspective on the Reasons Why and How to Address It'. *Health Policy*, 117(2): 210–215.

Isengard, B., König, R., and Szydlik, M. (2017). 'Money or Space? Intergenerational Transfers in a Comparative Perspective'. *Housing Studies*. doi:10.1080/02673037.2017.1365823.

Karagiannaki, E. (2011) 'Changes in the Living Arrangements of Elderly People in Greece: 1974–1999'. *Population Research and Policy Review*, 30(2): 263–285.

Lee, K. and Painter, G. (2013). 'What Happens to Household Formation in a Recession?'. *Journal of Urban Economics*, 76: 93–109.

Leventi, C. and Matsaganis, M. (2016) 'Disentangling Annuities and Transfers in Pension Benefits: Evidence from Greece'. 15th Conference on Research on Economic Theory and Econometrics Tinos.

Manacorda, M. and Moretti, E. (2006). 'Why Do Most Italian Youths Live with Their Parents? Intergenerational Transfers and Household Structure'. *Journal of the Euro-Pean Economic Association*, 4(4): 800–829.

Matsaganis, M. (2013). *The Greek Crisis: Social Impact and Policy Responses*. Berlin: Friedrich-Ebert-Stiftung.

Matsaganis, M. (2015). 'Youth Unemployment and the Great Recession in Greece'. In: J. J. Dolado (ed.). *No Country for Young People? Youth Labor Market Problems in Europe*. London: Centre for Economic Policy Research, 77–87.

Matsudaira, J. (2016). 'Economic Conditions and the Living Arrangements of Young Adults: 1960 to 2011'. *Journal of Population Economics*, 29(1): 167–195.

McElroy, M. B. (1985). 'The Joint Determination of Household Membership and Market Work: The Case of Young Men'. *Journal of Labor Economics*, 3(3): 293–316.

McGarry, K. (2016). 'Dynamic Aspects of Family Transfers'. *Journal of Public Economics*, 137: 1–13.

McGarry, K. and Schoeni, R. F. (1995). 'Transfer Behavior in the Health and Retirement Study: Measurement and the Redistribution of Resources within the Family'. *The Journal of Human Resources, Special Issue on the Health and Retirement Study: Data Quality and Early Results*, 30: S184–S226.

Mellor, J. (2001). 'Long-Term Care and Nursing Home Coverage: Are Adult Children Substitutes for Insurance Policies?' *Journal of Health Economics*, 20(4): 527–547.

Rogers, W. H. and Winkler, A. E. (2014) 'How Did the Housing and Labor Market Crises Affect Young Adults' Living Arrangements?' Institute for the Study of Labor. Discussion paper 8568.

Rosenzweig, M. and Wolpin, K. (1994). 'Parental and Public Transfers to Young Women and Their Children'. *The American Economic Review*, 84: 1195–1212.

Saraceno, C. (1994). 'The Ambivalent Familism of the Italian Welfare State'. *Social Politics: International Studies in Gender, State & Society*, 1(1): 60–82.

Schoeni, R. F. (1997). 'Private Interhousehold Transfers of Money and Time: New Empirical Evidence'. *Review of Income and Wealth*, 43(4): 423–448.

Wiemers, E. E. (2017). 'The Celtic Tiger and Home Leaving among Irish Young Adults'. *Review of Economics of the Household*, 15: 199–222.

Zilcha, I. (2003). 'Intergenerational Transfers, Production and Income Distribution'. *Journal of Public Economics*, 87: 489–513.

Conclusion

The last decade saw Greece navigate turbulent waters, both economically and socially, as well as politically. The sovereign debt crisis that hit the country in 2009 quickly evolved into a full-blown financial crisis with important consequences in all facets of economic and social life. Poverty and unemployment rose exponentially (as of 2017, the percentage of people at risk of poverty stood at 34.8%, an increase of 7.1 percentage points since 2010, and unemployment steadily remained the highest among the EU-28, at 21.5%); the political scene was reset, leading to the emergence of new players and the fading out of the old establishment. Political parties that were around at the beginning of the crisis either disappeared or were rebranded under new names and with new alliances (PASOK and LAOS), while new political forces came to the fore (SYRIZA, Potami, Enosi Kentroon, Golden Dawn). The crisis has been managed by four consecutive governments from all sides of the political spectrum. The socialist PASOK government signed the first Memorandum, followed by a short-lived national unity government in 2011 and a caretaker government in 2012, until the rise in power of the conservative New Democracy in 2012 and the signing of the second Memorandum. After two-and-a-half years in power, New Democracy was defeated in the 2015 elections by SYRIZA, the coalition of the radical left, which has governed the country since, forming a coalition government with the populist right-wing nationalist party of Aneksartitoi Ellines (Independent Greeks), albeit with a short interregnum in August 2015 (just before and because of the snap elections of September 2015).

Despite the different political manifestos of government parties throughout this period, all of them faced the same pressures from the creditors to comply with policies and implement measures that carried immense political cost with them. The traditional ideological divides – between Left and Right – started to disappear into thin air under the pressure to manage a crisis using tools and policies that transcended national political ideologies and conformed to a wider neo-liberal agenda.

As the contributions to this volume have revealed, however, the outcomes of these policies were highly contested, and the expected results did not always materialise – at least not in the way their initiators expected. On the contrary, several unintended consequences emerged, in line with Greece's institutional characteristics, which undermined the efforts to create a more competitive economy. This is particularly true in the case of employment relations and labour market outcomes. Although the programme of internal devaluation that was implemented to help increase Greece's competitiveness in the international markets eventually yielded some wage-related results, it also created a series of collateral problems that severely undermined the quality of employment relations. The decentralisation of collective bargaining that led to a reallocation of power in the labour market and a steep decline in wages, the rise in involuntary atypical employment, the huge brain-drain, and the feeling of desperation that characterised a whole generation of employees contributed immensely in undermining the productive potential of Greece's human capital. This describes only part of the impact of austerity policies on Greek employment relations. Several other aspects still remain under-researched, and their effects on the quality of the employment relationship are yet to be evaluated. The rise in undeclared work, the impact of the crisis and the new labour market environment on equality, the nature of the management of the employment relationship and the labour process, skills mismatch, and the impact of underemployment in employment relations and the wider economy are some of the crisis facets that are still not fully understood.

A typical characteristic of the Memoranda and their implementing measures was the almost monolithic emphasis on quantitative results at the expense of quality indicators. Reducing nominal wages to bring them in line with productivity, promoting the flexibilisation of the labour market, or increasing competitiveness were targets that were pursued without too much consideration of the consequences they would have on the quality of the employment relationship. This is hardly surprising, of course. The focus on quantity over quality characterises much of the EU policy agenda, as quantitative targets are easier to measure and to use in public debates. Despite a tentative shift towards qualitative indicators over the past years, the EU remained unshakably committed to the doctrinal and methodological teachings of economic orthodoxy, refusing to seriously consider any alternatives.

Yet, this quantitative approach is incapable of capturing the whole story. In determining the outcomes of the labour process and the types of social coherence in a society, the quality of the employment relationship is as important, if not more, as quantitative indicators. The existence of conflict and anger, of feelings of exclusion and desperation about one's present and future do not contribute to the development of a smooth employment relationship and feed into the emergence of reactionary politics, as eloquently portrayed by the rise of the extreme right in Greece. Greece is not an exception in Europe, as similar feelings are echoed across the EU, challenging the core of the European idea – as Brexit and the rise of nationalism across the various member states reveal. However, Greece experienced this situation in the extreme, primarily due to the adjustment programme policies that challenged the existence and effectiveness of traditional institutions and social structures – such as the ability of the family to provide and fend for its members.

In this context, in January 2015, the country saw the rise in power of SYRIZA, an anti-austerity radical left party, whose manifesto promised the renegotiation of the various adjustment policies and the country's eventual release from its Memoranda obligations. Having no previous government experience, and promoting a radical agenda, SYRIZA's election to power raised concerns in the markets and among Greece's creditors regarding the sustainability of the programme and the country's future in the Eurozone. Forming a coalition government with ANEL – a small party with a nationalist agenda – they initiated policies aimed at reverting the socially unpopular measures implemented in the country at the behest of the Troika.

Soon enough, however, the new government came to realise that change was not going to be easy within the framework of international politics. An attempt in early 2015, for instance, to re-instate the pre-2012 collective bargaining structure was blocked by the creditors, and discussions about a possible re-centralisation of collective bargaining were postponed until 2018. Political realism started to prevail, with SYRIZA gradually understanding that if the country were to avoid a potential default, an exit from the Eurozone, and further social and political instability, some reconciliation of its manifesto promises with the demands of the creditors was inevitable. The political high point of this realisation came on July 5, 2015, when the newly elected government held a referendum about the third adjustment programme that the creditors pushed through.

Calling a referendum was an ambiguous political choice, if not an outright miscalculation of significant proportions. The government invested heavily in a muddled rhetoric of direct democracy and anti-austerity politics, asking the Greek people to exercise their sovereign power and make a fundamental choice about their collective future. But both the process and the substance of the referendum were riddled with paradoxes. The Greek people were pressured into making a choice within an extremely tight timeframe (one week) and with very limited information, as the lengthy documents outlining the bailout agreement were hastily translated and publicised only a few days before the vote. The government campaigned in favour of a "No" vote, insisting at every turn that the question put to the Greek electorate was strictly whether the particular bailout package should be approved or rejected. At the same time, almost all Eurozone governments and several key EU officials came out with forceful public statements to suggest that a rejection of the bailout agreement in the referendum would be tantamount to a rejection of Greece's future as a Eurozone member state. The verbose referendum question, as eventually printed on the ballot, essentially presupposed that voters would have read and understood the bailout documents with all their technical jargon and complex economic indicators. Never before had the troubling relationship between democracy and technocracy been brought to such a sharp and immediate contrast in the context of a single public vote.

The result of the referendum was a resounding – and perhaps not entirely expected – rejection of the bailout agreement and a Pyrrhic victory for the government at home. In the immediate aftermath of the referendum, and despite the copious efforts to maintain a distinction between the Greek rejection of the specific bailout agreement and the unassailable commitment to Greece's place in the Eurozone, the Greek government was faced with a block of (some of) its Eurozone partners determined to push for a swift and hard Grexit. The outcome of a harsh negotiation was a third Memorandum package that would have to be ratified in principle by the Greek parliament in the space of a few weeks. And above and beyond all else, the most tangible and long-lived effect of the referendum was perhaps none other than the bitter division of the Greek people, which has reopened old wounds and left new scars yet to be repaired.

The third Memorandum was built on the same austerity rationale as the previous two, including a series of measures provided for interventions in public finances and the regulation of the markets. On the employment relations front, it was more "lenient" than its predecessors, primarily because the majority of the changes in the labour market had already been achieved during 2010–2012. Nevertheless, it still made provision for modifications in the field of collective redundancies (with a view to render them less dependent on state intervention) and for changes in strike legislation and in the management of undeclared work, while it reaffirmed the Troika's position that collective bargaining should remain decentralised, at least until the end of the programme.

The new demands by the Troika created obvious problems for the government, which found itself walking a tightrope between its ideological tenets and manifesto proclamations, on the one hand, and the political reality of securing further financial assistance on the other. In a move to ameliorate the situation and ease the political burden, it was agreed with the Troika that the government would seek the assistance of the ILO and an Experts Group, tasked with reviewing possible changes and proposing ways of satisfying the Memorandum commitments. This was the first time since the country entered the adjustment programmes that evidence-based policy could be created. In 2016, the ILO published two reports on the state of collective bargaining and undeclared work in Greece (Grimshaw and Koukiadaki 2016; ILO 2016), pinpointing the consequences of austerity and the deregulation of employment relations on the labour market, while making specific recommendations on how to improve the state of affairs. Around the same time, the Experts Group issued its report on the status of collective bargaining, strike legislation, and undeclared work, arguing that further changes with regard to industrial action were not required at this juncture. While a minority report argued that collective bargaining should remain decentralised, the majority claimed that the re-centralisation of collective bargaining could have beneficial effects in the labour market.[1] The findings of the report were further supported by a common declaration of the tripartite social partners, calling for the reinstatement of national collective bargaining to determine the National Minimum Wage and the re-instatement of sectoral collective bargaining. The social partners also reiterated the lack of need to change strike legislation and emphasised their commitment to tackle undeclared work.[2]

Politically, the common declaration of the social partners signified an important shift in the way capital and labour conceived of their relationship and their role in managing the employment relations environment. Having experienced the detrimental effects of deregulation on their organisational structure and institutional power as well as on the sectors of the economy they represented, a common front was formed to address the situation. In truth, this front was not as coherent or compact as the declaration would have one believe, as differences in opinions and policy directions still existed between and within the social partners. SEV (the employers' association representing large corporations), for example, although in favour of sectoral collective bargaining in principle, was still supporting decentralised firm-level negotiations over sectoral ones in practice. Both SEV and ESEE (the employers' association representing merchants), on the other hand, were in favour of changes in strike legislation. These splits and differences in opinion reflected specific class interests. SEV, which was primarily representing big, labour-intensive businesses (rather than sectors of the economy), considered firm-level bargaining better suited to its members, while ESEE, GSEVEE (which represented small manufacturers and artisans), and SETE (which represented the hotel and tourism industry), were in favour of sectoral bargaining in order to establish common rules across the market and, thus, avoid unfair completion and social dumping among their members (Voskeritsian et al. 2017).

In 2016, the first round of negotiations with the Troika began. The negotiations had a broad agenda, ranging from the re-centralisation of collective bargaining to changes in the legal framework for the regulation of strike action and collective redundancies. Eventually, some changes in the institutional framework were agreed upon, the most important being a change in the way strikes could be called by firm-level unions, with the introduction of a 50% turnout requirement of eligible (fully paid up) union members for the ballot to be valid (article 211 of Law 4512/2018); the abolition of the prior authorisation (by the competent Minister of Labour) requirement for collective redundancies to take effect, with said power now entrusted to the Supreme Labour Council (*Ανώτατο Συμβούλιο Εργασίας, ΑΣΕ*) in line with the decision of the Court of Justice of the European Union in *AGET*-Iraklis[3]; and the creation of a roadmap (in collaboration with the ILO) to tackle undeclared work (ILO 2017).

The outcomes of the negotiations traced a middle road between the Troika's demands and the government's agenda. For example, the government managed to avoid the introduction of the lockout in the Greek legislative framework (something that the Troika pushed for, contrary to the Experts Group recommendations and despite opposition from both the social partners and the government) but did not manage to secure an agreement regarding the re-centralisation of collective bargaining or the determination of the National Minimum Wage solely by the social partners. It was only in 2018, during the final negotiations with the Troika regarding the future of Greece after its official exit from the adjustment programme in September 2018, that the issue of collective bargaining was put on the table again. At the time of writing, the form that the collective bargaining framework will take in the post-memorandum era remains unknown.

No matter what the future holds, the new institutional realities will have to take account of and address many of the problems that 10 years of austerity brought to the employment relations system and the function of the labour market. Some of these issues were addressed in this volume, while others remain under-researched. Either way, in our view, the issue of quality of employment relations should take centre stage in every policy decision and direction, alongside considerations regarding quantitative outcomes. The fact, for example, that unemployment levels seem to be slowly declining, primarily because atypical forms of employment are on the rise, poses important questions about the quality of jobs in the Greek labour market, the efficient utilisation of human capital and skills, and the perceptions of workers about their own prospects in this labour market. The answers to these questions have important implications not only for the production and distribution of wealth, but also for the levels and quality of productivity. In a similar vein, the increased participation of women and migrants in the labour market raises pertinent questions about equality, non-discrimination, and diversity, topics that are only gradually being dealt with by the Greek legal system and are still underappreciated by the Greek society. The way the employment relationship is being managed at the shop floor, and the treatment of employees by management, should also be part of the wider discussion. The low unionisation rates in Greece, coupled with the low union presence in the vast majority of Greek businesses, raises important questions about the kind of "voice" that employees have in their work environment. Although this has been a diachronic issue in Greek employment relations, it has become more important in the past decade due to the reallocation of power in the labour market. The country's journey out of the crisis and towards growth is still at an embryonic state. But if Greece is to come out of its recent adventure as unscathed as possible, it should strive to create an employment environment that will work for everyone rather than for the benefit of specific actors or powerful veto players. If this entails sacrificing quick growth for a slower – but fairer and more sustainable – development, then it is a sacrifice worth making.

Notes

1 See www.ieri.es/wp-content/uploads/2016/10/Final-Report-Greece-September-2016. pdf (accessed July 2018).
2 See www.gsevee.gr/deltiatupou/690-2016-07-19-13-59-50 (accessed July 2018).
3 C-201/15 – Anonymi Geniki Etairia Tsimenton Iraklis (AGET Iraklis) v Ypourgos Ergasias, Koinonikis Asfalisis kai Koinonikis Allilengyis, December 21, 2016. In *AGET Iraklis*, where the Court found that the prior authorisation regime for collective redundancies envisaged by Article 5(3) Law No 1387/1983 was incompatible with EU law insofar as the grounds upon which the Minister of Labour could refuse authorisation for the collective redundancies scheme were not appropriately and specifically defined.

References

Grimshaw, D. and Koukiadaki, A. (2016). *Evaluating the Effects of the Structural Labour Market Reforms on Collective Bargaining in Greece.* www.ilo.org/travail/whatwedo/publications/WCMS_538161/lang–en/index.htm (accessed 4 May 2018).
International Labor Organization (2016). *Diagnostic Report on Undeclared work in Greece.* Geneva: ILO.
_____ (2017). *Road Map for Fighting Undeclared Work in Greece.* Geneva: ILO.
Voskeritsian, H., Veliziotis, M., Kapotas, P., and Kornelakis, A. (2017). *Between a Rock and a Hard Place: Social Partners and Reforms in the Wage Setting System in Greece under Austerity.* London: Hellenic Observatory, LSE.

Index